# FLIRTING WITH DANGER

## QUALITATIVE STUDIES IN PSYCHOLOGY

This series showcases the power and possibility of qualitative work in psychology. Books feature detailed and vivid accounts of qualitative psychology research using a variety of methods, including participant observation and field work, discursive and textual analyses, and critical cultural history. They probe vital issues of theory, implementation, representation, and ethics that qualitative workers confront. The mission of the series is to enlarge and refine the repertoire of qualitative approaches to psychology.

GENERAL EDITORS
Michelle Fine and Jeanne Marecek

Everyday Courage:
The Lives and Stories of Urban Teenagers
by Niobe Way

Negotiating Consent in Psychotherapy
by Patrick O'Neill

Voted Out:
The Psychological Consequences of Anti-Gay Politics
by Glenda M. Russell

Inner-City Kids:
Adolescents Confront Life and Violence in an Urban Community
by Alice McIntyre

Flirting with Danger:
Young Women's Reflections on Sexuality and Domination
by Lynn M. Phillips

# FLIRTING WITH DANGER

Young Women's Reflections on Sexuality
and Domination

## LYNN M. PHILLIPS

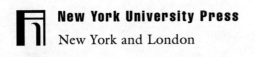

**New York University Press**
New York and London

NEW YORK UNIVERSITY PRESS
New York and London

Library of Congress Cataloging-in-Publication Data
Phillips, Lynn M.
Flirting with danger : young women's reflections on sexuality and
domination / Lynn M. Phillips.
p.   cm.
Includes bibliographical references and index.
ISBN 0-8147-6657-9 (cloth : alk. paper) —
ISBN 0-8147-6658-7 (pbk. : alk paper)
1. Young women—United States—Sexual behavior. 2. Young
women—United States—Interviews. 3. Man-woman relationships—
United States. 4. Sexual harassment of women—United States.
5. Discrimination against women—United States.   I. Title.
HQ29 .P49 2000
306.7'08352'0973—dc21          00-009877

New York University Press books are printed on acid-free paper,
and their binding materials are chosen for strength and durability.

Manufactured in the United States of America

10  9  8  7  6  5  4  3  2  1

*To my family, for giving me the support*
*and courage to wonder out loud.*

# Contents

■   ■   ■   ■

# Preface

I recently came upon a lapel button that said, "What is it about 'no' that confuses you?" Having worked for many years on combating violence against women, I rushed to buy the pin, delighting in the question as I imagined it posed to men. With one simple rhetorical question, this pin seemed to capture the messages I had learned and tried so hard to communicate as a feminist researcher, teacher, and advocate. It pointed out that *of course* "no means no and yes means yes." And it asked smugly, "Why don't men understand this?" "Perfect," I thought, "clear and to the point!" But as I waited in line to make my purchase, the pin's words began to take on other meanings. After I initially imagined a male audience, it occurred to me that this same question, when posed to women, is neither straightforward nor rhetorical. In fact, it is a central question that drives my work.

As my attraction to this button reveals, I often feel the impulse to make clear-cut statements about women's desires and their responses to male domination. Indeed, in a society where women's charges of rape and harassment are still frequently met with questions about what they did to "lead men on," it has been critical to stress to lawmakers, employers, juries, and men in general that consent and coercion are inherently distinct. Yet at the same time, having listened for many years to young women's reflections on their own experiences, I am increasingly persuaded that, in fact, *their own* answers to the question, "What is it about 'no' that confuses you?" are often multiple, murky, and dauntingly complex. I am further persuaded that greater understandings of the apparent contradictions and ambiguities in women's experiences are vital to a social analysis of sexuality and domination. Indeed, as I have found in my work with adolescents and young adults, even the notions of male domination and male aggression, which have long been central to feminist analyses (including my own), become problematized in light of young women's nuanced articulations of their own stories. Although it has been politically essential to assert, simply, that "no means no and yes means yes," it is also important to explore what is *not so clear* in women's experiences of their relationships and sexualities if advocacy efforts are to effectively help young women prevent and make sense of the various manifestations of sexualized aggression in their lives. This book is intended as a step in that ongoing exploration.

Based on an in-depth, qualitative study with a diverse group of young women in the northeastern United States, this book probes women's complex understandings of sexuality and violence, as well as their development of what I call "hetero-relational subjectivities," in a cultural context of gendered power asymmetries. By "hetero-relations" I mean the interactions, both sexual and seemingly nonsexual, that women have with men and masculinities. Hetero-relations may include serious love relationships, casual sexual encounters, nonsexual/nonromantic interactions across genders that involve elements of domination, exploitation, or coercion based on gender, and interactions that one person intends to be nonsexual/nonromantic but into which others introduce elements of uninvited sexuality or romance. Hetero-relations include interactions that are explicitly sexualized as well as those that are more ambiguous, such as interactions between women and men in which the goal is nonsexual, but in which participants call on dynamics such as flirting to "facilitate" the interaction. Such interactions may occur at work, at school, at home, or on the street. Hetero-relations may be wanted or unwanted, delightful or painful, consensual or forced. And, as we will see, they can be all these things at once.

My interest in the development of young women's hetero-relational subjectivities involves exploring the processes by which women construct understandings of their relationships to gendered power and domination, as well as agency, through their thinking about their various relationships with men, male-centered institutions, and culture.[1] I use the term "hetero-relational" rather than "hetero-sexual" because I believe that all women, regardless of sexual orientation or sexual identity, are engaged in hetero-relations of some sort. Certainly hetero-relationality may play a greater or lesser role in the construction of women's subjectivities, depending on the amount and kinds of time they spend with men. But since women in a male-centered society must spend enormous amounts of energy sifting through complex and pervasive messages about pleasure, danger, and entitlement regarding sexuality and male power, it follows that all women in Western culture (even if they express their sexualities exclusively with women) are involved to some extent with a process of constructing hetero-relational (as well as "homo-relational") subjectivities. It is the dialectical relationship between young women's development of hetero-relational subjectivities and their experiences in their hetero-relations that this book explores.

My exploration of these phenomena is based on the life experiences of thirty young women who have graciously shared their stories with me. In the chapters ahead, I invite readers to witness these women's hetero-relational encounters and understandings through their own eyes and in their own voices, and then to consider my own theorizing about what these voices say back to us, as a culture, about sex, power, violence, and gender. It is my hope that by listening carefully to young women's intricate reconstructions of their own experiences, we may gain greater understandings of women's developing hetero-relational subjectivities, and the meanings of male domination and sexualized power in their lives.

In chapters 1 and 2 I discuss the questions and concerns that prompted me to conduct this research. I also offer a theoretical framework to guide our understandings of the culturally constructed nature of subjectivity, power, choice, and desire, and I provide a description and rationale for the methodology I used to study these issues. In chapters 3 and 4 I examine the cultural and developmental contexts in which young women's hetero-relational subjectivities are constructed and situated. Here I consider the complex web of early messages women received about gender, sexuality, aggression, and victimization. In chapters 5 and 6 I discuss how young women apply their hetero-relational understandings to their perceptions, decisions, and attributions about their own and other women's hetero-relational experiences. Central to this discussion is an examination of the sometimes paradoxical strategies they develop to explain their victimizing encounters without losing a sense of self. In the final chapter I consider broader political and theoretical implications of the findings and suggest possibilities for envisioning and creating more satisfying, safe, and reciprocal hetero-relational experiences. For those readers interested in questions of qualitative research and feminist politics, I provide an afterword that explores the dilemmas and possibilities of conducting feminist, participatory, activist-research on issues of sexuality and violence against women.

# Acknowledgments

Writing a book is a profoundly personal endeavor, but thankfully, I was never in it alone. Many friends, colleagues, students, and family members helped to bring this work to its present form. It is a pleasure to thank them here.

I must first express my indebtedness to the thirty young women who were gracious enough to share their very intimate stories with me so that, together, we might give voice to aspects of women's lives too often kept private. Although their names have been changed in this text, their identities are forever etched in my mind and my heart.

I am deeply appreciative of the time and energy that several people put into reading drafts of the manuscript, helping me work through the data, and offering feedback and encouragement. Michelle Fine has been a supportive mentor, a critical reader, and a cherished friend. She helped me give birth to this project, and has seen me through to its completion. Her wit and wisdom have stretched my thinking and inspired me to move from "what is" to "what could be." Jeanne Marecek provided thoughtful feedback on the manuscript and made important suggestions that strengthened this work. Her insights and enthusiasm for this project helped propel it forward. Demie Kurz and Vicki Smith gave generously of their time and insight, pointing me in valuable directions, offering supportive feedback, and helping me clarify my thinking about complex and politically provocative issues. Sara Ruddick read my work with care and offered valuable insights; I am grateful for both her camaraderie and her intellectual rigor.

Many friends deserve thanks (and merit badges) for their encouragement and insights. Lisa Handler challenged my thinking and refueled my energies, lending her brilliant mind, good humor, and constant support. Nancie Zane reminded me to trust my own process and engaged with me in countless stimulating conversations about research, ethics, and social change. Jackie Cunliffe Emini offered helpful insights and was always ready with a pep talk at a moment's notice. Rhoda Unger's generous friendship and rich, provocative scholarship both deepened my thinking and warmed my heart. Arnie Kahn's enthusiasm for this project helped keep me motivated, and our conversations about sexuality and violence enriched my work. Jennifer Milici, Deb Tolman, and Maria Torre enhanced my thinking about gender, power, and sexuality through ongoing and delightful conversations about our work and our commitments to social change. Pearl Rosenberg and Dana Kaminstein helped me think through issues of power and subjectivity and made the research a much friendlier process. Elizabeth Sayre and Maureen Cotterill provided much-appreciated intellectual, emotional, and technical support during the research phase of this project. And throughout the process, Scott VonRhee provided a welcomed sense of balance with his warmth and humor.

My colleagues at Eugene Lang College of the New School have provided me an invigorating intellectual home. In particular, I wish to thank Nancy Barnes, Jennifer Fondiller, Jerma Jackson, Trace Jordon, Gary Lemons, Suzanne Obeler, Ann Snitow, René Alexander, and Gregory Tewksbury, both for their inspiring work and for our conversations about the intersections of scholarship and social justice. Bea Banu, Toni Oliviero, and David Rosenberg have given me tremendous support in my work and helped create a space where teaching, theory, and research can thrive. Gail Persky has been a true comrade and an enthusiastic reader of my work. All researchers should be so fortunate as to have access to the expertise and support of Gail and her staff at the New School's Fogelman Library. Thank you to Amos Himmelstein, Verna deLaMothe, Monica Kassan, Joe Chartier, and Amy Funes for everything from help with the photocopier to keeping me laughing throughout the process of data collection and writing. I am especially grateful to my students at Eugene Lang College and the University of Pennsylvania for their invaluable contributions to my thinking about the interview data. Their critical reflections enhanced my own understandings of young women's negotiations of complex and difficult life circumstances.

A special thank you goes to Lynne McMahon, who took gentle care of my mind and my spirit, and prodded me to keep moving when times got tough. She has been an inspiring role model, a careful reader, and a compassionate teacher. I also wish to thank Judy Eidelson, whose warmth and insights helped me work through both my excitement and anxieties about this project, and kept me focused on the important things.

I have been very fortunate to work with two skilled and supportive editors at New York University Press. Tim Bartlett greeted my ideas with enthusiasm and respect and helped me envision the completed book. Jennifer Hammer has seen it through from an early draft to its final stages; I am forever grateful to her for giving me the space and encouragement needed to bring it to life. Thank you, as well, to Laurie Kimbraugh, not only for her excellent transcription skills, but also for our lively conversations about the data.

Finally, I wish to thank my most generous and loving family. My mother, Geri Phillips, has given me support beyond measure. She has read my work with enthusiasm, encouraged me to pursue my passions, and given me both the practical and emotional support to do so. My father, Stanley Phillips, encouraged critical thinking, nurtured my creativity, and taught me to reach for excellence. His strength, love, and belief in me live on in my heart and inspire my work. My grandparents, Lawrence Soucy and Doris Soucy, provided me with the best example I can imagine of mutual love and respect in hetero-relationships. My grandfather's support and enthusiasm throughout the research process meant more to me than I could ever have expressed to him. My uncle, Robert Soucy, both encouraged me to do my best and reminded me to keep things in perspective. Their memories fortify my spirit and my work. My sister, Leigh Phillips, and my brother-in-law, Bruce Beauregard, have encouraged me with warmth and wit and always provided me with a sense of homecoming. Barbara and Tom Jackson have taken an active interest in my work and offered much-needed support and encouragement throughout the research and writing process. Together with their children, sons- and daughters-in-law, and grandchildren, they have encouraged me to work and reminded me to play.

I am delighted to be able to acknowledge my daughter, Lauren Emma Phillips-Jackson, who was born during the final stages of preparing this manuscript. Although her arrival may have slowed things down a bit, her presence in my life has only fueled my sense of urgency to work toward a more gender equitable world. Most of all, I wish to thank my husband, Mark Jackson, for being an anchor to steady me, and a scaffold to help me climb. In solidarity, he and our dogs, Shaynah, Carrie, and Jason, slept more than one night on the floor by my desk as I worked on this project. Whether supplying me with coffee or putting down his own work to read through mine, he has been a vital part of this book, from the first interview I conducted to the last word I typed.

# 1

■　■　■　■　■　■　■　■　■

# Introduction

DURING THE LAST FIFTEEN YEARS I have listened with increasing concern and attention to young women's struggles to make sense of their relationships and sexualities. I have seen how an awareness of male aggression filters through young women's experiences and understandings of their own hetero-relational lives. Scenes such as the following have been common in my experience:

## Scene 1

*The classroom is buzzing with animated conversation about women's experience of street harassment. I am teaching an introductory course in Psychology and Women, and the students, almost all undergraduate women, are discussing the objectification and anxiety they feel when men make comments about their body, their attire, or their mood. Without exception, the comments are about how terrible that feels. After extended discussion, a male student comments that he too has been whistled at by females on the street, and he, for one, has always taken it as a compliment. "Don't women really see it that way too?" Discomfort fills the room—women students squirm, some nod their heads with embarrassment. Yes, some women acknowledge reluctantly, even if they're not proud of it, sometimes it does feel good. Finally a woman names an important distinction: "It may feel good for both of us. I can even find it a turn-on. But as a man, you never have to wonder if that 'compliment' is going to lead to you getting into trouble. As a man, you can play up the compliment or reject their attention. But you don't have the anxiety of making sure you don't either lead them on, getting you into trouble, or get them pissed off, getting you into trouble. Women always have to straddle that fine line. . . . Still, though, I guess I'd have to admit . . . there is something exciting about* flirting with danger—*and about* straddling those fine lines."

## Scene 2

*I am in a battered women's shelter, interviewing a battered woman who has left her abusive husband. She is responding to my question of when and how her husband first began to be violent: "You know, they say hindsight is 20/20, and that's the truth. They [the shelter] have these posters hanging on the walls here that say the warning signs, you know, of if a man may be somebody who's going to be a batterer. Don't you know, my man had all of the symptoms—all of the warning signs were right there. But I didn't see them as that. When he was always in control, control over me, it just looked pretty normal, like what do you expect? It's not to say I liked it. In fact if you had asked me, I would have said with a straight face that I would never put up with being dominated or abused by a man. But I would never have considered what I got as abuse or as even leading up to abuse. Looking back on it now, I can see where he was* going over the lines, *but at the time, all I can tell you is that it didn't look that way. What I can see now as me being set up to be victimized, at the time just looked like normal marriage."*

## Scene 3

*I am walking through an urban park with two undergraduate women. We have just left a workshop on sexism in which they voiced both their anger about men's objectification of women and their constant fear, as women, of male aggression. A man, whom none of us knows, walks toward us. As his eyes scan us in an exaggerated way from head to toe and back again, he says, "Well hello there girls, you sure are looking fine tonight—my, my, my." I say to my companions, "I can't believe he just said that" (read: I'm annoyed by the intrusion, by his presumption that his assessment of our appearance has value for us, by his calling us girls, etc.). The woman next to me replies, "I know, me either. I wasn't thinking I looked that good." I suddenly realize that we are having two different conversations, based on two very different experiences of the interaction. Both women tell me that they find such attention affirming and exciting, and that they sometimes consciously solicit it. Asked if they ever worry that a man's attention could "go too far," the second woman replies, "I guess so, but it's playing around where those lines are that's all the fun. It makes me feel really desirable and kind of powerful to know that I've got what a man wants really badly—to sort of play around the edge."*

I have listened to such reflections across many settings—in the classes I teach, in battered women's shelters, while playing and studying with adolescent girls in my urban community, in discussion groups with teens, and in streets, subways, and restaurants, as I eavesdrop on women's "private" conversations. I have found myself nagged by a growing realization that the stories I hear do not mesh with the dominant themes in the mainstream social science literature and, surprisingly, even much of the feminist research literature on women's sexualities, relationships, and experience of male aggression. And they certainly do not mesh with current popular portrayals of rape, battering, and harassment. These literatures generally portray women's perception of male aggression as relatively straightforward and unidimensional—either exclusively erotic and sought after, or exclusively demeaning and terrifying. Yet women's own accounts are often much more textured and complex, filled with apparent internal contradictions that have not yet been sufficiently explored in the social science or popular literature.

Scenes such as those above offer glimpses of the variability and murkiness of the boundaries, or "edges" and "fine lines"—between seduction and domination, pleasure and danger, responsibility and exploitation, agency and objectification, consent and coercion—that women interpret and negotiate as part of the "normal" experience of their daily hetero-relational lives. In these scenes we see women, enmeshed in the ever present context of male power and their own potential violation, constructing multiple and sometimes contradictory meanings of pleasure, choice, and objectification in their experiences of relationships and senses of their hetero-relational selves. The tensions in the above scenes suggest that women may perceive the same sets of interactions as simultaneously annoying and complimentary, unfair and normal, dangerous and enticing.

Intrigued by the gap between what I thought I knew as a feminist social and developmental psychologist and what I was hearing from the women and teens around me, I set out to learn more about the textures and contradictions in hetero-relational experiences from young women themselves. I had previously interviewed battered women and rape survivors quite extensively and written about the lack of resources, constrained options, and victim-blaming attitudes that often prevented them from escaping abuse. In an effort to combat popular assumptions that women who do not "just leave" must either enjoy abuse or not know any better, much of my research focused on the failure of social systems to protect women and on identifying external material and social conditions that compelled women to endure male aggression (Phillips, 1989). While I continue to believe that such a research focus is critical to counter woman-blaming societal attitudes and is relevant to many women's experiences, I began to realize that the external forces I was stressing did not apply to many of the young women I encountered in my everyday life—particularly those in the classes I taught—who shared stories of their experiences of male aggression. Indeed, many of these women did possess the material resources to leave abusive relationships, and many of them voiced a political and psychological sense of entitlement to be treated well and taken seriously. Yet they spoke of domineering boyfriends, coercion and force in their sexual encounters, harassment by their male professors, employers, and doctors. They spoke of being pushed, hit, and verbally abused in their intimate relationships. Of course, I was troubled (although, unfortunately, not altogether surprised) that young women still experienced such abuses. But I was equally troubled by their insistence that theirs were basically "good" relationships and that the men who treated them this way should not be confused with "real" batterers, harassers, or rapists. Despite the availability of material resources and social supports that could help them find alternatives to these relationships, these women chose to stay in them and found ways to make their mistreatment seem tolerable.

Clearly, the materialist analysis I had relied on previously could not explain these young women's perspectives or decisions. And so I became concerned with understanding the more subjective factors that inform women's hetero-relational decision making. I wanted to know more about how young women conceptualize the distinctions between good relationships and bad ones, between consent and coercion, and between agency and victimization. I wanted to understand how young women make sense of the violence and manipulation that all too often invade their hetero-relationships. And I wanted to learn what they tolerate, what they resist, and what they perceive as "normal" or inevitable in their own and other women's hetero-relational encounters. As I turned to the literature for insights, I found that some feminist theorists (see, for instance, Bartky, 1990; Benjamin, 1988; Butler, 1990; Collins, 1991; Espin, 1984; hooks, 1984; 1990; Kitzinger and Thomas, 1995; Kitzinger, Wilkinson, and Perkins, 1993; Mohanty, 1992; Sawicki, 1991; Snitow, Stansell, and Thompson, 1983; Valverde, 1987; Vance, 1984; Weeks, 1985) had grappled admirably with complex questions about sexuality, power, and paradox in women's subjective experiences. Yet the voices of young women themselves were generally absent from this literature. Looking for research studies on the complexities of young women's experiences, I found that social scientists had explored women's responses to "clear-cut" instances of rape, battering, and harassment. Yet these studies generally did not explore the paradoxical nature of young women's perspectives or incorporate the textured understandings generated by feminist theorists (see Brodkey and Fine, 1988; Hollway, 1984; 1995; Kahn and Mathie, 1999; Fine, 1983; Halson, 1990; Stanko, 1985; 1990; Thompson, 1995; and Tolman, 1996, for some notable exceptions). Inspired by my reading, but not entirely satisfied, I decided that I needed to interview young women to bring together the insights and questions I was developing from reading social research and feminist theory and from listening to the thoughts and concerns of young women themselves. I wanted to ground feminist theoretical insights by developing research that went directly to the source and asked young women themselves to explore the wrinkles and contradictions in their lived experiences. I also wanted to situate my research design and analysis within a feminist theoretical framework that honors complexity and paradox, rather than reducing young women's perspectives to mere variables or trying to find one, coherent explanation for their discrepant experiences.

In order to move past a materialist analysis and into an exploration of women's subjective experiences, I needed to speak with young women whose decisions were not necessarily constrained by a lack of resources, social supports, or senses of possibility for equality in relationships. I was also interested in speaking with young women outside contexts such as shelters or rape crisis centers where they would already have been labeled (by themselves and/or others) battered women or rape survivors. I wanted to hear women describe themselves and their experiences in their own terms in a context that did not already suggest that they were victims of abuse.

With these concerns in mind, I decided to interview undergraduate women in a large city in the northeastern United States. Since a quarter to a third of all women experience sexual abuse by the time they are eighteen years old (Benson, 1990; Finkelhor and Dziuba-Leatherman, 1994), I expected that an undergraduate sample would include both women who had encountered male aggression and those who had not. I located a small, progressive, liberal arts college that has a reputation for providing a non-traditional, profeminist, politically and intellectually challenging learning environment. Seventy percent of the students are female, and the student body is more diverse than most private colleges in terms of race and social class. Consistent with the emphasis on feminism at the college, students have access to considerable resources to help them find their way out of and seek redress for violent or exploitive circumstances they may encounter. Discussions of gendered power and male violence flourish in classrooms and student groups, and the intimate setting and small teacher-to-student ratio insure that students can find help in working through personal problems and finding solutions.

With the permission of school administrators, I placed letters in the campus mailboxes of all female students, inviting them to be interviewed about "power and intimacy in various relationships." Throughout the course of a spring semester, thirty women spoke with me in great depth about their relationships, their expectations, and their thoughts about the distinctions between "normal" hetero-relations and those that are "over the line." In a private lounge on campus, in students' off-campus apartments, and in their dorm rooms, the women spoke of romance, passion, pain, and possibility. They shared stories, punctuated by both laughter and tears, that many said they had never uttered before. Some in hushed tones, others with bold animation, the women spoke at great length about the intimate details of their hetero-relationships and the strategies they developed for managing them. They recalled how they approached their relationships and sexual encounters, how they negotiated power and voice once inside those encounters, and how they managed to get out when things ran amok. While I had expected the interviews to last about an hour and a half, most lasted from three to five hours. In some cases, we became so engrossed that it was not until we finally turned off the tape recorder that we realized it had become dark outside and our afternoon appointment had run well into the evening.

To my surprise, although I had carefully steered away from any mention of violence or victimization in my description of the study, twenty-seven of the thirty women (90 percent) described at least one encounter that fit legal definitions of rape, battering, or harassment.[1] Yet also to my surprise, only two women ever used such terms to describe a personal experience, and both of these women went on to describe other violent or coercive personal experiences that they did *not* consider rape or abuse. The young women were eager to talk about the pain and mistreatment they had endured, and they were quite willing to use words like "rape," "battering," "victimization," and "abuse" to describe *other* women's experiences. These women expressed great concern about violence against women in general. Indeed, several offered rather eloquent analyses of gender and victimization. But when it came to naming what they had gone through personally, women tended to say things like "let's just call it a bad night" or "things just went really badly." Furthermore, their explanations for why things "went badly" involved a great deal of self-criticism: "I should have known better," "Why did I go with him?" or "What was I thinking?" While many expressed anger at the men involved, their attributions for their painful experiences focused primarily on their own behavior. And even as they recounted stories through teary eyes and clenched teeth, they were quick to remind me that what they experienced was not so bad—not *really* abuse.

As I listened to women's experiences and their strategies for managing them, I struggled to make sense of what I was hearing. Everything I knew as a social psychologist seemed turned on its head. I had studied attribution theory and learned that people tend to attribute other people's negative experiences to personal flaws or poor behavior, but that they attribute their own negative experiences to forces outside themselves (Ross, 1977). I had learned that naming an injustice is an important step in coming to terms with it (Kidder and Fine, 1986). I had learned that self-blame interfered with one's ability to cope (Peterson, Schwartz, and Seligman, 1981). And from feminist activism, I had learned that women see the lines between pleasure and danger, between "yes" and "no," very clearly. Yet here were young women who were active agents in their own lives, expressing a general sense of entitlement, but also blaming themselves, blurring the lines, and seeming to dilute the severity of their own experiences. Throughout their interviews, women spoke of confusion, of contradictory emotions, of not knowing what to think.

I became consumed with a need to know more. How can we understand young women's struggles to negotiate gendered power, and to what can we attribute their reluctance to label their experiences abuse?[2] Why did they seem to apply different standards when evaluating their own experiences compared to those of others? And why did they seem to hold themselves accountable for their own victimization, even as they spoke sympathetically about other women who had experienced abuse? As I have pored over young women's stories and grappled with their nuances, I have become convinced that there are no straightforward answers to such questions. But I am also convinced that deepened understandings may be gleaned from an examination of the complex weave of cultural messages young women have encountered throughout their development, as well as through an analysis of the gendered power asymmetries that contextualize their hetero-relational experiences. Young women's stories can teach us much about the multiple meanings of such concepts as power, domination, intimacy, danger, seduction, responsibility, victimization, and desire in their hetero-relational experiences. And an exploration of young women's cultural and developmental *contexts* can help us situate our understandings in a framework that embraces contradiction and acknowledges the culturally constructed nature of their experiences. This book represents my own attempt to seek out and honor the complexities of young women's lived hetero-relational experiences, and to develop deeper understandings of the strategies they use to negotiate and make sense of gender, power, and sexuality in those experiences.

The search for greater understandings of these complexities has several important implications. Theoretically, such an exploration may deepen insights into cultural constructions of hetero-sexuality, male entitlement, male aggression, femininity, and the objectification of women within these constructions. While much of the existing literature *presumes* women's hetero-sexuality or explores hetero-sexual *relationships,* too little work has been done with women that interrogates and unpacks the multiple meanings of power and danger within, and the contours of, hetero-relationality as an element of their own subjectivities. Further, while feminist social research has addressed women's experiences on either side of the presumed lines between "normal" hetero-relationships/encounters and those that are "dangerous," "exploitive," or "objectifying," we have insufficient knowledge about how women conceptualize these lines for themselves. Thus, the women's stories recounted in this book can push forward our theoretical understandings of women's sexualities and gender development.

Clearly, though, this exploration does not speak simply to abstract, theoretical concerns. While many women, like those in the opening vignettes, may sense something deliciously empowering about "flirting with danger," the danger in such "flirting" is entirely too real. Indeed, in the midst of multiple and contradictory cultural messages about hetero-sexual intimacy and male aggression, girls and women are daily exploited, harassed, raped, battered, and killed at the hands of both men they encounter casually and men they know very well. Seduced by the excitement of "straddling those fine lines" and "playing around the edge," young women may enter into situations that put them at risk, thinking, erroneously, that they have the ultimate power over men.

Moreover, when women are violated, be it through rape, harassment, or battering, the popular culture typically blames them for their own victimization. Women are asked what they did to bring it on themselves, or why they didn't "just leave"; society (including women) presumes clear lines and stands ready to hold women responsible as gatekeepers for men's actions (White and Niles, 1990). During the years that I have been studying hetero-relationality, there has emerged a raging public debate about the nature of women's victimization and sexual agency, and about women's responsibility to name, leave, and seek redress for supposedly clear-cut crimes involving sexuality and abuse. Beginning in the early 1980s with academic debates about political correctness and the so-called thought police, fueled by the unprecedented public attention to Anita Hill's allegations of sexual harassment during the Clarence Thomas hearings, and catapulted to new levels by the investigations of President Clinton's sexual "misconduct," questions of men's and women's responsibility in hetero-relations have soared into public consciousness.

While such public attention is potentially helpful, a troubling consequence has been that important discussions about *complexities* in
women's experience are too often shut down before they begin, col-
lapsed under the weight of what Michelle Fine (1990) terms "a context
of zero-sum guilt"—the idea that if women's victimization is acknowledged as *at all* related to their own behavior, they are vulnerable to
being assigned full responsibility, while the men who hurt them are ex-
onerated. This notion, embraced by the very woman-blaming, and unfortunately quite popular, positions of some contemporary women authors,[3] speaks loudly to the need to carve out spaces in which we dare to
talk about agency, confusion, power, desire, and the murkiness of consent, without blaming women for their own violation (Lamb, 1999;
Maglin and Perry, 1996; Morrison, 1992).

Finally, as the participants' stories will make clear, the generation of
young women currently coming into adulthood may have quite different
understandings of gendered power than those of second-wave feminist activists and scholars, perhaps twenty to fifty years their senior. Unlike most
feminists who write about women's experiences of male domination, the
current generation of young women came through childhood and adolescence in a climate where violence against women was discussed (although
oversimplified) in the popular media, where girls were often led to believe
that their society would view and treat them as equals to boys, where
women's sexuality was acknowledged (although still constricted and exploited), and where, in some cases, their own caregivers were second-wave
feminists. At the same time, these young women were raised in an era of
Reagan/Bush conservatism, the Religious Right, and antifeminist backlash that told them that gender inequity had been "solved," that feminists
were simply whiny, angry man-haters, and that feminist analyses were
therefore irrelevant to their present lives. Clearly, these shifts in social climate have not replaced the oppressive gender ideologies experienced by
the women who came before them. However, they have added new dimensions to young women's experiences of themselves and their hetero-
relations—dimensions that may complicate their understandings of male
domination beyond those discussed in the feminist literature. Whereas
feminist scholars may speak of male domination and women's victimization as rather obvious phenomena, younger women, raised to believe in
their own independence, invulnerability, and sexual entitlement, may not

so readily embrace such concepts, even as they are raped, harassed, and battered by men.

If we are to take steps toward *preventing* women's victimization, we must grapple seriously with young women's understandings of male domination, in all their complexity. Researchers, theorists, advocates, and activists need to listen to the next generation of young women, to learn *their* understandings of domination and aggression in hetero-relations. Young women need to hear one another's stories, too often kept privatized, if they are to come together to disrupt dominant notions that constrict their options, promote their victimization, and compel them to take responsibility for their own abuse. And young men need to hear young women's experiences of violence and coercion if they are to play a part in ameliorating hetero-relational victimization. If a normalizing of dangerous male behavior and an eroticizing of women's objectification and commodification are woven into the very construction of traditional hetero-sexuality for women as well as for men, then we must understand how this plays out in the minds of young women if we are to explore more agentic visions of hetero-relations.

# 2

• ■ • ■ • ■ • ■ • ■ • ■

## Contextualizing the Study

*Establishing an Interpretive Framework*

THE YOUNG WOMEN in this study are entering adulthood at a time of profound social and political change. The last thirty years have seen traditional gender roles talked about, teased apart, and, to some extent, renegotiated. Whereas not so long ago, Lucy and Desi couldn't be seen sleeping in the same bed on television, explicit sexuality now appears everywhere from music videos to toothpaste ads. Popular magazines encourage young women to accept nothing less than fascinating careers, fulfilling relationships, and wildly exciting sex lives. More and more, the public voices shock and outrage when cases of woman abuse come to light. And new laws address rape, harassment, and battering in ways these young women's mothers may only have dreamed about.

Yet despite some evidence of societal progress, in other ways little has changed. Women are still beaten, raped, and harassed at alarming rates, and they are more likely to be injured at the hands of a battering partner than from muggings, rapes, and automobile accidents combined (United Nations, 1995). Examples of continued cultural tolerance of male aggression abound, along with a persistent refusal to take women's complaints seriously. For instance, when a group of high school athletes raped and sodomized a retarded girl in Glen Ridge, New Jersey, in the early 1990s, community members rushed to the young men's defense, claiming that they were good boys, model citizens who were sowing wild oats and having some fun (Fine, Genovese, et al., 1996; Lefkowitz, 1997). In 1991, when Anita Hill accused the Supreme Court nominee Clarence Thomas of sexual harassment, the Senate Judiciary Committee—all white men—expressed incredulity, concluding that she surely would have left her job and filed a complaint immediately if such events had really occurred. In cases where fraternity members have repeatedly gang raped unconscious and intoxicated women, university officials have looked the other way, and many students and parents have defended the boys' behavior as crass, perhaps, but certainly not criminal (Sanday, 1990). When the sportscaster Marv Albert was accused recently of sexually assaulting his lover, public discussion focused more on his penchant for wearing lingerie than on the seriousness of the woman's accusations. Indeed, we need only read the sports page of our newspaper to find sympathetic stories of athletes who have beaten their wives or raped their dates but are now facing this adversity (as though it was they who were victimized) with grace and courage. Such highly publicized cases are often sensationalized and treated as aberrations. Yet they barely scratch the surface of publicly condoned woman abuse.

In the last three decades feminist researchers, theorists, and activists have generated a critical and politically provocative body of literature that debunks long-held myths about male aggression and challenges social acceptance of violence and harassment (see, for instance, Adisa, 1997; Bartky, 1990; Blackman, 1990; Browne, 1987; Dobash and Dobash, 1992; Fine, 1983; 1989; Fine, Genovese, et al., 1996; Gordon, 1988; Hollway, 1984; 1995; hooks, 1984; 1996; Jones, 1994; Jones and Schechter, 1992; Koss, 1985; 1993; Kurz, 1990; Riger, 1991; Russell, 1982; Sanday, 1990; 1996; Stein, 1995; Sunday and Tobach, 1985; Walker, 1979; 1989; Warshaw, 1988; Yllo and Bograd, 1988). This work has played a vital part in disrupting common assumptions that male sexuality is inherently aggressive, that women "ask for it," that violence is a private "family matter," and that what women call harassment is simply good-natured flirting. Many feminists have stressed that "normal" relationships do not involve violence, coercion, and degradation—that the lines between sexuality and abuse are sharp and clear and that it is men who misunderstand or choose to ignore them (Sanday, 1996). Combating traditional conceptions of women as masochistic, and thus bringing on their own abuse and exploitation, feminist researchers and activists have maintained that no woman asks to be victimized, that male domination is demeaning and threatening, and that women endure abuse because they lack the resources to escape or because they are unable to perceive other options (Blackman, 1990; Browne, 1987; Ewing, 1987; Jones, 1994; Kurz, 1990; Walker, 1979; 1989).

By distinguishing "normal" hetero-relations from those that are abusive, feminists have offered powerful counterarguments to the woman-blaming assumptions woven throughout mainstream discussions of violence against women. Yet for all their value, those very arguments present a troubling dilemma. On the one hand, we live in a society that bases advocacy and legal decisions on clear-cut (and often unrealistic) definitions of victimization and that stands ever ready to presume women's responsibility for male aggression. Very often, those who advocate for women's sexual safety and equality are required to defend sharp lines and make unambiguous arguments—such as "No means no" and "Rape isn't about sex, it's about violence"—in order to debunk victim-blaming myths and defend women's rights and safety. On the other hand, it is not possible to advocate fully and effectively for women if the complexities of their lived experiences are ignored. Often those experiences seem to defy the very straightforward arguments many feminists have worked so hard to promote. For instance, for many of the young women in this study, rape *is* about sex, *as well as* about violence. Often it involves coercion, manipulation, or threats, but falls short of physical aggression. Many women report saying yes when they want to say no, and saying no when they want to say yes or maybe. And some say nothing, even when they want a painful encounter to end. For instance, Rachel,[1] who described herself as a white, hetero-sexual, twenty-one-year-old, recalled her response to her boyfriend hitting her, calling her a slut, and acting out his rape fantasies during their sexual encounters. "This is going to sound really sick," she said, "because it just sounds so weak. And it's like I brought it on myself because I never said, 'this is disgusting and degrading and it hurts!' I didn't know how to handle it, so I thought I should just pretend I enjoyed it too. I just never thought I could say something."

■

How can we maintain the important gains made by feminist research and activism, and yet still do justice to the complex realities young women express? If we speak faithfully to the textures and contradictions in their stories, do we risk fueling dominant assumptions that hold women responsible for their own mistreatment, casting them as fickle, confused, or sending mixed messages? Yet if we ignore their complexities, are we not also erasing young women's realities? To work responsibly through this dilemma, we need a theoretical framework to guide our understanding. To appreciate the meanings of the participants' actions and the integrity of their perspectives, we must begin from an understanding of the cultural construction of subjectivity—or how cultural contexts, practices, and assumptions inform young women's thoughts and decisions. We must look critically at issues of subjectivity, sexuality, power, and choice.

In my own struggle to understand how young women construct their experiences as active and evolving subjects, I have drawn on insights from research and theory across several disciplines.[2] In the remainder of this chapter I lay out the theoretical framework that guides my analysis and work through some key concepts needed for a critical understanding of the women's narratives. I also offer an overview of the study and the questions that shaped my work.

## Theorizing Subjectivities

My framework for understanding the participants' stories is based on the idea that our subjectivities—our senses of ourselves and our social realities—are inseparable from the cultural contexts in which we live. This notion may sound straightforward on its surface. Yet it can actually be quite challenging to grasp if we are used to Western concepts of identity that frame the self in opposition to—rather than as part of—the social world. Traditionally, psychologists who want to understand personality extract individuals from their social contexts, attempting to determine the characteristics of some essential self (Farganis, 1989; Hare-Mustin and Marecek, 1990; Meyer, 1988; Narayan, 1989; Shweder, 1995; Unger, 1988; 1989). Mainstream psychology conceptualizes identity as a collection of relatively stable, internal characteristics that are separable from the larger social, cultural, and historical contexts in which the person develops (Henriques, 1984). Accustomed to such a framework, we may find it difficult to envision the intricate and dynamic interplay between culture and subjectivity. Yet this is essential if we are to understand how young women's experiences and perceptions are formed.[3]

To clarify the interdependence of self and context for my students, I like to start with the metaphor of a lava lamp—those glass vessels filled with colorful globs that float and stretch gracefully in a clear liquid background. While at first glance the "lava" appears separate from the substance in which it is suspended, its ever-shifting contours are actually shaped in dynamic relation with the substance that surrounds it. As the lava moves around the glass container, heat from the lamp and pressure from the surrounding liquid gradually change the lava's shape in various ways. And as the lava's shape changes, so too must the liquid's. Often, when looking at this phenomenon, we look past the clear background and the warming and cooling of the lamp, ignoring their relationship to the lava on which we are focused. But their impacts on the lava are, nonetheless, constantly there. Similarly, in Western culture we tend to focus on individual identities, not mindful of the ways those identities are shaped and transformed by the cultural conditions in which they are immersed. But we are never without context, for our lives do not exist in a social vacuum. Like the lava, our selves are fluid and dynamic. Whether or not we are consciously aware of their influence, social messages, practices, and power relations impact on who we are and how we move through our lives.[4]

While this metaphor can help us understand how we are embedded in our cultural contexts, our analysis must go at least one step further. Not only are our identities *impacted by* our social contexts, but also we construct our identities *from* those contexts and the competing discourses that circle within them. Discourses represent sets of prevailing ideas or cultural messages about the way things are and the way things should be. They promote certain values and perspectives (and marginalize others) that tell us what is natural, inevitable, desirable, and appropriate in human behavior and social phenomena (Foucault, 1981; Gee, 1987; Hare-Mustin, 1991; Hare-Mustin and Marecek, 1990; Sawicki, 1991). Discourses both reflect and give shape to the ways we conceptualize, question, and talk about things. Both produced and reproduced by the institutions and social practices with which we live, discourses subtly instruct us how to think, speak, and act in ways that identify us as part of some socially meaningful group (e.g., a "woman," a "student," a "good citizen") (Gee, 1987).

We do not simply live inside our cultures. In many ways, our cultures live inside us. Immersed in a sea of competing expectations and complex social relations, we develop our subjectivities in dynamic tension with the discourses that surround us. Our relationships to those discourses shape not only *what* we see, but *how* we see—what we imagine is possible and what we take for granted. Since we are exposed to multiple and often contradictory discourses that shift across time and place, our senses of our social realities are not static, nor are they independent of the contexts in which we live. Just as a plant is shaped by the various nutrients and pollutants in the water it drinks and the soil in which it grows, so too are our identities constituted by the various discourses—the messages and meanings—we absorb from our cultures.

Subjectivities may be understood as the site of tension among multiple and competing discourses (Britzman, 1988). If only one discourse existed for any given aspect of social life, our realities might be relatively straightforward. But for any social phenomenon there exist multiple possible discourses, all of which may compete for our attention. For instance, we are not exposed to only one discourse about how to be a "successful individual." Rather, we are bombarded with conflicting sets of messages about what a "successful individual" is. On the one hand, in Western culture, capitalist institutions teach us that we should be competitive, independent, wealthy, and influential. On the other hand, many Western religious institutions promote a discourse of the "successful individual" as one who is compassionate, humble, and concerned with social justice. Increasingly we hear from the self-help movement that a "successful individual" strives for self-awareness, intimacy, and personal fulfillment. Each of these discourses may be compelling and folded into our consciousness, yet we must somehow deal with the tensions among them. Confounding things even further, if we are women, we may be told that to be "successful" is to be soft and nurturant and to sacrifice our own wants for those of our families. Yet we are also told that we should be passionate, sexually sophisticated, and alluring to men. And these days, we are told that a "successful" woman "has it all"—in addition to our loving families and exciting sex lives, we should have fast-track careers and financial freedom. Not only must we negotiate the tensions among these images of a "successful woman," we must also reconcile them with the competing notions of a "successful individual." Even more complicated, we may face still other discourses of a "successful individual" depending on our race(s), sexualities, class, or other aspects of our social identities. Say, for instance, we strive to be a successful-individual-wealthy-religious-bisexual-Caribbean-American-woman. The bombardment of competing expectations becomes dizzying. All may be compelling, yet they stand in many ways at odds with one another. We cannot simply choose one and reject all others, for they seep into our consciousness in subtle and pervasive ways. Rather, we are left to negotiate among these and countless other competing messages as we make our way through our worlds as multiply positioned individuals.

In applying these notions to the perceptions and experiences young women across racial, ethnic, class, and sexual lines have shared throughout this book, we can see that they develop their hetero-relational subjectivities in a culture saturated with contradictory discourses of hetero-sexual sex, love, and male aggression. Young women are simultaneously taught to solicit and feel flattered by male sexual attention, to protect themselves against it, and to control men so that they do not express it. They are told that any self-respecting woman would "just leave" at the first sign that a man is dominating or aggressive. Yet they are taught to "stand by their men," and they are bombarded with movies, television, women's magazines, advertisements, and romance novels in which "normal" passion and romance involve coercion, domination, and physical force. They are taught that "today's woman" is her own person. Yet they are encouraged to aspire to objectified images of women in which they are more sexual or nurturant commodities than active agents in their own personal and sexual development. To further complicate the matter, they are flooded with classist, racist, and hetero-sexist messages that tell them that only certain women (white, hetero-sexual, middle-class or affluent women) are entitled to speak out, worthy of advocacy, or even believed when facing injustice in their personal lives.

In the midst of these complex, pervasive, and discrepant messages, perhaps the one thing that is clear is that the meanings of domination, agency, aggression, entitlement, and desire are, in Western culture, *anything but* clear. Although differently situated with regard to race, class, and sexual orientation, all the young women in this study are constructing their hetero-relational subjectivities in an environment filled with tangled messages about their own power and entitlement, and about the lines between normal and dangerous relationships, sexual encounters, and male behavior.

It is important to note that this framework does not preclude an acknowledgment of young women's agency. To say that women's subjectivities are comprised of the cultural discourses in which they are immersed is not to say that they are passive recipients of these discourses. Indeed, collectively, it is possible to reshape popular discourses, as evidenced by the feminist movement's success in pushing for the establishment of laws against battering, acquaintance rape, and sexual harassment, as well as the rape shield laws that ban the once common practice of using rape survivors' sexual histories against them in court.[5] Rather, my point here is to acknowledge that these discourses represent the available materials from which women are able to form their ideas of what is possible, desirable, or inevitable in their hetero-relational lives. It is not so much the case that discourses are imposed *on* young women, but rather that they operate *through* them (Gee, 1987). Individuals are the "carriers" of cultural discourses, both producing and reproducing them through our language, beliefs, and social practices. Young women may or may not grapple consciously or explicitly with the tensions among the various discourses they encounter. But I will argue throughout this book that they nonetheless simultaneously use and resist them, often actively and skillfully, as they negotiate their way into gendered young adulthood.

## Theorizing Power and Choice

If we are to understand the strategies young women devise to position themselves in their hetero-relations and the attributions they form to make sense of their experiences, we must also look critically at issues of power and choice. It is not enough to recognize that subjectivity is constructed from social practices and cultural discourses, for those practices and discourses are woven with and from broader power relations (Marecek and Hare-Mustin, 1990; Sawicki, 1991). We must therefore probe critically the complex interplay of subjectivity with power, desire, and choice.

People in Western cultures often talk about power as a commodity possessed by an individual—something to be held over those who do not have it (Gatens, 1992). And we often think of choice as something one exercises freely, based on a range of unlimited options (Hare-Mustin, 1991). Accustomed to thinking in this way, we may fail to appreciate the ways power infuses our relationships, our social contexts, and the choices we make within them. Take, for instance, Rachel's experience referred to earlier in this chapter. Viewed in one way, she has the power to leave her boyfriend, to refuse to have sex with him, or to tell him she does not wish to be hit and demeaned. He is not, after all, holding a proverbial gun to her head. Based on a narrow understanding of power and choice, we might say that Rachel is to blame for her circumstances because she is not choosing to put an end to her boyfriend's behavior. Indeed, most of us can look back on elements of our own past decision making and, with the comfortable distance of hindsight, blame ourselves for not exercising other choices.

But power is far more complex than that. Power is enacted within, but also transcends, particular moments or particular relationships. Power is not simply something we have, but rather something we exercise in relation to others, through both resistance to and compliance with the discourses available to us (Bartky, 1990; Foucault, 1978; 1980; 1981; Lips, 1991; Sawicki, 1991). Our ability to exercise power in a particular context depends, in many ways, on the number and types of choices available to us in that context. And the choices available to us determine, in many ways, whether and how we exercise power. Since we are differently positioned with regard to power across our various social relations, our sense of power and choice is context-dependent. Consider, for a moment, an example that is not complicated by issues of sexual intimacy: when delivering a lecture, I exercise considerable power and choice in setting the agenda. But when sitting in my car, about to receive a speeding ticket, I may experience considerably less power. In the first case, my relationship to the people in the audience, the context we are in, and the social rules and expectations we have internalized about the relative roles of lecturer and listener help determine the power I can exercise. It is not that the audience is powerless, but rather that they have agreed, in this context, to allow me to speak my mind and set the terms of the discussion. In the second case, I could, in fact, fight with the officer giving me a speeding ticket or try to run off, avoiding the citation. My feelings and expectations might vary considerably, depending on my assessment of our relative positions in terms of race, class, and/or gender, as well as my (and my community's) prior experiences with the police (Fine and Weis, 1998). But my understanding of the structured status difference between officer and motorist, as well as my expectations of the consequences of disobedience, would likely render me willing to acquiesce (however grudgingly) to the officer's demands.

Knowing that the officer has socially sanctioned power in this context and would be likely to prevail (whether through use of a weapon or use of the courts) if I "got out of line," I might feel very little power while sitting in my car. Now imagine that the officer were also a member of the audience to which I was lecturing. It is not that one of us is a powerful individual and the other is not. Rather, our sense of options and relations to power shift, according to our own biographies and understandings of the social conventions that inform the various contexts in which we interact.

In a similar fashion, young women like Rachel (as well as the rest of us) make decisions in their relationships based on the contexts (both interpersonal and cultural) and socially constructed understandings they bring to their interactions. Rather than holding them individually accountable for making what may appear, on the surface, to be problematic *decisions*, we must understand the ways they are embedded in problematic *contexts*—both immediate and societal—that constrain their choices and senses of possibility. If we view it this way, we may interpret Rachel's situation quite differently. Rachel and her boyfriend do not operate as autonomous entities taking part in a discrete encounter. Each partner brings to the relationship a collage of ideas based on their prior experiences and the discourses they have encountered in their surrounding culture(s). They make sense of their relationship not as isolated individuals, but rather as contextualized subjects who have learned cultural scripts and incorporated messages about the nature of gender and hetero-relations. Those scripts and messages position them differently as a man and a woman in their relationship and shape their senses of power and choice accordingly. As we will see in later chapters, Rachel can certainly critique the notion that women should subordinate their needs to those of men. But like many women, she has also internalized powerful messages that privilege male pleasure, that stress the importance of preserving relationships, and that normalize a certain amount of male aggression in hetero-sexual encounters. She does not like the physical and verbal abuse she endures from her boyfriend, and she can exercise power to do something about it. But *what* she does—how she exercises that power—is shaped by her sense (as well as her boyfriend's sense) of what is possible, appropriate, and desirable in hetero-relations, as well as by the particularities of this specific relationship. Like the rest of us, Rachel's very sense of what is possible, appropriate, and desirable is constrained by the available discourses in the cultural contexts in which she lives.

Indeed, our very desires—sexual and otherwise—are informed by our accommodation and resistance to the discourses coursing through and around us. Our senses of pleasure, intimacy, and eroticism are not biologically predetermined. Rather, they take shape through an intricate weave of cultural images, roles, expectations, and taboos, with all their complexities and paradoxes. Leonore Tiefer (1995) puts it quite poignantly in the title of her recent book, *Sex Is Not a Natural Act*. As Jeffrey Weeks (1985) writes,

> The erotic possibilities of the human animal, its generalised capacity for warmth, intimacy and pleasure, can never be expressed "spontaneously" without intricate transformations; they are organised through a dense web of beliefs, concepts and social activities in a complex and changing history. We cannot hope to understand sexuality simply by looking at its "natural" components. These can only be realised and given meaning through unconscious processes and via cultural forms. "Sexuality" is a historical as well as a personal experience. (4)

With an understanding of the socially constructed nature of subjectivity, power, choice, and desire, we can interpret young women's perceptions and decisions against a backdrop of the powerful and often contradictory cultural messages they have encountered. As we listen to the stories they share throughout this book, we must remember that they never form their perceptions and attributions in a social vacuum. Rather, we will see them absorbing, resisting, and attempting to transform cultural discourses that do not fully speak to their lived experiences. Attempting to make sense of their often painful relationships and encounters, these young women, like all of us, use the cultural materials available in an attempt to position themselves, as much as possible, as active agents in their own experiences.

## Exploring Women's Hetero-Relations: The Methodological Framework

The theoretical framework described above has informed not only my way of understanding young women's stories, but also my way of collecting

them. Interested in the possible contradictions in young women's perceptions, I approached this study with a commitment to honoring women's
voices and the complexities of their experiences. I was not trying to dis-
cover whether young women *really* see male aggression as normal or enticing or *really* view it as dangerous and unacceptable. Nor was I interested
in classifying women's responses into neat, internally consistent "types." I
had no intention of getting to the bottom of things, once and for all. Instead, I hoped to explore the range and multiplicity within and across
young women's understandings and experiences of sexuality, agency, and
male aggression in their hetero-relations. Of course, I expected I might see
certain themes or patterns emerging across women's stories. But I entered
with an open mind as to what those patterns might be, and with a commitment to analyzing them against the backdrop of women's textured realities (for a fuller description of the procedure used to analyze the data,
see appendix C, "Analysis: Working with the Data").

Similarly, my goal in this book is not to draw conclusions about all
young women, or even about all women who share some general characteristics with those I interviewed. I do hope that the participants' stories
will shed some valuable light on other women's experiences and help push
forward public discussion of sexuality and aggression. Their relationships
and the cultural messages they articulate will no doubt resonate with many
readers. But since subjectivity takes shape within the specificities of our
own particular lives, the stories recounted here must be understood as ultimately about the relationship between the young women who have nar-
rated them and the contexts in which they live.

With this in mind, I did not set out to locate a research sample that
would generalize across the entire population of young women in the
United States. I wanted to interview women of various races, ethnicities,
social classes, and sexualities so that I could learn more about the range of
experiences and expectations to which young women have been exposed.
But I have no illusions that the participants speak for all young women of
their particular race(s), class background, or sexual identity. Indeed, I
would not want them to try, because each woman is positioned uniquely
in relation to the complex web of discourses she has encountered, as well
as the particularities of her own experiences. As such, I do not make any
claims in this book that women of a certain race, class, or sexual identity
experience or interpret their encounters differently than (or the same as)

women of other social backgrounds. I have tried, in my writing, to allow the women to speak for themselves, drawing connections to their backgrounds and social identities as they see fit.

Before I began the interviews I sent out a short survey, attached to a letter describing the study and inviting young women to participate. The survey asked women their age, year in school, major, country or region where they were raised, and type(s) of relationship (if any) they were in. Using open-ended questions, it also asked how they describe their race(s) and sexual orientation(s). Frustrated by social conventions that collapse individuals' complex race, ethnic, and sexual identities into narrow, predefined categories, I wanted young women to speak for themselves—to describe these aspects of their identities in their own words and with their own concepts. While some of the women responded to the question about race with more typical descriptions like "Black," "African American," "white," or "Asian," others used less conventional language, such as "Mixed" or "MUTT." And one woman simply responded, "I cannot." Similarly, when asked how they describe their sexual orientation(s), most women used terms like "heterosexual," "lesbian," or "bisexual." Others, however, offered such descriptions as "heterosexual/bisexual," or "mostly heterosexual, with a healthy bisexual curiosity, but with no experience." Rather than trying to translate these nuanced descriptions into more traditional categories, I have kept each participant's self-definition intact and included them in the table below. I have also included their own descriptions of their ages, races, and sexualities after each quote throughout the text so that readers may be reminded of these aspects of their identities as they listen to their words. Since we will be hearing a great deal from these young women in subsequent chapters, it is important to understand them as embodied subjects, and to keep that understanding in mind while reflecting on their stories. As we can see from reading their self-descriptions, the sample included eighteen- to twenty-two-year-old women across a broad range of race and sexual identities.[6]

| Name | Age | Sexual Identity | Race(s) |
|------|-----|-----------------|---------|
| Alicia | 22 | Heterosexual | Asian |
| Andrea | 20 | — | Mixed (Lebanese/Chinese/Swedish/American) |
| Chloe | 22 | Heterosexual/Bisexual | Caucasian |

| Name | Age | Sexual Identity | Race(s) |
|---|---|---|---|
| Claudia | 21 | Heterosexual | Caucasian |
| Cynthia | 22 | Bisexual | White |
| Darla | 19 | Heterosexual | White |
| Diana | 21 | Bisexual | White |
| Elaina | 22 | Lesbian/Bi | White |
| Evelyn | 21 | Heterosexual | Caucasian |
| Frances | 21 | Heterosexual | American Indian/French |
| Gloria | 20 | Heterosexual | African-American |
| Heidi | 21 | Bisexual | White |
| Henna | 21 | Heterosexual | Korean |
| Jeanne | 18 | Heterosexual | Black, Indian, White |
| Jocelyn | 19 | Hetero | Mutt (Mother Vietnamese, Chinese, French; Father English, Irish, German, Italian, Mexican, Danish, Swiss, French) |
| Laura | 22 | Bisexual | Bi-racial/West Black Indian, White American |
| Louise | 21 | Hetero | White |
| Martha | 19 | Female | White |
| Melissa | 21 | Heterosexual | Eastern European-American Jew |
| Natalie | 19 | Bisexual | Unimportant |
| Olivia | 22 | Heterosexual | Caucasian |
| Paula | 20 | ? | Spanish-American |
| Rachel | 21 | Heterosexual | White |
| Robin | 21 | Heterosexual | I cannot |
| Sara | 20 | Mostly heterosexual with a healthy bisexual curiosity, but with no experience | White |
| Sondra | 19 | Heterosexual | Afro-American/Native American |
| Stephanie | 21 | Heterosexual | White |
| Theresa | 19 | Heterosexual | Biracial |
| Tonya | 18 | Straight | Jewish/White by race and religion |
| Wendy | 22 | Heterosexual | Puerto Rican/Italian |

My understanding of subjectivity helped determine how I interviewed the participants. Since I wanted to learn about contradictions, I needed to create a context that encouraged women to reflect on the complexities of their lived experiences. Aware that in interviews or surveys participants often feel compelled to smooth out apparent incongruities and articulate a clear and consistent perspective, I began by telling each woman that I was interested in hearing what was confusing, complicated, or counterintuitive—that I did not expect her to have just one set of opinions or one type of experience. If young women considered particular experiences straight-forward, I was, of course, interested in hearing about that. But I wanted them to know that I both expected and valued the nuances in their stories and that I did not see them as "wishy-washy" for having multiple perspectives or for being unsure. During the interviews, when women seemed to focus on just one aspect of their experiences, I asked questions such as "How else did it feel?" "Did you ever have an experience where it went differently?" or "Were there any parts of it that felt good/bad?" Almost inevitably, the women would offer a different facet of their thinking or share another story that seemed to counter, in some ways, the example they had just given. It is important to note that I was not trying to "lead" participants by suggesting that what a woman had just told me was untrue or deliberately partial. Rather, I attempted to create a safe space that prompted women to reflect on the full range of their perspectives and experiences, hopefully secure in the knowledge that I viewed all aspects of those perspectives and experiences as authentic and meaningful.

Our conversations were long and intense. While I brought a list of questions to guide discussion (see appendix A), each interview took on a life of its own. Women shared stories of first kisses, sex education classes, and early stolen glimpses of parents' pornographic magazines. They recounted their struggles and dilemmas in deciding whether, when, and with whom to have sex. Most told of experiences marked by pain, betrayal, or humiliation, of trusting too much, of demanding too little, of trying to come to terms with their own and others' responsibility in relationships and encounters where things had "gone badly." They spoke of their hopes and expectations, their fears and disappointments, their convictions and doubts. Their recollections were peppered with anger, disgust, and disappointment, with laughter, excitement, and possibility. Throughout the interviews, many women expressed frustration that they lacked spaces in their lives to muse on these issues—to tell their stories and have them heard.

Many participants told me they wanted to share their perspectives in the hopes that they would help others by bringing women's difficult experiences to light. But it quickly became clear in our conversations that the interviews also served a more personal need for reflection and confirmation of their most intimate experiences. Women left saying things like "This felt really empowering"; "It's such a relief to finally talk about this stuff—I'm going to think a lot more about it now"; or "This has made me want to go out and talk with my friends about these things." This, it seems to me, is the essence of qualitative, feminist research. It is clear that many social researchers are committed to conducting studies that help women through the benefits of their *findings*. But deeply feminist research also strives to provide empowering opportunities for participants to reflect critically on their experiences through the very *process* of the research (Fine and Phillips, 1990; Ladner, 1971; Lather, 1986; 1991; LeCompte and Bennet, 1988; Linton, 1989). Patti Lather (1986), for instance, argues that social research must have "catalytic validity," that its design must prompt participants to grapple with the issues they are raising through the research process. Feminist research entails a collaboration between researcher and participants, so that "through dialogue and reflexivity, design, data and theory emerge, with data being recognized as generated from people in a relationship" (Lather, 1991, 72).

With this in mind, I also invited participants to take part in group discussions where they could grapple with hetero-relational issues collectively with other young women, and where they could analyze the findings along with me. After completing the thirty interviews, I sent out another letter to all participants, inviting them to engage in a discussion group about the issues we had discussed in the individual interviews. I hoped that the discussion group would create an ongoing context where women could bounce ideas off one another, listen to peers with different perspectives, and explore these issues even more fully than we had in the individual interviews. Six women agreed to take part in the group, which met one evening a week, for approximately two hours per session, over a four-week period. We sat in a small, private lounge on the college campus, munching on snacks, sharing stories, and spinning ideas. Although I introduced topics and asked probing questions, my role quickly became more of a facilitator than an interviewer, as group members asked and responded to one another's questions and built on one another's ideas. The conversation took on vibrant and supportive tones. Participants shared anger and sadness over each other's pains and laughed together over the sometimes funny or stilted messages they had received from families, women's magazines, or sex education (see appendix B for an overview of group interview discussion topics).

In both the individual and group interviews, I asked young women to reflect on hetero-relations across multiple levels. For instance, I asked them their thoughts on rape, harassment, and battering in general, as well as their thoughts on violence or domination in their own experiences. I was interested in whether they distinguished between their own and other women's experiences when considering whether force or coercion was acceptable in hetero-relationships. I was also interested in knowing the extent to which their abstract convictions (such as "I don't think a woman should ever put up with a domineering man" or "It's never a woman's fault for being raped") meshed with their personal experiences (such as "He's sort of controlling, but it's not that bad" or "I really only have myself to blame"). Each interview thus included discussion of young women's general attitudes about how hetero-relations "should" be, their personal standards and expectations for their own relationships and encounters, and their lived experiences as they actually played out in their intimate relations with men.

## Interpretive Dilemmas

In addition to taking part in individual and group interviews, I had wanted young women to collaborate with me in analyzing the data they had produced. At the beginning of this project, I envisioned a fully collaborative process of data analysis in which most, if not all, of the participants would engage in the reading and interpretation of their own interview transcripts. As I formed ideas about themes that emerged across the interviews, I wanted to see what young women had to say about the stories they had told and the perspectives they had shared. To my disappointment, however, the participants expressed an overwhelming reluctance even to read through their own transcripts. Some of the women indicated that they simply lacked the time, that they found themselves too caught up in the pressures of the semester to participate in this aspect of the study. I came to see that what I had considered a genuine gesture of reciprocity and respect was, understandably, perhaps too much to ask for some of the research participants. More disturbing, however, was the finding that several women experienced considerable dissonance at the thought of reviewing their own transcripts. While these women indicated that they had found their interviews helpful for exploring their own experiences, as one young woman put it, she "couldn't bear to see them in black and white." I found such statements particularly provocative. I had asked women to collaborate in their own analysis in an effort to give them more control and to invite complexity and multiple layers of meaning, even beyond those articulated in the original interviews. And yet, rather than seeing such collaboration as a welcomed opportunity to gain and share insights, some women viewed the prospect of reading their own words as too time-consuming, at best, or, worse, as threatening or otherwise disturbing. To say the least, I was humbled and prompted to rethink my own assumptions about the collaborative possibilities of feminist, qualitative research.

While I continue to be committed to the idea of catalytic validity (Lather, 1986), I am also concerned about the implications of opening up possible new understandings with women, only to have us each walk away at the end of the interview. Although all the participants described the interview experience as helpful and enlightening, and although I provided each woman with my telephone number, an invitation to call if she wished to speak further, and a resource sheet including hotline numbers and counselors in case she wanted to discuss these issues with someone else, I worry about the implications for women who said such things as "I guess it really was a little like acquaintance rape, although I never thought of it as that until just now." I also wondered how to make sense of women's reluctance to read their own transcripts. Was it that the interview had been sufficiently satisfying that they felt no need to revisit these issues? Were they really just too busy? Or did the interviews somehow open up new ideas and dilemmas they found too disturbing to contemplate further? No doubt, the "truth" lies somewhere in between for various women. I certainly do not mean to imply by my concern that these young women are incapable of incorporating any new insights gained through the interview into their own lives and their own thinking. But I do remain conflicted about the balance between the obvious benefits and the possible costs of asking questions and introducing ideas that may create dissonance for participants. I take seriously the participants' statements that they found both the individual and group interviews positive and empowering. But I believe that qualitative researchers need to grapple further with these issues if research is to have truly empowering impact for participants.

One of the implications of women's decision not to interpret their own data is that I have analyzed the narratives without the benefit of their input. I did fold many questions into the interviews that asked women to reflect critically on what they had just said. For instance, I asked women, "What sense do you make of that?" or "How do you describe that to yourself when you're thinking about your experience?" I also asked the participants in the discussion group to grapple with the themes I was hearing in the individual interviews. While my promise of confidentiality precluded me from sharing individual transcripts with the group, I did ask them to "try on" various interpretations I was considering based on women's stories across the transcripts. I also discussed my conclusions with friends, students, and colleagues from a wide range of backgrounds in an effort to see past any "blind spots" I may have as a white, middle-class, academic, feminist woman in a long-term hetero-relationship. While I have endeavored to incorporate as many perspectives as possible and to preserve women's own meanings and understandings unearthed in the interviews, the process of qualitative data analysis ultimately requires theorizing—that is, interpreting women's words, choosing some stories over others, and using terms to describe women's experiences that they may or may not find appropriate. For instance, I sometimes refer to experiences that fit legal definitions of rape, harassment, or battering as "victimizing" or "abusive," even though individual women might wish to distance themselves from such terms. To some extent, such interpretive license is necessary—otherwise we would simply be left with a stack of unanalyzed transcripts in which many women do not analyze power in their own relationships (even though they do so when reflecting on other women's relationships). Left untheorized, their words might easily be misconstrued or misused as evidence that they have not been victimized when, in fact, their experiences fit not only legal definitions, but also their own definitions of abuse when they examine other women's encounters. I have tried to strike a balance through my decision to quote women extensively in their own words, to note instances where their interpretations may be different from my own, and to theorize about what those differences might say about the hetero-relational contexts in which they experience and make sense of their own encounters.[7]

Finally, although I have endeavored to position both the women's stories and my own interpretations in a larger analysis of complex power dynamics and social-cultural constraints, I am concerned about the dangers of writing about young women's confusions, ambiguities, and contradictions in a context of "zero-sum guilt" (Fine, 1990). In a social and political climate where women are too often assigned full blame (while men are excused) for their own violation if they can be shown at all complicit in their victimization, I worry that revealing the sometimes nebulous nature of consent, coercion, agency, and domination may be misused to suggest that young women somehow "ask for," deserve, or don't mind their own abuse. However, this worry competes with an even stronger concern that if we *do not* explore the textures and nuances of young women's experiences, we may actually help perpetuate women's victimization by failing to acknowledge and appreciate the complexities of their real hetero-relational circumstances, as they live and understand them. As Snitow, Stansell, and Thompson (1983) remind us, if we are to understand women's sexual experiences and work toward sexual justice, we must dare to examine what we may not want to know:

> Intercourse can be rape; it can also be profoundly pleasurable. Sexual experience with men or women can be abusive, objectifying, and degrading, but it can also be ecstatic, inspiring, illuminating. It can also be—and here the inadequacy of a polarized discourse becomes clear—a peculiar mixture of all these things: objectifying and pleasurable, degrading and inspiriting. We must bring together the complexities and contradictions: we must integrate what we know with what we don't want to know. (42)

I have attempted to resolve my dilemma by presenting the multiple layers of meaning in young women's experiences, while continually reminding readers how these sit within a larger context of cultural constraints and gendered power asymmetries. By demonstrating how young women's choices and perceptions of their hetero-relations are embedded in larger sexist and individualistic cultural contexts, I hope to do justice to the women's stories while also warning against any tendency to blame the "victim."

In the remaining chapters I will discuss the hetero-relational lives of the young women I interviewed, teasing apart their stories and highlighting connections among them. Throughout the analysis, I attempt to draw some coherent theoretical conclusions while simultaneously embracing the complexity and contradictions of women's experiences. My attempt to strike a balance between theoretical coherence and rigorous attention to women's contradictions may pose a particular challenge to readers. The preceding discussion of subjectivity notwithstanding, in a culture that tends to categorize individuals into particular "types," it may be tempting to try to figure out the *real* story of these participants. Are the young women critical agents, actively and heroically resisting abuse and objectification? Or are they really victims, internalizing the terms of their own oppression? I ask that we consider that they may be both and neither—that, in fact, there is no one, *real* story of women's hetero-relational experiences. Throughout the following chapters I will ask readers to suspend preconceived notions about victimization and coping, subjectivity and objectification, consent and coercion, denial and choice. I will ask, instead, that we listen closely to the multiple voices in which women articulate their experiences, and understand that the contradictions in women's stories do not cancel each other out, but rather reveal the intricate textures and nuances of women's hetero-relational lives.

Most important, I ask that readers resist any tendency to distance themselves from the women who have shared these stories. Although sometimes confusing or painful to contemplate, their experiences are, unfortunately, not anomalies. Indeed, theirs are the very types of experiences that I had heard in my classrooms, in my office, and in my casual conversations with other women, which first prompted me to explore these issues in greater depth. Although, of course, we are all "unique," these are, in many ways, "average" women. They are the daughters of plumbers, doctors, homemakers. They are undergraduates studying history, psychology, science, women's studies, and the arts. They might be our sisters, our classmates, our students, or our daughters. As they share their struggles to make sense of male aggression and to find meaning in their hetero-relationships, we need to understand them as embodied young women using the cultural categories available to them to interpret their experiences. In short, we must remember to problematize the constraining social practices and cultural discourses that have informed their (and perhaps our) gendered development, rather than problematizing the women themselves.

3

■　　■　　■　　■　　■　　■　　■　　■　　■

# What's a Young Woman (Not) to Think?

*Sifting through Early Messages about
Hetero-Relations*

It's funny how you just pick up these messages so early on. I mean, it's
not like anybody even necessarily has to teach you directly, but you get
these messages all growing up, and whether you believe them in your
conscious mind or not, . . . they kind of stick. Sometimes you try to fight
against them with what you think now, but they still nag at you from the
back of your mind. Those early messages . . . it's hard to put your finger
on them exactly, but they're a lot more powerful than you'd like to think.
—Diana, 21, "bisexual," "white"

I BEGAN THIS STUDY seeking clearer understandings of the nuances and apparent contradictions in young women's contemporary thinking about their hetero-relations. In conducting the interviews, however, I
came to understand that their current perceptions and relational decisions
were rooted in lessons learned in childhood and early adolescence.[1] As
women spoke, stories about these early lessons wove in and out of their reflections on both their past and present experiences. Consistent with my

understanding of the social construction of subjectivity, it quickly became clear that I could not do justice to women's fluid and multifaceted subjective experiences without first backing up to examine the cultural messages that, early on, began to contextualize their current perceptions.

Eager to understand these early influences, I asked them what kinds of messages they had received from their families, their teachers, their peers, and the media. What did their caregivers or siblings tell them (through their words or their actions) about sex, gender, and romance? What had they learned in sex education? What kinds of books, magazines, TV shows, and videos were they drawn to, and what did these sources have to say about hetero-relations? What about pornography? How did their friendships and adolescent sexual experiences help to shape their early understandings? I wanted to learn what types of images and ideas they found most compelling, what they resisted, and what they accepted as simply "the truth." As I asked such questions, women's memories came pouring forth. At times they were comical, as when Andrea laughingly told of her childhood penchant for *Brady Bunch* reruns, and of how she came to believe that the kind and virtuous Carol Brady (the mother on that show) was the ideal image of a "good woman." Sometimes they were painful, as when Robin described the sense she got from her sex education teacher that women's bodies were dirty and that normal women did not feel desire. Often messages that seemed troubling to women in retrospect had simply seemed like "a given" at the time, as when Wendy recalled her grandmother's cautions that when it comes to relationships, "men don't come through." Like Diana, women noted that they were not always conscious of receiving these messages at the time. But those early ideas and images had clearly made a strong impression, and often they had left them feeling deeply conflicted about male and female entitlement and responsibility in their hetero-relationships.

The young women I interviewed felt a strong need during adolescence for information and spaces to talk about sexuality and relationships. Yet few expressed satisfaction with the types of information they received or the forms in which they received it. Since the women in this study came through middle school and high school during a time when HIV/AIDS was well known (although still often misunderstood) and teenage pregnancy was framed as a public emergency, I had hoped that their educators would have been more forthcoming about sexuality and relationships than my own were some twenty-five years ago. However, the participants' early educations also took shape during the conservative Reagan/Bush era of the late 1980s and early 1990s. While liberals and conservatives engaged in heated debates regarding the distribution of condoms, access to information about birth control and abortion, parental notification/consent, and the inclusion of gay and lesbian sexualities in the curriculum, schools increasingly chose or were forced to retreat from discussions of "controversial" issues like abortion or birth control, let alone desire.[2] Never particularly progressive from its inception, school-based sex education became ever more watered down in the face of mounting pressures from the Right. As the participants' experiences confirmed, sex education in many districts has been largely reduced to "disaster control" (Sears, 1992), restricted to endorsing abstinence and teaching students to "just say no."[3]

I had also hoped that the participants would have reaped the benefits of the women's movement's efforts to enhance girls' and women's options and sense of entitlement (both sexual and nonsexual), to bring violence against women to light, and to critique the androcentric, racist, and hetero-sexist assumptions underlying long-standing norms regarding relationships and sexual practices. I found that, in many ways, they had. Two-thirds had taken at least one gender studies course in college, and many had read the important and provocative works of such writers as Toni Morrison, Alice Walker, Cherríe Moraga, bell hooks, and Chandra Mohanty in their literature and cultural studies courses. The participants spoke often and easily about feminist politics and gender, race, class, and sexual inequalities. They were outspoken about violence against women and seemed remarkably uninhibited about telling me, an adult researcher, the details of their sex lives—something my friends and I would never have considered doing when we were in college. Some also spoke of their mothers as second-wave feminists with whom they could discuss questions about their bodies and their sexualities. They recalled reading about women's sexualities and girls' sexual development in such books as *The New Our Bodies Ourselves* (Boston Women's Health Book Collective, 1984) and *Are You There God? It's Me, Margaret* (Blume, 1971). And all were able to critique the sexist (and often racist, classist, and hetero-sexist) images they encountered in their women's magazines, in movies, and on TV.

Yet in other ways, they seemed as affected (if not more) by the backlash against feminism as they were by the gains of the movement itself. Even as they spoke with outrage against male violence, they admitted to having internalized many victim-blaming assumptions when it came to explaining their own experiences. They discussed their convictions that they could be smart, independent, and sexually assertive, yet they worried about being seen as unfeminine or as coming on too strong. They were told by their mothers or other adults to diet, to hide their periods from their fathers and brothers, to laugh sweetly at boys' jokes, and to refrain from "giving in" to men's sexual "advances." They often bought into the suggestions from their teen magazines that if only they had the right hair, the right makeup, the right body, or the right boy, they would be not only be more attractive but also somehow more worthy as women.

As I listened to the women's stories, it became clear that they had received a great deal of information from families, sex educators, friends, and the media; it was just not necessarily the information they were looking for. At first glance, the messages they received often seemed individualized or arbitrary as they were being presented to young women. Strikingly, they never received just one set of clear-cut messages about sexuality, bodies, relationships, or potential victimization. As Frances noted toward the end of her interview, it sometimes felt like she was navigating a "minefield."

> I'm not sure I ever consciously went through them, but now that I'm thinking about it, I feel like I got a whole bunch of mixed messages. Do this, do that, be like this, be like that. You want to be a good girl, but there's a million ways to be that, and a million booby traps along the way. You want to expect a lot from a relationship, from a man, but then you get all these messages that that's not how it turns out. It's hard to know what to think. It feels like a minefield. (Frances, 21, "heterosexual," "American Indian/French")

Across the interviews, the women's stories revealed a subtle, and often not so subtle, flood of conflicting messages about how they should act and what they should expect from themselves, from men, and from their hetero-relationships. Indeed, the contradictions and "booby traps" were dizzying. Yet as I read and reread the interview transcripts, I began to discern certain patterns emerging across the messages these young women took away from the early hetero-relational lessons they had encountered. Although I did not enter into my analysis looking for evidence of particular *types* of messages (I simply wanted to know what messages they had received, rather than seeking to confirm any preconceived categories), I found that these messages seemed to cluster around four dominant themes: how to be a "good woman"; what constitutes "normal" male sexual behavior; what counts as "real" victimization; and what should be expected from men and hetero-relationships. As I looked further into the interview data, it became clear that for each of these themes or questions, two overall sets of largely opposing messages were being conveyed. It also became clear that the participants were not able simply to choose one set of messages and reject the other. As Diana and Frances suggest in their quotes above, even though women were able to critique some of the information they learned, these messages were still quite powerful. As Diana put it, "they still nag at you from the back of your mind."

Sifting through the themes in the interview data, I began to see connections between the lessons they had learned and larger, pervasive cultural discourses regarding gender, sexuality, victimization, and hetero-relationships. Again, I did not enter into this study with these discourses in mind. Rather, listening to the women speak, and poring over their transcripts, I heard echoes of larger cultural assumptions and societal practices in the stories they were conveying. As I noted in chapter 2, discourses reflect dominant ideas and practices that tell us what is normal, natural, or simply "the ways things are" or the way they "should be." Like the clear surrounding fluid in the lava lamp, discourses help shape our thinking, often without our awareness that they are even there; they also provide the raw materials from which we form our perceptions and interpret our experiences. Conveyed through cultural institutions (such as the law, the media, and disciplines like psychology that normalize certain behaviors and pathologize others), they are also transmitted to us (and we, in turn, reproduce them, by consent or by silence) through our personal experiences with our families, educators, partners, and friends.

Rather than speaking to any one, dominant discourse, these women's narratives gave voice to four pairs of *conflicting* discourses, about "good" womanhood, "normal" male sexuality, "real" victimization, and "typical" hetero-relationships. In order to appreciate the political, cultural, and personal implications of the contradictory messages participants have encountered, we may find it helpful to look more closely at each of these discourses and examine the larger cultural institutions and practices through which they are conveyed. It is important to note that although I have isolated each of these discourses in an effort to understand them better, they did not sit neatly in isolation from one another in women's stories. As we will see, the messages girls and women received from one source (such as sex education) often conflicted with messages they received from another (such as the media or friends). And participants often received opposing messages from any given source (as when their women's magazines told them to be coy and demure, and yet also to be bold, independent, and sexually adventurous). Indeed, it is the very tensions among these messages that make them so powerful and so difficult for young women to ignore.

In later chapters we will see how these discourses compete for young women's attention as they endeavor to make decisions and make sense of their experiences. In particular, I will examine how women both draw on and resist these discourses as they form attributions for encounters that have "gone badly." We will also see how the troubling *absence* of certain cultural discourses places these women in often stifling double binds and limits the field of interpretive options available as they attempt to define, manage, and understand their experiences of agency and domination in their hetero-relations. In order to illuminate the compelling and often troubling nature of these pervasive discourses, in the present chapter I draw extensively on excerpts from women's interviews to demonstrate the complex twists of experience and cultural interpretations they encountered as they were forming ideas about what is normal, acceptable, or inevitable in their hetero-relationships and sexual encounters.

## Who Is a "Good Woman"?

The participants' stories of their early lessons about hetero-relations reveal a set of two discourses about good womanhood that emerged in the 1970s, 1980s, and early 1990s: a good woman can be "the pleasing woman," or she can be "the together woman." Both of these discourses address women's agency, desires, entitlement, and "proper" roles, particularly within their hetero-relationships and encounters. Although they offer nearly opposite visions of the ideal woman, these two discourses snarl together to pose a series of dilemmas or catch-22s for young women attempting to forge their gendered and sexual identities. As we will see throughout this study, the participants cannot simply choose one discourse and disregard the other. Rather, they typically feel compelled to accommodate themselves to the expectations of both, despite their apparent mutual exclusivity.

### The Pleasing Woman Discourse

The more traditional discourse regarding good womanhood, the "pleasing woman discourse," holds that integral to women's proper gender roles is the desire and ability to be pleasant, feminine, and subordinate to men. Like Victorian prescriptions for the genteel woman, the pleasing woman role stresses morality, sexual "purity," and service to men and children. The pleasing woman is typically portrayed as white, middle- or upper-class (Espin, 1984; hooks, 1981; Robinson and Ward, 1991; Ward, 1996), fragile, and "innocent" (a notion that, of course, equates women's sexual expression with guilt). As feminist theorists have long noted (Bordo, 1989; Brownmiller, 1984; Miller, 1986, Steiner-Adair, 1990), mainstream Western culture associates femininity with passivity, softness, and martyrdom. In the pleasing woman discourse, then, women are assumed to lack, or at least to ignore, their own desires. Instead they are urged to cherish the feminine "virtues" of modesty, attractiveness, and sacrifice to others, particularly men. Embedded in this discourse is a compelling contradiction. On the one hand, women are not portrayed as active subjects in their own decision making, relationships, or sexualities. Rather, their job is to sit sweetly in wait for a man to act, and they derive their sense of power from being needed. On the other hand, women are *expected* to act—not passively, but assertively—in their quest to satisfy the wants and needs of men. In other words, the pleasing woman is somehow supposed to be *actively selfless*. While she is expected to tailor her appearance and behaviors to the desires of men, she should not be a desiring sexual subject herself.

The pleasing woman discourse was readily apparent in the teen and women's magazines that the majority of the participants read regularly throughout their adolescence. Often focusing heavily on "how to get a man," these magazines made clear that this should be done without seeming aggressive or "slutty"—a pleasing woman is always discreet. The participants' recollections suggest that these magazines communicated the pleasing woman discourse rather explicitly through such tips as how to tilt one's head, smile coyly, and dangle one's foot while listening attentively to boys and laughing demurely at their jokes. Suggestions that women should have "baby-soft" skin, long, flowing hair, smooth underarms, and genitals that smell like flower gardens revealed a presumed connection between femininity and youthful "innocence," as well as a suggestion that women's faces and bodies are flawed and in need of enhancement, reshaping, and camouflage. These messages conveyed the notion that women's bodies are not the sites of active desire, but rather objects to be admired and kept under control.

Claudia learned from women's and teen magazines that she should strive for a "sophisticated look" at the office (although, reading these magazines as an adolescent, she had no office to go to), while still managing to be coy, charming, and innocent in her relationships. Like many women in the study, she got mixed messages about how to present herself, yet she found each of these messages compelling and wanted to incorporate all of them into her own persona. One theme that stood out, though, was that even when presenting themselves as professional and sophisticated, women should always endeavor to appear "soft" and "very female." Even as she tried to envision herself like the models in her magazines, she struggled with the realization that none of them seemed like her.

> They would have these do's and don'ts for dressing and hair and makeup. . . . But the other thing that drew me in was that the clothes and makeup and hair they showed for romance were mostly soft and sheer, or maybe whites and pastels. You just got the impression you were supposed to be strong, but not too strong, during the day, and sweet and innocent by night. You saw these models who looked coy and charming and innocent, you know, who looked up out of the corner of their eye and had pouty, soft lips. I struggled a lot to find the right look, because none of them seemed like me, and yet I wanted to be all of them. (Claudia, 21, "heterosexual," "Caucasian")

Olivia, describing her early experience with women's magazines (and confessing to still having a "secret stash"), indicated that she feels compelled to read them, and yet typically feels bad about herself when she does. She described the pleasing woman discourse's assumption that those who do not achieve the proper "look" have somehow failed as women:

> There's this new thing you can put on your face, and there's this new diet program, and it's just somehow implied you failed, you haven't fixed it by

now. But you know, in all of my magazines, every month there was something new that I could do to myself to fix these things, whether or not I could afford it. But I have no right to complain about it because why don't I just put ten pounds of makeup on my face and it will fix it. . . . *Self* [magazine] sort of makes me feel guilty, but damn it, I can't afford these new two-hundred-dollar running shoes, therefore I can't complain that I can't do anything about it. I'm not a wealthy person who can spend three hours a day at a gym with a personal trainer. . . . I have done one thing that I think has helped me a bit lately, that I don't have as many mirrors in my apartment. I think for too long as an adolescent I had too many mirrors, and that really just cut yourself down. (Olivia, 22, "heterosexual," "Caucasian")

As Olivia's experience with popular women's magazines suggests, the pleasing woman discourse presupposes not only the willingness, but also the financial capability to change one's shape, cover one's "flaws," and adorn oneself with expensive clothes and accessories. Unable to afford the magazines' recommended wardrobes, health club memberships, or makeup, Olivia was left feeling bad about herself. Interestingly, she attributed her dissatisfaction with herself as much to her own image in the mirror as to the unrealistic images presented in her magazines. Sadly, rather than deciding not to look at the magazines, she got rid of her mirrors, deciding, instead, not to look at herself.

The women's magazines' rendering of the pleasing woman discourse implies not only a certain socioeconomic status, but also a privileging of certain race-related characteristics that cast "whiteness" as the ideal. Gloria discussed the pain she felt as an African American teenager looking through women's and teen magazines and finding no images to which she could relate.

I used to go through all the magazines for tips on how to improve my appearance, you know, my posture, my complexion, my hair, my clothes. Oh yeah, and my body. Don't even get me started on my body. And all the pictures and articles and ads in those magazines, all they address is white women. And even most of the magazines that target Black women don't necessarily look like real Black women. I mean, those models, that may be Black skin, but that is not a Black nose and that is not a Black mouth, and that certainly isn't natural Black hair. And all my friends as a teenager, they would look at white women's magazines, and when I looked at them, which I did a lot, all I would feel was bad about myself and my Blackness. I felt like, you know, I just didn't come close to fitting the ideal and I would never be able to be beautiful. (Gloria, 20, "heterosexual," "African American")

In addition to promoting very narrow, often unhealthy, and classist and racist standards of physical beauty, the pleasing woman discourse emphasizes selflessness and deference to men as essential elements of good womanhood. This message can be seen in the "good woman" role portrayed in movies, television programs, and commercials, where the adoring female martyr wins the love and devotion of her man and her family. The participants' romance novels promoted the idea that, to the extent that women do experience their own desire, it is fulfilled as they, passive and demure, are ravaged by strong and lustful men whose passions they have aroused through their impeccable femininity. Beauty pageants, watched avidly by most of the women in this study from a very early age, further the message that women should find fulfillment in being beautiful, "congenial," and desired by men.

Despite its focus on sexual "purity," ironically, elements of the pleasing woman discourse were incorporated into the pornography some participants found hidden away in their parents' basements or in their siblings' drawers. Natalie, for instance, remembered seeing pornographic images of women who were certainly seductive, but also quite docile. Not unlike the "fairy tale princess" many participants described seeing in beauty pageants, these models represented an unclothed version of the coy and objectified woman posing for the male gaze. In the pornographic version, however, these soft, "perfect" women were, as Natalie put it, "inviting men to do something naughty."

> The women were in these garter belts and everything, but they were just laying around in the bathtub or on satin sheets and what have you. They were very sexy, but they were just lying there in these seductive poses, or bending over, holding their breasts and sticking their asses out. Like a come-fuck-me pose, but also coy and sex kitten–like. They all had perfect bodies and faces, which now I know they're all airbrushed. But it was like the peachy, docile little sex kitten, inviting men to do something naughty. (Natalie, 19, "bisexual"; asked to describe her race(s), she wrote, "unimportant")

Beyond prescribing women's "proper" appearance and demeanor, the pleasing woman discourse sets clear rules for women's sexual behavior.

This discourse both draws from and reproduces the classic madonna/ whore or virgin/whore dichotomy still prevalent in Western culture. The participants encountered this discourse quite clearly in the emphasis their teachers and caregivers placed on virginity as a prerequisite for female respectability.[4] Describing her teachers' attitudes toward female sexuality, Theresa noted that the overall message was one of shame.

> They talked in this judgmental tone. They made it clear that girls who did it didn't care about themselves and that they were dirty little tramps or something. And I just sat there so ashamed. I felt like I was bad and they probably knew it. I would die if they knew I was having sex already because they would be so disgusted or disappointed in me. They didn't even try to hide their feelings about girls who gave in or anything. They made it very clear, just through their tone of voice and the look on their faces and their choices of words that they thought those girls were weak and shameful. And I was sitting there listening to them and, I mean, that was me. (Theresa, 19, "heterosexual," "biracial")

Throughout the women's sex educations, they heard messages that "good girls" are essentially asexual, at least until marriage, and that young women who respect themselves will find ways to fight off boys and men who "only want one thing." Although approximately half of young women in the United States have had intercourse by the time they are eighteen (Abma et al., 1997), there clearly continues to exist a strong pressure to believe that "good girls don't," and that those girls who "do" should be ashamed of themselves.

Just as the pleasing woman discourse reveals classist assumptions about women's appearance, it often uses classist language to describe young women's sexuality. Sara's teachers, for instance, made it clear that "sexually advanced" girls were "dirty" and "lacking class"—certainly not images this discourse associates with a pleasing young woman. Apparently intending to dissuade their students from sexual expression and the negative repercussions associated with it, Sara's teachers transported into their classrooms the pleasing woman discourse's classist notion that young women who express their sexualities are somehow "cheap" (as though women's sexualities are commodities that should command a high price?). It is interesting to note that her teachers made no such association with male sexuality.

> I remember my teachers saying that girls who sexually were advanced, that was their word for it, were seen as cheap. They kept using these expressions to scare us, like we would be perceived as cheap and easy and loose, or dirty. Seen that way by boys. Certainly seen that way by our teachers, they made that much clear. Girls who were classy were supposed to be discriminating and proper. Girls who had sex were lacking in self-respect and lacking in class. It was like they turned up their noses at you when they even talked about it. Like something stinked or something. (Sara, 20, "mostly heterosexual, with a healthy bisexual curiosity, but with no experience," "white")

In addition to linking sexual behavior with social class, the pleasing woman discourse conveys the message that white women are somehow more sexually "pure" than women of other races. As bell hooks (1981) notes in her classic book, *Ain't I a Woman*, this racist and sexist assumption underlies the centuries-old practice of distinguishing "good" women from those who are "fair game" for sexual encounters. In this way, white men are encouraged to "sow their wild oats" with sexually "loose" women (read: women of color and poor or working-class white women), while acting chivalrous toward "good women" (read: middle-class or affluent Caucasian women). While no one in the study reported hearing this message explicitly, they did recall subtle gestures that let them know that adults in their lives held such assumptions. Laura remembered the pain and frustration she and her African American classmates felt as their high school sex education teacher revealed her underlying racist assumptions through her body language.

> I'm sure she wasn't even aware of it, but whenever she would talk about the fact that some girls were probably already doing it, she would always look in the direction of the Black students. She never looked at the white girls when she talked about promiscuity, except when she talked about how good it was that smart girls were willing to wait. But whenever she talked about how some girls were already sexual at a really young age, her eyes would turn to the Black girls, which was all the more annoying because the white girls were doing it just as much as anybody else. I don't think she knew what she was doing, I think it was probably more just subliminal. But we all knew what she was doing. I'm sure the white girls knew it too. (Laura, 22, "bisexual;" "bi-racial/West Black Indian, white American")

Regardless of the types or extent of young women's actual sexual experience, the pleasing woman discourse teaches them that they should not *appear* too "forward," "loose," or "advanced." As Jocelyn's parents warned her, even eating lunch alone in public could suggest a woman's "availability," a message that good girls should never convey. Sondra learned that simply by developing physically more quickly than her peers, a girl could develop a reputation as "unfeminine" or "easy," or both.

> It was embarrassing because all the boys would talk about my breasts, because I had to wear a bra in fifth grade, which was way before any of the other girls in my class. So I got sort of this reputation as easy, even though it wasn't true, and both the boys and the girls in my class treated me like I was different. But the other girls, they would be talking about things they learned in their magazines or from older girls or wherever, about how you should cross your legs and dangle your foot and tilt your head and giggle a lot when a boy is talking to you. You know, like, you should act coy and feminine and show how delicate and dainty you are. But, see, I wasn't delicate or dainty, I was a big girl, and I wasn't ever going to look coy and feminine. So I felt like this overdeveloped cow or something, like I was a horse and all of the other girls were these petite little feminine beauties. I was always alienated and hating my body for what it was, and really resenting the other girls for what they had. (Sondra, 19, "heterosexual," "Afro-American/Native American")

It is important to understand that the pleasing woman discourse takes shape not only through the explicit negativity toward girls who express their sexualities, but also through the relative absence of any positive messages at home or school about female pleasure and desire (Fine, 1988; Phillips and Fine, 1992; Sears, 1992). In most cases, sex education classes revolved around what Frances referred to as "what the instruments are." Significantly, though, none of the young women could remember ever hearing of the clitoris as one of those "instruments." Although Jeanne's teacher made an attempt to discuss the "biology of an orgasm," she failed to entertain any notion of human feelings and desire.

> [My teachers] thought it was like a big radical deal that they would say the word "orgasm" and pretend to tell us about it, but they didn't say anything real or anything we could relate to. We wanted to know what it meant, what

it felt like, if girls got them too, if it was normal to have them or not, things like that. But there was no way they were ever going to deal with stuff on that kind of level. (Jeanne, 18, "heterosexual," "Black, Indian, white")

It is interesting to note that even after her lesson about orgasm, Jeanne was left questioning whether "girls got them too" and whether or not it was "normal" for her to have them. Such residual questions suggest that while her teacher approached an important topic that many educators simply ignored, the lesson still revolved around *male* orgasm and was not contextualized by any discussion of desire. To the extent that any of the participants' teachers considered desire, they framed boys as the sexual actors, and girls (if they respected themselves) as the ones who should resist males' advances. Girls' pleasure and entitlement in their own right clearly fell outside the realm of the sex education classroom. Heidi's sex education discussion of orgasm was the closest any came to acknowledging female pleasure, and even this fell short.

They just said, "You're going to want to do this, and you know, you should wait as long as you can." Boys had orgasms, but I don't know, they said boys come and girls come, so I said, "What do you mean? What happens? I know when a boy comes he ejaculates and this white stuff comes out. What happens when a girl comes?" They never explained. They couldn't explain. I was a little confused. (Heidi, 21, "bisexual," "white")

The *silence* surrounding female pleasure and desire, juxtaposed with the *presumption* of male sexual desire, suggests that young women's active sexualities are inconsistent with "normal" womanhood. As many participants noted, the absence of discussion of female desire, coupled with the hushed tones (and often the sex-segregated classes) surrounding discussions of female bodies, suggested to them that female sexuality must be kept hidden, and that their own desires were somehow trivial, dangerous, or abnormal.

The pleasing woman discourse is troubling not only in its denial and attempted suppression of young women's desires, but also in its recasting of inequalities to look like equality and its casting of women as responsible for sustaining those inequalities (Haavind, 1984; Hare-Mustin, 1991). By encouraging young women to aspire to an "ideal" that constricts their sexual agency and promotes a sense of dissatisfaction and shame with their own gendered and racial embodiment, the pleasing woman discourse endorses women's subordination and objectification in the name of "good womanhood." Essentially, if men do not deem a young woman pleasing, she has failed as a woman.

## The Together Woman Discourse

Competing with the pleasing woman discourse, the more contemporary, but still problematic "together woman discourse" promotes the notion that a "together" woman is free, sexually sophisticated, and entitled to accept nothing less than full equality and satisfaction in her sexual encounters and romantic relationships. Accepting uncritically the liberal, androcentric "ideals" of total autonomy, self-direction, and entitlement to sex and relationships without personal responsibility, this discourse is, in some ways, an offshoot of liberal feminism. It urges that women can (and must) "have it all" and that they can, with sufficient determination, refuse to let anything hold them back from their own sense of pleasure and fulfillment.

The together woman discourse lurked alongside the pleasing woman discourse in the participants' magazines, movies, and conversations with friends. Magazine articles conveyed this discourse quite clearly by teaching young women how to be sexually sophisticated and suggesting that they should freely seek out sexual and other pleasures. Aspiring to be grown-up and independent, participants often found this discourse particularly intriguing. As Claudia's experience suggests, the together woman discourse promises a sense of freedom, excitement, and a certain power over men.

> The looks were always about how to either look sweet and innocent, and those were your pastels, your angora sweaters, your Bambi eyes, or they were about how to look sassy, together, flirty, and sophisticated. Sexy, you know, alluring. We all wanted to be that woman who just oozes sexuality, the one who has all the exciting affairs and wears bold lipstick and attracts men through her amazing sexual flair. We were into the little miniskirts and the tight clothes, and we wanted cleavage. There was something about those women who were mysterious, unpredictable, sassy, and they were always fickle and sort of frustrating to men who wanted them so bad. She was the knockout ditz who would get flowers from a man and then throw them in his face. (Claudia, 21, "heterosexual," "Caucasian")

Ironically, as Claudia's experiences indicated, the together woman often comes across as one who is "sassy," "flirty," "mysterious," and "fickle." Unfortunately, while the message supposedly promotes independence and unbridled sexual pleasure, the sexually "together" woman often is still portrayed as possessing childlike qualities. Whereas the pleasing woman discourse promotes "baby-soft innocence" as a marker of good womanhood, the together woman discourse often promotes "sassiness," an equally childish quality, as the embodiment of female sexual liberation.

While this discourse maintains that full sexual freedom indicates strong womanhood, women who have sex *too* freely are often criticized as being desperate and lacking self-respect. Thus, a together woman is sexually competent and satisfied, but never "cheap" or "needy." In its appeal to classist language in the definition of "good womanhood," we see an overlap between this discourse and the pleasing woman discourse. But while the pleasing woman discourse describes a "classy" young woman as someone who turns down boys' advances, the together woman discourse portrays a "classy" woman as one who is discriminating and "together" enough to find sexual satisfaction without appearing desperate.

A further irony in this discourse is that while it tells women that they, as much as men, deserve the "ideals" of individuation, such ideals are very often put forth as an effective new way of *attracting men*. Such notions were fueled quite explicitly by the participants' women's and teen magazines, which spoke of the sexiness, allure, and mystique of today's strong, independent woman. Men, they were told, are mesmerized by a woman who knows her own mind and body, and is not afraid to take control. Olivia remembered encountering this message in her magazines and romance novels as a teen.

> Some of the articles in my magazines and even some romance novels were about how bold, independent women drive men wild. Of course, they still had to be pretty and sexy, but it was like the women were the ones that had this allure, this charm. Even though a lot of the articles and pictures were about women being kind of sweet and coy to attract a guy, other ones were about women having these wild sexual appetites, and men loving that. (Olivia, 22, "heterosexual," "Caucasian")

Whereas the pleasing woman discourse contends that women should be desirable *without* being sexual agents, the together woman discourse suggests that in order to be desirable, women *must* be sexual agents. Although this discourse appears, on the surface, to promote complete sexual freedom, that "freedom" is confined to *hetero*-sexuality. At no point in their interviews did the participants recall any images that promoted women's sexual freedom with other women. Indeed, the together woman is still assumed to want, and to have, a man. As Melissa apparently learned, even providing sexual pleasure for oneself will not do; a sexual woman must be "pathetic" if she does not have a male partner. Recounting her discovery of a vibrator and erotic books in her mother's bedroom when she was thirteen, she recalled very mixed feelings about using and enjoying them.

> There was this whole ritual like finding it and sneaking in there and using it. . . . I had fun, but then I'd feel guilty and I'd feel like something is wrong with me and . . . yeah, I think I figured out what an orgasm is. But you never feel just one way about something. I think I was feeling really bad. That's how my mother is, this sort of wonderful woman who's smart and successful, who had her shit together in so many ways, but couldn't be happy with love and couldn't be happy with men, and here she was with her vibrator. It was like, this is really pathetic. (Melissa, 21, "heterosexual," "Eastern European-American Jew")

Although this was potentially an opportunity to see herself and her mother as sexually self-sufficient, Melissa's feelings of pleasure were tainted by the sense that both she and her mother were "pathetic" for exploring sexual pleasure on their own. While she said she had fun and enjoyed experiencing orgasms, she nonetheless assumed that something was wrong with her, and with her mother. She had incorporated the ironic notion that "together" women must not be on their own—that they must have a man. The idea of women finding pleasure by themselves meant they couldn't get their "shit together."

Like the pleasing woman discourse, the together woman discourse incorporates certain racist assumptions as well. As Sondra's experience suggests, the association of race with together womanhood is not straightforward. Growing up in a predominantly African American urban neighborhood, she received empowering messages from her mother, her aunts, and her female community members about African American women's strength. Consistent with research on families of color who raise their daughters to be "resisters" (Collins, 1994; Robinson and Ward, 1991;

Taylor, 1996; Ward, 1996), the women in Sondra's life had raised her to critique racist stereotypes and trust her own voice. Yet she also attended a predominantly white school outside her neighborhood. There she learned that strength, for African American girls, was often interpreted quite differently than in her own community. Although her white classmates were able to talk with their friends about their sexual encounters, Sondra felt she would be stereotyped as "a promiscuous Black girl" if she spoke about her own.

> I learned from the women in my community that Black women are strong and independent. It's always known that it's better if you have a man, but it's okay if you don't. Women are the strong ones. And I remember feeling good about myself and the women in my family. Now that I'm older, I really do. But then at school, I figured out that if Black girls are too strong or outspoken or whatever, you're seen as pushy or out of line. Even if you're going after the same things white girls are. They're ambitious, but I'm pushy or mouthy. And then, you know, everybody expects Black girls to be promiscuous, so you can't let people know if you're having sex. Not if you still want to be respected by your white friends. Because even though they're your friends, everybody still has that stereotype that Black girls are easy, you know, "Oh, that promiscuous Black girl," so you don't want to feed into that. (Sondra, 19, "heterosexual," "Afro-American/Native American")

Although Sondra and the women in her home life were able to see and critique the racist double standards underlying societal prescriptions for "pleasing" and "together" womanhood, those at school simply reproduced the sexism and racism woven through these "ideals." Valuing the respect of her white friends and teachers, the onus was thus on Sondra to censure her own behavior and storytelling so as not to fuel the stereotypes already lurking in the minds of those outside her home community.

While elements of the together woman discourse can be seen in the early lessons provided by some teachers and parents, their support of young women's entitlement was generally limited to academic and professional pursuits. Although some adults did convey to young women that they were entitled to fair treatment in their relationships with men, these messages seldom included a promotion of young women's *sexual* entitlement. Rather, to the extent that adults conveyed the together woman discourse, it focused more commonly on the idea that a self-respecting woman should leave abusive relationships, and that she should refuse to put up with anything less than total respect from her male partners. Evelyn's mother, who had experienced physical and emotional abuse in her former marriage, stressed that Evelyn should be independent enough always to be able to leave a relationship if a man showed any abusive tendencies.

> We never talked about sex, per se. I don't think my mother could have handled that. But she did tell me, "Evelyn, don't you ever let a man raise a hand to you. If he ever touches you, or degrades you, I don't care what, you just leave. You're worth more than that." I knew that because that's why she got out of her marriage, because he hit her. That's why it was so important to her that I be my own person and not depend too much on a man. (Evelyn, 21, "heterosexual," "Caucasian")

Although adults often modeled relationships based on inequality, and although some parents, such as Henna's, taught their daughters that a woman's place was behind/beneath her man, several parents promoted the message that women should insist on being treated with respect. The support of women's entitlement to respect in their hetero-relations is, of course, encouraging. However, this support failed to include acknowledgment of gendered power relations or women's sexual entitlement, and it typically was not backed up by any concrete mechanisms (beyond "just leave" or "just say no") for attaining the self-determination parents and teachers advocated.

Throughout its various articulations, the together woman discourse poses problems for young women. First, by insisting that women can be completely autonomous agents, this discourse fails to consider oppressive gendered, racist, hetero-sexist, and classist social structures and practices that deny women's equality and punish them for expressing their own sexualities. As such, the together woman discourse places full responsibility on the individual young woman to overcome any barriers placed in her way. She must somehow "transcend" her gender (and often her race, social class, and sexual identity) and her society's gendered, racist, classist, and homophobic expectations. When she (inevitably) fails to do so, the terms of this discourse would suggest that she simply is not sufficiently "together." The together woman discourse further promotes the notion that since women are presumed able to exert complete control over their own life circumstances, women who are victimized are somehow weak, inept, or lacking in self-respect.

Perhaps most problematic, this discourse also supports an illusion that young women's supposed autonomy and entitlement somehow insulate them from the possibility of victimization. While it is certainly positive for young women to feel entitled to explore and find pleasure in their own sexualities (Fine, 1988; Phillips and Fine, 1992; Phillips, 1996; Tolman, 1996; Tolman and Higgins, 1996), as we will see in later chapters, a false sense of power may also lead them into victimizing situations where men exploit the very real cultural and personal power they can exercise over women.

## What Is "Normal" Male Hetero-Sexuality?

Overlapping the discourses about good womanhood is a second set of discourses concerning the nature of "normal" male sexual behavior. Here, two competing discourses vie for women's attention. The first suggests that healthy and abusive relationships are mutually exclusive. The second discourse contends that aggressive male behavior is a normal and inevitable component of their sexualities—that "boys will be boys." Although these discourses promote vastly different images of male sexuality, they sit alongside one another in the early lessons young women received.

### The Normal/Danger Dichotomy Discourse

Across the various sources of women's early hetero-relational educations, we can hear strong echoes of a particularly powerful cultural discourse that I call the "normal/danger dichotomy discourse." This discourse suggests that Western society abhors violence and holds that "normal" hetero-sexual encounters, relationships, and men are inherently distinct from those that are "dangerous" or "exploitive." Although research by the feminist historian Linda Gordon (1988) suggests that the lines distinguishing "normal" and "abusive" shift across both history and context, the normal/danger dichotomy discourse presumes that clearly perceptible, static, and enforceable lines separate these two (supposedly) obviously different types of relationships. Essentially, there are "good guys" and "bad guys," and the two categories do not overlap.

The normal/danger dichotomy discourse is presumed, perpetuated, and formalized by larger cultural institutions that dichotomize consent versus coercion, and normal versus deviant behavior. The United States' legal system, for instance, tends to criminalize only male aggression that is "clearly" violent, thereby normalizing other, more typical forms of aggressive or exploitive male behavior (Stanko, 1985; 1990). Newly enacted legislation, such as "Megan's Law," reflects the belief that sex offenders are clearly separable from "normal" men, by suggesting that police (and sometimes community) notification by convicted sex offenders will allow parents to protect their children from the dangers "out there."[5] Such laws have received popular support, despite U.S. Bureau of Justice Statistics data indicating that among girls who were reported raped in 1992, 96 percent of those under twelve years old, and 85 percent of those twelve to seventeen years old, were victimized by a family member, friend, or acquaintance (Langan and Harlow, 1994). The discipline of psychology similarly reflects and reproduces this discourse when it labels "sexual deviants," "aggressives," and "dysfunctional families," as distinct from "normals," the presumed nonexploitive/nonaggressive majority, and when it separates studies of "normal" relationships and sexuality from studies of aggression, rape, and family violence.[6]

Compounding these more formal practices, the normal/danger dichotomy discourse is conveyed in popular media and literature. From movies to soap operas to romance novels, we can see images of the strong and heroic man rescuing the helpless woman from a ruthless villain. Indeed, one can turn on the television almost any night and see police dramas featuring women being stalked, raped, and brutalized by evil men, only to be saved by the handsome and benevolent male detective. Unfortunately, these images often draw on racist stereotypes of who is a "good guy" and who is a "bad guy." For instance, reflecting on the TV shows she watched with her family while growing up, Cynthia, a white woman, noted with some embarrassment that the programs were filled with racist assumptions that helped shape her notions about whom to trust and whom to fear.

We watched a lot of TV in my house, that's what we mostly did every night. We watched detective shows, and I realize now that it was always the white woman who was raped or in some kind of trouble, and it was always a white guy who was the hero. And when they caught the guy who did it, it seems like it was always a Black man. Maybe things have changed some, but when I was a kid, that's what you saw. I don't think it registered that that's how it was scripted, but I know it made me fearful of Black men, more so than white men. That's really hard to admit, and now, in my cultural studies class, that's one of the things we're talking about, like how that stuff sort of gets to you, and how it's a real problem. (Cynthia, 22, "bisexual," "white")

Along with their awareness of these broader societal practices, the participants received both warnings and assurances from families, friends, and teachers that were based on, and simultaneously reproduced, the normal/danger dichotomy discourse. Most girls received warnings regarding "perverts," "dirty old men," and the type of boy who "only wants one thing," revealing adults' sense that dangerous males were clearly identifiable and separate from "normal" boys or men. Wendy's experience points vividly to the normal/danger dichotomy discourse in messages from families. Although she was sexually abused by her uncle while growing up, Wendy recalled that her aunts' and grandmother's warnings focused only on danger from strangers or acquaintances outside the family who wanted to harm or take advantage of her. Dangers lurking in the family remained unspoken.[7]

I was supposed to guard myself from the type of guy who would take away my virginity and exploit me. My aunts and my grandmother would warn me that some guys were sexual predators, and that I was to stay clear of those men. But the thing I realize now is so crazy is that all the time they were warning me to stay away from those kind of men, my uncle was sexually, you know, molesting me, but they never warned me that the bad guy could also be the good guy. It's like they assumed that just because people were in the family they were safe. But my grandfather beat me and my grandmother, and my uncle raped me, and I'm sure my grandfather sexually abused my grandmother, like when he would come home drunk and everything, but somehow those men were never talked about as possible sexual abusers. Even though, in reality, they were probably more dangerous than any stranger would be. (Wendy, 22, "heterosexual," "Puerto Rican/Italian")

Interestingly, despite the physical and sexual violation eleven of the young women and/or their female caretakers experienced from family members and friends, only one young woman, Robin, received warnings about potential abuse from those close to her. The focus on danger from strangers, coupled with the lack of apparent concern about danger from acquaintances, suggests that only particular men rape or abuse women, and that these men are distinct from the men with whom women share their everyday lives.

Like Wendy, Chloe received strong warnings not to associate with "the wrong type of boy," and her parents encouraged to seek out a "nice" boy to protect her rather than walking home alone. Having been told of the dangers of male violence, she asked a boy from her church youth group to walk her home one night from an evening meeting when she was thirteen. Although she expected him to protect her from "stranger danger," that same boy forced himself on her and raped her.[8] As Chloe's experience suggests, the normal/danger dichotomy discourse may not only set women up to be unsuspecting victims, it may also deepen the sense of disillusionment and betrayal from that victimization when the very men expected to protect women from danger become the ones who ultimately violate them.

> The thing that was most disillusioning about the whole experience was that this was a boy I thought I'd be safe with. He was supposed to be a good, upstanding boy from a respectable family, but it wasn't true. I was coming home from a CYO meeting, and it was dark out, and I knew my parents didn't want me walking home alone because it might be dangerous. So when this boy from CYO offered to walk me home, I thought it was a really good idea, because I sort of knew him. It never occurred to me that he might be the one who was dangerous, because all the warnings I had always gotten were about strangers who leap out at you from the bushes or lure you into their cars or something. So I thought this guy would protect me, but instead he forced himself on me and made me do things to him sexually. It was so humiliating. I felt so stupid. I felt afterward like I should have known better, but I was always led to believe that you should have a nice boy walk you home, and that the boys in my church group qualified as nice boys. (Chloe, 22, "heterosexual/bisexual," "Caucasian")

When I asked Chloe whether she ever reported the incident or told her parents about it, she explained that her parents would have no category in their minds that would let them believe that she had been victimized by a "nice boy." So strong was the pull of the normal/danger dichotomy discourse, that either they would maintain their belief that he would not do such a thing (and therefore she must be at fault), or they would transform their image of him into a "dangerous" type that she should not have trusted in the first place (again, making her at fault).

> No, I couldn't. I don't think my parents would ever have believed me, that I hadn't done something to go along with it. Either that, or they would have decided all of a sudden that he wasn't actually such a nice boy, even though they thought he was, and they would have told me I should have known better than to go with him. One way or the other, they wouldn't be able to believe me. So I never told anybody about it. I just kept it to myself and dropped out of the CYO.

The normal/danger dichotomy discourse was perpetuated not only by adults in the participants' lives, but also by their peers. As Andrea recalled, she and her friends were actually quite frightened by their parents' warnings about the dangers of accepting rides with strangers and of men hiding in the bushes who wanted to do bad things to little girls (although not, apparently, to little boys). Attempting to conquer and make light of their fears, they made up scary stories to tell one another. In this way, they were able to give voice to their anxieties, to share them with others, and then to laugh at themselves and the stories. This ritual represented both an attempt to deal with, and a reproduction of, the normal/danger dichotomy discourse. Of course, the stories always involved "crazy-looking" strangers, rather than "normal-looking" men or people they knew.

> I remember it was really scary, like you heard about these scary old perverts hiding in the bushes who leap out and abduct little girls. We were too young to know about the sexual stuff, but we knew something really awful could happen to little girls like us. So we used to make up these scary stories, sort of like ghost stories, about these crazy-looking guys in trench coats with peglegs or eye-patches who would steal little girls and kill them or something. We'd all get really scared, and then we'd laugh at each other for being scared, and then we'd tell another story. In a way, it was kind of a way of letting off steam, I guess, because I know we were all really scared. (Andrea, 20, "Mixed–Lebanese/Chinese/Swedish/American"; asked to describe her sexuality, she wrote, "—")

The normal/danger dichotomy discourse appears in a wide range of cultural messages and practices that hold women responsible for acting as gatekeepers of men's actions (White and Niles, 1990). Young women are admonished by sources ranging from women's magazines to "after-school specials" to families, friends, and educators that they can and must "just leave" relationships, jobs, and interactions with boys or men at the first sign that they are dangerous or exploitive. Like the together woman discourse, these messages obviously overlook the lack of resources and the very real physical and material threats that keep many women from "just leaving" or controlling men's aggression (Browne, 1987; Castelano, 1996; Ewing, 1987; Fine, 1983; 1989; Jones, 1994; Phillips, 1989; Walker, 1979; 1989). They also reveal the implicit assumption that there exist two separate kinds of relationships and two separate kinds of men—those that are aggressive/dangerous and those that are normal—and that women are in a position to discern clearly one from the other.

Such practices give the impression that a dangerous or exploitive relationship/man/situation would be visibly identifiable as abnormal, suggesting that women who do not leave, avoid, or prevent such encounters must either be responsible for their own victimization (because they used poor judgment) or not be victimized at all (because they must have "asked for" or chosen to tolerate the behavior). It is important to acknowledge that women's opinions, as well as men's, may be deeply influenced by this discourse. This was frighteningly evidenced by many women's victim-blaming public reactions to the high-profile cases brought against Clarence Thomas, Mike Tyson, and William Kennedy Smith, as well as complaints by some contemporary women authors that women "whine" too much about their own victimization.[9] As Chloe's decision not to tell her parents of her rape reveals, the woman-blaming tendencies fueled by the normal/danger dichotomy discourse find their way into young women's consciousness and help to inform their decision making.

## The Male Sexual Drive Discourse

Compounding and confounding the problems of the normal/danger dichotomy discourse, a second discourse twists the knot of contradictory messages young women inherit about the roles of power, danger, and objectification in their hetero-relations. Indeed, the same culture that claims to abhor violence also eroticizes hetero-sexual male aggression and embraces what Wendy Hollway (1984) has termed the "male sexual drive discourse." This discourse tells us that men possess a natural sexual drive that is inherently compelling and aggressive in its quest for fulfillment.

The male sexual drive discourse is both fueled by and reflected in countless implicit and explicit messages, practices, and priorities woven throughout mainstream Western culture. It is what assures women (and men) that sexualized male aggression, from street harassment to gang rape, is neither a crime nor an act of violation, but just another case in which "boys will be boys." It is what tells us that "working a yes out" (Sanday, 1990) from a nonconsenting woman is not rape, but merely what any "red-blooded American male" would do when aroused. It is what allows defense lawyers to "justify" such behaviors as fraternity gang rape on college campuses and acquaintance rape of women who are drunk or unconscious (Sanday, 1990; 1996; Warshaw, 1988).

As Gloria found when she and her third-grade classmate were assaulted in the school gym by a group of young boys, both adults and peers often regard sexual violation as normal male experimentation. Even though the boys were smaller and younger than the girls they were attacking, they had apparently already learned that they were entitled to violate female bodies. And even though Gloria's teacher saw what happened, he apparently saw no need to address the sexualized nature of the boys' violent behavior.

> And I remember all these little boys. They were all smaller than we were, and they started to proceed to sort of like, rape me. It was very violent. When I look back at it, it's like they weren't getting any sexual pleasure. They were far too young. It must have been something they saw or something, you know? What was scary about it was not having any power because basically the gym teacher actually came in and saw it and broke it up, and he didn't pursue it. It was something that [he] just didn't want to deal with, you know? That was the scary part about it. (Gloria, 20, "heterosexual," "African-American")

Compounding the denial of male responsibility, boys' "experimentation" is often seen as being provoked by girls and young women. By warning young women, "Don't start what you're not willing to finish," the male sexual drive discourse serves to remind them of their vulnerability and subordinate status relative to men (Hare-Mustin, 1991; Frye, 1983; Brownmiller, 1975). As Robin's experience suggests, boys and men often invoke this discourse in their efforts to persuade young women that they must "follow through." She noted that more than one young man had pleaded with her to have intercourse so that they would not have to experience "blue balls" (the supposedly unbearably painful sensation in a man's testicles if he does not ejaculate once aroused).

> Guys will be like, "Come on, you know, if we don't do it, I'm gonna have blue balls! You don't know what it's like! I need it! Why'd you get me so hot if you weren't going to follow through? Come on, this is painful!" And, you know, [*laughing*] I was persuaded by that. I didn't know it was just a myth guys use so they can get what they want. It works! (Robin, 21, "heterosexual"; asked to describe her race(s), she wrote, "I cannot")

The male sexual drive discourse extends beyond the normalizing of aggressive male sexuality. So pervasive is the privileging of male entitlement that aggression moves well beyond merely being naturalized as inevitable; indeed, male domination is often posed as something positive—erotic, flattering to women, an indication of the powers of desire. Such messages are communicated clearly—to women as well as to men—in the eroticizing of women's powerlessness and objectification in pornography (Stoltenberg, 1990; Griffin, 1981; Dworkin and MacKinnon, 1988). Jeanne recalled reading stories in pornographic magazines in which women who were deemed "teases" were "put in their place" by being sexually assaulted. She also learned that women secretly desire to be raped, and that if they led a man on, they deserved it.

> I remember reading this letter from a guy bragging about how this woman was a cock tease and how he put her in her place by fucking the shit out of her. The gist was that she had been leading him on and getting him excited. Then she wouldn't have sex with him, she was just teasing him. But supposedly she really did want to, because he talked about her like she was a slut and really wild and she wanted it, you know? So he forced it on her, and the letter goes on to brag and say how he had her screaming in ecstasy and begging him for more. Anyway, the moral of the story that I took out of it was that if a woman is a cock tease, it's okay, and hot even, to put her in her place and make her pay. That, and that women really like to be raped. (Jeanne, 18, "heterosexual," "Black, Indian, white")

We can also observe the male sexual drive discourse in the romanticizing of movies, soap operas, and novels that collapse categories of love and

male domination (Christian-Smith, 1993; Peiss and Simmons, 1989; Snitow, 1983). Much like the classic scene in *Gone with the Wind* in which
Rhett Butler sweeps Scarlett O'Hara off her feet and carries her, against
her protests, up the stairs and off to bed, passion and love are everywhere
confounded with women's objectification and male aggression. Such images suggest that domination and aggression are not only inevitable male
privileges, but actually natural and desirable elements of hetero-relations,
even for women. Soap operas, watched daily by many of the participants,
convey this message quite poignantly. Although Cynthia noted that she actually learned some valuable information about date rape and AIDS from
her soap operas, her overall impression was that the story lines often characterized lust as synonymous with male aggression.

> But even still, a lot of the messages, I guess most of the messages are about
> men taking control, and passion is about lust and aggressive men having
> their way with the female character, and that's what women see on the TV
> as being about good romance. . . . Lots of times it's the man is pressuring
> the woman really hard, and she's saying, "No, stop, we can't do this," and
> then his passion takes over and he picks her up and puts her on the bed and
> gets on top of her, and then she gives in and she loves it. It's like, that's pretty
> much what happens. Of course, you never see it the other way around
> though. (Cynthia, 22, "bisexual," "white")

Young women found similar messages in romance novels, which the
majority of the participants acknowledged were a particularly compelling
source of entertainment and hetero-relational images during their teenage
years. Stephanie, who read "probably a couple a week, for awhile there,"
now laughs at the predictable plots and the "corny" stories. But she acknowledged that the images left lasting impressions, both appealing and
distasteful.

> The story's always something about a woman and a guy who are attracted to
> each other, but she kind of tries to reject him. And then there's whatever
> other silly stuff in between, but the upshot is, there's always a hot sex scene
> where he grabs her and presses against her, she's overpowered by his manli-
> ness, his shirt's always open to show his great body, and it's so electric, and
> then he takes her and it all works out great. I have to say, they're really stu-
> pid, but it did sort of leave an imprint. I have this feeling, and I don't like it,
> like a man's supposed to sort of conquer me or something. God, that sounds

pathetic, but it's sort of something I fantasize about. (Stephanie, 21, "het-erosexual," "white")

Unfortunately, as we will see in the chapters ahead, this confounding of aggression and romance may encourage young women to experience, paradoxically, a sense of power (however illusory and dangerous) through their own objectification. If male arousal is considered inherently aggressive, and if hetero-sexual women are taught to evaluate their self-worth by their ability to please men (Miller, 1986), then it follows that many young women would be taught to interpret men's aggressive sexual overtures and objectifying behavior as not only threatening or inevitable, but *simultaneously* as flattering and seductive, confirming their desirability and hence their "success" as women.

## What Counts as Victimization?

A third set of discourses addresses the question of what actually "counts" as victimization. Drawing from the preceding discourses regarding "good womanhood" and "normal" male sexual behavior, two other discourses, which I call the "(hetero)sex as female victimization discourse" and the "true victim discourse," offer simultaneously overlapping and conflicting messages about the types of hetero-relational behaviors that should be regarded as victimizing. On the one hand, the (hetero)sex as female victimization discourse suggests that any hetero-sexual activity by girls or young women inevitably leads to their victimization. By contrast, the true victim discourse offers an extremely narrow view of victimization, contending that certain criteria must be met in order for women to "qualify" as true victims in hetero-relational encounters.

### The (Hetero)Sex as Female Victimization Discourse

Threading throughout the participants' early educations, a pervasive set of messages links adolescent female sexual expression with victimization. The (hetero)sex as female victimization discourse warns young women that sexual involvement will lead, inevitably, to "disaster," whether through disease, pregnancy, rape, loss of self-respect, or the development of a bad reputation (Fine, 1988). This discourse is typically framed in terms of threats and warnings, and it is typically presented to young women in attempts to dissuade them from expressing their sexualities. Theresa heard elements of this discourse (as well as the male sexual drive discourse) in her brother's warnings about men who only want "one thing." Although she said he and his friends were proud to "get anything they can" from other women, he was ready to do bodily harm to any man who touched his sister. Extrapolating from his own behaviors, he assumed that other men would want to exploit Theresa. Apparently, he had no sense that Theresa might be a sexual agent who would actually want to have sex with a man. To him, Theresa's sexuality meant her inevitable victimization.

> My brother is so girl crazy, and he and his friends, all they think about is "How much did you get?" But then he would talk with me, like, "If some guy lays his hands on you, I'd fuckin' kill him." And "Don't let a guy ever get away with shit, because guys are only looking to get one thing." So here I am with this horny older brother who will get anything he can from other girls and then brag about it with his friends, and yet he's telling me he'd fuckin' kill a guy who wanted to do the same thing with me. (Theresa, 19, "heterosexual," "biracial")

Particularly prevalent among the lessons provided by sex educators and adult caregivers, the (hetero)sex as female victimization discourse typically takes the form of disaster prevention and control (Sears, 1992). Focusing on the evils that befall young women who engage in sexual relationships, many of the messages young women received from adults went beyond the pleasing woman discourse's tendency to equate sexual involvement with a lack of class, femininity, or self-respect. Rather, the messages of the (hetero)sex as female victimization discourse warn that once a young woman steps over the line into the realm of sexuality, she will become victimized, damaged, or tainted.

In some cases, parents appealed to girls' desires for fulfilling relationships, stressing that girls who were not virgins would be unappealing to "nice" boyfriends. As Tonya's mother summed it up (in a rather unfortunate, but frequently heard, metaphor), "Why would a man buy the cow when he can milk it for free?" Henna's parents put it in more dire terms, telling her that a young woman who was no longer a virgin would forever be unwanted, regarded as a "whore." Raised in a traditional Korean household and community, Henna learned,

> For a Korean woman, to lose your virginity before marriage meant you would shame yourself and shame your family. You would be an outcast from the community for the rest of your life. No man would ever want you, and your family wouldn't have you either. You'd be all on your own and scarred for life. (Henna, 21, "heterosexual," "Korean")

Other participants encountered the (hetero)sex as female victimization discourse in adults' warnings that girls would be violated if they expressed their sexualities. Like Henna's parents, they often suggested that once girls "lost" their virginity, terrible things would happen that they could never rectify. But these adults' warnings focused on physical danger. Louise's teacher cautioned, "Once you cross that line, you can't control what happens to you." Diana's teacher also stressed to her students that sex, for girls, was dangerous. Rather than preparing young women to become empowered *within* their sexual relationships with men, such messages suggest that the only way to maintain their physical and psychological integrity is to deny, avoid, and resist their sexual desires.

> My teacher only really touched on sex in terms of it was dangerous. In terms of actually talking about sex itself, all she would really say was that once you had sex, sex really opened up a whole can of worms. Interesting choice of words, I really remember that. It was like opening Pandora's box, and who knows what evil things will pop out. (Diana, 21, "bisexual," "white")

The (hetero)sex as female victimization discourse is reflected and perpetuated through popular media images as well. As Clover (1987) argues, "slasher films" follow a formula in which a teenage woman is inevitably mutilated and killed by a maniacal man while she is having sex; not surprisingly, only the virgin is spared. The participants' teen magazines, while sometimes promoting independence and self-determination, also promoted the (hetero)sex as female victimization discourse through articles and letters about girls who "went too far" and "got in trouble" by becoming pregnant, contracting sexually transmitted infections, or being raped. Alicia recalled reading advice columns in which teen girls were advised to "wait." Apparently never entertaining the possibility that sexual relationships might be satisfying, meaningful, or empowering for young women, these columns instead focused on the tragedies that could befall a girl who participated in a sexual relationship.

> I liked the advice columns, because even though they usually didn't relate to me, I sort of felt like I could learn something and see what kinds of problems other girls had. There was stuff on pregnancy, like, "Help! I missed my period! What do I do?" And there was even stuff on STDs and "How do I protect myself from herpes or AIDS?" But it's funny how you asked me were there any positive messages about pleasure or sex, because I don't remember any. Getting boys, yes, but having sex with them? Not at all. (Alicia, 22, "heterosexual," "Asian")

The (hetero)sex as female victimization discourse attempts to prevent young women not only from having intercourse, but also from experiencing or demonstrating their sexualities in any way. We see this message (as well as the pleasing woman discourse) in Jocelyn's parents' warnings not to eat alone in public. As her parents told her, a young woman sitting alone would be considered "fair game" by men, language linking men with hunters and women with prey. Similarly, in parents' warnings not to dress "provocatively," we see young women's gendered and sexual expression through clothing linked with the likelihood of provoking an attack. Paula saw this connection through her mother's very angry reaction when she wore a miniskirt at fifteen.

> I wanted to wear miniskirts so bad, but when I borrowed my girlfriend's one once and wore it home, my mother threw this major fit. Totally. Major fit. Like, "What do you think you're doing with your bottom hanging out like that? Just what are you looking for? Do you want to get in some kind of trouble?" She was real clear on that, real clear. I said, "Mommy, why can't I look how I want to look? It's not my problem if some guy wants to look." And she said, "Oh yes it is your problem. And it's not the looking I'm worried about." (Paula, 20, "Spanish American"; asked to describe her sexuality, she wrote, "?")

It is certainly worth noting that the (hetero)sex as female victimization discourse was invoked only to discourage the participants from engaging in sexual relations with men. It was not the case that adults or the images in popular culture told young women that sexual expression with other women was safe or acceptable. Rather, messages about lesbian sexuality or bisexuality were missing entirely. Indeed, not a single woman in the study could recall hearing about same-sex partnerships from the adults in their lives. If hetero-sexual sex was dangerous, lesbian sexuality was nonexistent.

Laura described her amusement over the fact that her middle school sex education teacher presumed, first, that the girls in her class were not yet exploring their sexualities, and second, that when they did, they would be thinking only about boys. In warning her students about the dangers of "sex," she was clearly thinking of *hetero*-sexuality.

> They were assuming we were all these little girls and they were preparing us for that big day in the future when we started thinking about sex. I had already had sex with one boy, and I had been fooling around with other girls for a couple of years, having orgasms and loving it. But they never imagined any of us were already having sex with boys, and I'm sure it never occurred to them that we would ever think to have sex with other girls. So me and my girlfriends just sat there rolling our eyes and laughing at the teacher and all the ridiculous shit she said. And we'd be like, "Oh yes, I'll have to remember that when the time comes!" (Laura, 22, "bisexual," "bi-racial/West Black Indian, white American")

It is also important to recognize that this discourse is invoked in the popular culture, and particularly by parents and other concerned adults, only as a *preventive* measure. It provides adults a reason to give young women for *not* expressing their sexualities, rather than giving them a way to understand and deal with young women once they have done so. In other words, the (hetero)sex as female victimization discourse does not suggest that young women who have already had intercourse should be regarded with sympathy or seen as victims. Once young women have decided to engage in a sexual relationship or encounter, this discourse stops short, and "sexually active" young women are often regarded with the same contempt, mistrust, or sense of failure implied by the pleasing woman discourse. Whereas "virgins" are seen as potential victims of sexual desire, young women who choose to "give in" to those desires are held individually responsible, guilty of not heeding the warnings of the (hetero)sex as female victimization discourse.

## The True Victim Discourse

The true victim discourse distills the messages of the preceding discourses into an overarching notion that there exist two distinct types of victims—those who deserve social respect and advocacy, and those who are undeserving of sympathy or support, because they are presumed responsible for their own victimization. In this discourse the only true victims are those who were "clearly" victimized through physical threat or violence, who did everything they could to avoid or prevent their victimization, and who used every socially acceptable channel available to them to cope, once their victimization occurred.

Like the pleasing woman discourse, the true victim discourse draws on and promotes the classic virgin/whore dichotomy. And like the normal/danger dichotomy discourse, which divides men into the supposedly distinct categories of "normal" versus "dangerous," this discourse presupposes that there are two separate kinds of women—those who are "loose," "dirty," or "masochistic," and thus deserving of abuse and exploitation, and those who are "pure," "virginal," and "innocent," and thus true victims, deserving of sympathy and respect. Picking up where the (hetero)sex as female victimization discourse leaves off, this discourse operates in the popular assumption that prostitutes or other women with "sexual pasts" cannot really be raped because they have already decided to sell or give their bodies away freely. These women are thus considered "fair game," and they must forfeit their right to sympathy or redress. It can be seen further in public reactions to sexual harassment cases in which women are stripped of their right to complain if it can be shown that they participated in any way in the behavior in question. In such cases, despite structural power or status differences between the complainant and the accused, the woman is often treated as a greedy "gold digger" or vindictive troublemaker rather than a true victim.

The participants were exposed to this distinction very early in their hetero-relational educations. As we saw from Jeanne's description of the messages she took away from the stories and letters in pornographic magazines, a woman who is a "cock tease" apparently deserves to have sex forced on her. While such an act was portrayed as "putting her in her place," the woman was not portrayed as a victim of rape, presumably because she was "loose" and had therefore asked for it. Robin's mother conveyed this discourse in her warnings that "sexually active" or "promiscuous" women "deserve what they get." Recounting a conversation with her mother when she was in eighth grade, Robin remembered being struck by her mother's response to a newspaper article about a case of acquaintance rape.

She just said that girl must have deserved what she got. She said if you're going to be promiscuous, you're asking for it. It was like she had no sympathy for this girl at all. Even though the rape, if I remember, was pretty brutal, it was like her being victimized wasn't surprising, or wasn't even relevant. It was like it was her fault, not the guy's. I still remember it, because I wasn't sure what to think. (Robin, 21, "heterosexual"; asked to describe her race(s), she wrote, "I cannot")

The true victim discourse defines not only who can be considered a victim, but also what types of behaviors and circumstances can be considered victimizing. Here we see remnants of the normal/danger dichotomy discourse. As Elizabeth Stanko (1985; 1990) has noted, dominant notions of normal hetero-sexual interactions tend to define normal or acceptable male behavior as that which is typical. If we follow this notion, only clearly aberrant behaviors are considered problematic. In such a construction, "everyday violence," "little rapes" (Stanko, 1985; 1990), and insults to women's hetero-relational autonomy—which the women who are targeted might consider street and workplace harassment, acquaintance rape, and battering—are cast as normal, because they are, unfortunately, so typical. Significantly, according to Stanko, the lines separating normal and aberrant behaviors are culturally constructed from a male point of view (hence, the "reasonable man standard," which was traditionally used in courts of law), so that only those behaviors men deem abnormal are taken as such. As a consequence, behaviors or interactions that are not clearly aberrant to men are taken as unproblematic or normal, even if the women involved experience them as oppressive or exploitive. This distinction was made clear to Gloria through her gym teacher's refusal to address her attack as a case of gendered violence. Apparently assuming that "boys will be boys," he broke up the "fight," but did not question the boys' enactment of a rape scene on Gloria and her young friend.

When she was ten years old, Elaina learned from her friends' behaviors that a girl who engages in sexual activities, even if forced, may be judged to be a whore rather than a victim. She also learned that girls as well as boys made this distinction. Elaina's first exposure to sexualized violence came through frightening and alienating experiences with her first boyfriend, whom she now describes as "a really violent, crazy-looking fucker [who] would chase me around with an ax." Held down by a female friend while her boyfriend assaulted her in front of their male and female peers, she was not defended as a victim, but rather, branded with a bad reputation. When I asked whether she looked to adults for help, she responded that the adults in her life would likely have made the same assumption as her friends—that it was her fault. The incident left her feeling not only embarrassed and angry, but also guilty.

> I remember my best friend holding me down, but they didn't even know what they were doing. It wasn't like "We're going to rape you," because I don't think they even knew how to have sex. It was, "We're going to take off your pants," and it was more about, "We're going to imitate something, but we're not sure what it is." So I had this reputation as a whore, because everybody knew about this. It was more humiliating than anything else. I remember being angry and embarrassed and I felt very guilty. (Elaina, 22, "lesbian/bi," "white")

The true victim discourse is further supported by a sexist society's fear that women wish to falsely accuse men of physical and sexual abuse. Though technically the victim's sexual past is no longer admitted as evidence in court cases, rape victims/survivors continue to be asked what they were wearing, whether they fought back, and whether they had ever been known to be "promiscuous" (Fine, Genovese, et al., 1996). Such questions imply that if a woman is deemed "sexually active" and/or if she failed to fight off an attacker, she must have somehow asked for her own sexual violation; thus, she is not a true victim. Similarly, battered women are asked why they did not "just leave" an abusive partner, suggesting that if a woman stays, she must have consented to her own abuse. This is the case despite the fact that women are most likely to be seriously injured or killed by their batterers when they attempt to leave (Browne, 1987; Ewing, 1987; Castelano, 1996). Nonetheless, such a woman is held to be complicit in her own victimization, and thus she fails to qualify as a true victim. As we saw so clearly in the responses to Anita Hill's accusations of sexual harassment in the Clarence Thomas Judiciary Committee hearings, if victims do not seek immediate redress in the ways nonvictims suppose they would (e.g., pressing charges, filing complaints with superiors, removing oneself from the victimizing situation immediately), they are not considered to be true victims. Indeed, such women are typically seen as trying to set men up, accusing them of victimization where none exists. Not fitting into the true victim category, such women are, in fact, seen as victimizing men by exaggerating normal (i.e., typical) hetero-relations out of proportion.

## What Should Women Expect from Hetero-Relations?

A final set of discourses concerns the overall nature of hetero-relationships, giving young women very mixed messages about the role such relationships should play in their lives. The first discourse, which I have termed "the love hurts discourse," gives women the sense that male irresponsibility (both sexual and nonsexual) is inevitable, and that even the best of hetero-relationships are fraught with difficulty and dissatisfaction. Competing with this discourse is what I call "the love conquers all discourse," which suggests that relationships with men are the key to women's overall life satisfaction. This discourse maintains that if a woman can simply find the right man, she will certainly live happily ever after. These two discourses come together to provide important elements of the backdrop against which young women define and assess their own hetero-relationships.

### The Love Hurts Discourse

Consistent with the male sexual drive discourse, the love hurts discourse lets young women know that they should not expect too much from men in their relationships. This discourse expands on the male sexual drive discourse, however, to include nonsexual as well as sexual behavior. The love hurts discourse is conveyed both through explicit lessons and through young women's own observations of the relationships around them. By casting women's disappointment and mistreatment as inevitable in hetero-relations, this discourse simultaneously normalizes men's misbehaviors. Inherent in this discourse is the expectation that women must compromise themselves and their needs in order to compensate for men's apathy, neediness, or misconduct.

The love hurts discourse is promoted through novels about unrequited love and through tortured love songs that call on women to "stand by their men." As Ann Snitow (1983) notes in her analysis of mass-market romance novels, "Cruelty, callousness, coldness, menace, are all equated with maleness and treated as a necessary part of the package" (248). In my previous work with battered women, I heard this discourse expressed as women told me stories of turning to family, clergy, and counselors for help, only to be told to go home, try to be more understanding, and work on becoming better wives (Phillips, 1989). We can hear undercurrents of this message in advice columns for the "lovelorn," as women are essentially advised to lower their expectations and try to be more patient if they want to find satisfaction. Significantly, the love hurts discourse condones *men's* irresponsibility while holding *women* accountable for coping with this. It does not suggest that women are expected or entitled to be emotionally distant, selfish, or abusive, nor does it suggest that men should have to accept that love hurts.

Many of the women in this study got the message that love hurts from their own observations of the relationships around them. Although Martha said she "wouldn't mind" finding a fulfilling, long-term relationship with a man, she considered herself "cynical" about hetero-relationships at this point in her life. She described her father as an alcoholic, addicted to cocaine, and the son of an emotionally and physically abusive father. Having witnessed her father's emotional abuse toward her mother, and having experienced his anger toward women in general, she said she did not envision finding a stable and responsible male partner.

> My dad used to just curse at my mom all morning. He would wake up to go to work and spend an hour, "You fucking bitch, you whore!" and I would hear this every morning, and my dad, when my mom wasn't home, would take it out on me, like, "You women are all the same!" And when my parents first got divorced, my father used to call me Peggy, which is my mother's name, and yell at me. . . . He would be in a fit of screaming at me as Martha, and then it would turn into Peggy. And it was like he didn't even see me anymore. (Martha, 19, "white"; asked to describe her sexuality, she wrote, "female")

Whereas Martha's mother eventually left her husband, other women watched as their mothers stayed in abusive relationships. Interestingly, in each of the cases where a mother stayed, the participant attributed her unwillingness or inability to leave to religious or cultural values. For instance, although Andrea described her father as "a tyrant," she said her mother would never leave, for fear of her father's and her grandparents' wrath. Despite her mother's unhappiness and her parents' refusal to communicate with one another for eight years, her cultural and religious values, as well as the fear of family humiliation, kept her mother committed to remaining married.

> You just know that she will never leave him. Even though he's such a tyrant and even though they'll probably never speak another word to each other as long as they live, they'll never officially separate. It's just not done in my culture, even though my culture is actually a mix of cultures, or whatever. But like, my mom will stay upstairs, and my dad will live in the basement, and they'll pretend to the outside world like they're really married, even though they haven't been for years, in my opinion. There would just be too much shame for my mother to tolerate if she left him. And if my father or grandparents didn't kill her for leaving, the shame and embarrassment probably would. (Andrea, 20, "mixed—Lebanese/Chinese/Swedish/American"; asked to describe her sexuality, she wrote, "—")

Unlike those who tried to keep their families' unhappiness or abusive male behaviors hidden, Henna noted that her family and her community considered male violence acceptable. Indeed, Henna was the only one among her Korean friends who thought that her father's violence toward his wife and daughters was unacceptable. Whereas she considered her father's behaviors unjustified, she had been taught explicitly that Korean men are entitled to use violence to "discipline" their wives and children. Based on her belief that Korean hetero-relationships are inevitably based on an acceptance of inequality, she stated that she is now unwilling to date Korean men, much to her parents' and friends' dismay.

> Men chose and did, and women followed and listened, and as far as sex, only bad women were sexual. I mean the wife is basically, it's her duty, or it's her gift to him, men need it. And as a woman you're not really supposed to enjoy it. And when men beat women and children, it was just called discipline, like that's something that Korean men are just entitled to and expected to do. None of my Korean friends even understand why I have a problem with that. (Henna, 21, "heterosexual," "Korean")

Like Henna, Wendy attributed the physical, verbal, and sexual abuse she witnessed toward her grandmother, who raised her, to what she sees as the sexism woven into her culture. Describing the concepts of *machismo* and *marianismo*, Wendy recalled learning that Latina women were to aspire to emulate the Virgin Mary—to be clean, pure, and subservient—while Latino men were encouraged to be selfish, domineering, and irresponsible. Like Henna's mother, Wendy's grandmother taught her that unhappiness in hetero-relationships was simply inevitable. Unlike Henna's mother, however, she taught Wendy how to use these cultural expectations for her own survival.

> I basically learned from my grandmother that women are treated badly by their men, and they're not allowed to complain about it. Women are supposed to be virtuous and keep the home together. But even though I used to think this kept women weak, I learned that it's the women who really are the stronger ones. I learned that even though men beat us and sexually abused their wives, women learned to provide just enough sex and comfort to keep your man around to work and pay the bills. And even though my grandfather was irresponsible and drunk most of the time, my grandmother actually benefited from that. As long as you can keep him drunk and amused with other men, he stays out of your way. (Wendy, 22, "heterosexual," "Puerto Rican/Italian")

Although she and her grandmother learned ways to manage her grandfather's abuse, it was only by keeping him drunk that they were able to control his behavior (and thus ensure their own safety). Leaving him or demanding that he change appeared beyond the realm of consideration. According to the love hurts discourse, male irresponsibility is a given, and it is women's responsibility to tolerate or work around it.

Significantly, whereas women of color often attributed the abuse they, their mothers, or their neighbors experienced to the values of their cultures, none of the white women in the study attributed their own experiences or observations of abuse to their "whiteness" or their ethnicities. The "dominant culture" is certainly a powerful source and carrier of the love hurts discourse, and white women as well as women of color witnessed male violence in their families and communities. Yet perhaps because "whiteness" is an unmarked category in American society (Fine, Powell, et al., 1996; Fine and Weis, 1998), it was left unproblematized in the white women's stories of their own families' experiences of abuse.

Although most of the participants did not witness such severe abuse, many nonetheless learned that hetero-relationships were inherently unstable. For instance, growing up in both a family and a neighborhood where few men lived for long with their children or their children's mothers, Robin got the impression that "relationships don't last."

> I really formed the idea that relationships don't last because my father has so many other sons and daughters that he stays with them until they reach the age that I was [when he left], which was nine, and then goes, you know? I really decided that's the way it is, you know? People don't really stay together, and everybody, nobody in that neighborhood has a father, hardly, that lives there. Very few people. (Robin, 21, "heterosexual"; asked to describe her race(s), she wrote, "I cannot")

In the midst of all these unstable and unhappy relationships, six women did describe their parents and/or their stepparents as being in healthy and fulfilling relationships. Although these women were clearly a minority in the study, they described their parents as "hopelessly in love," "disgustingly happy," or "all over each other." Interestingly, however, these women tended to express surprise and even embarrassment at their parents' affection for one another. Apparently aware that her parents' happiness countered the norm (and the love hurts discourse), Rachel noted,

> Not only are my parents still married, which is weird enough compared to all my friends, but they're actually still in love with each other, which is really strange. It's almost embarrassing. (Rachel, 21, "heterosexual," "white")

## The Love Conquers All Discourse

Whereas the love hurts discourse suggests that women's disappointment in hetero-relationships is inevitable, the love conquers all discourse offers the opposite message, maintaining that hetero-relationships are the key to women's happiness. This discourse is communicated to women from a very early age through fairy tales in which the charming young prince carries his true love off into the sunset to live happily ever after. Posing hetero-relationships (and ultimately marriage) as central to women's well-being, this discourse suggests that every woman needs a man in order to find true fulfillment.

The love conquers all discourse does not limit itself to the notion that long-term hetero-sexual relationships are necessary for women's fulfillment in love. Indeed, it suggests that finding the right man will somehow solve all of life's problems. Like the fairy tale images of "happily ever after," romance novels and so-called feel-good movies promote the idea that a man will come along and take a woman away from any difficulties she may have experienced previous to finding her ideal man. This message was epitomized in the film *An Officer and a Gentleman,* which was extremely popular among my women students for over a year after it was first released. In the film, a woman is "rescued" from her factory job and her difficult life by an officer who, in the last scene of the movie, walks into the factory, literally sweeps her off her feet, and carries her away to happiness (as the other women in the factory applaud and shed tears). Women's overwhelmingly positive response to this movie suggests the power of the love conquers all discourse. It also suggests the sexism and hetero-sexism implied in this discourse, as my students' shock and laughter revealed when I asked them whether the movie would have been so moving if the female character had swept the male character off his feet and saved him from his working-class woes, or whether the movie would have "worked" if the characters had been of the same gender.

The participants encountered the love conquers all discourse in their parents' (and particularly their mothers') hopes and visions for their daughters' futures. Although none of the women could recall conversations with their parents about sexual desire, many remembered discussions about romance and future marriage. Natalie described the sentimental expression on her mother's face as she was showing her her wedding gown, and musing that some day Natalie might wear it in her own wedding. Not having told her mother of her attraction to other girls, Natalie described a flood of mixed emotions, ranging from "panic" to "some kind of romantic hopefulness."

> So I'm like, thirteen, right? And we're in the storage closet, and she's showing me her wedding gown. And she says, "Maybe you'll wear it at your own wedding," or something like that, right? She has this far-off, dreamy look on her face, and it's clear she wants to see me married in this dress. And here I am, realizing maybe I like girls, but of course, God knows I haven't told her that, and I'm feeling like this feeling of panic. And I'm also feeling like maybe I should get married, like some kind of romantic hopefulness that this is what you're supposed to do. Like this is what makes you happy. And I did like boys, too, and so I'm just standing there feeling really confused and like I kind of just want to run away. (Natalie, 19, "bisexual"; asked to describe her race(s), she wrote, "unimportant")

Other women were more willing to buy into the love conquers all discourse. Evelyn acknowledged with some embarrassment that she had been planning her wedding for as long as she could remember. Although well aware, on one level, that marriage was no guarantee of happiness, she noted that on another level, she was unable to let go of the notion that love conquers all.

> In this day and age, I know it's really stupid and sappy, but I really do sort of have this idea in the back of my head that I'm supposed to have the fairy tale wedding and the fairy tale life. I've been basically planning my wedding all my life. Since I was a little girl, I've known what I would look like and how it would be, and how this handsome, adoring guy would be at the end of the aisle waiting for me, and how we'd live happily ever after [*laughing*]. I know it's a long shot in this day and age, but I still really have that image. I still always cry at weddings, even on TV. (Evelyn, 21, "heterosexual," "Caucasian")

Whether or not they accepted the love conquers all discourse, all the participants encountered it growing up. Among the most common endorsers of this discourse were women's and teen magazines. Along with tips on how to dress, diet, and act, were suggestions on how to get, and keep, a man. Implicit in these recommendations was the notion that women must want a man, and must be involved with one in order to be completely fulfilled. Although some of the magazines promoted an image of independence and individual success, they nonetheless emphasized hetero-relationships as central to women's life satisfaction. As Olivia noted, these messages were often woven across various topics.

> Even though they said in one place, "You can be self-reliable and strong and independent," they'd still have the articles about how love is great and how it's all really about relationships and men. That's what they all really come down to, I think, is that you do all these things, whether it's great recipes or how to lose twenty pounds or what to wear this season, it's that you do all these things to get a man, and then you'll be all set. (Olivia, 22, "heterosexual," "Caucasian")

It is evident from these messages that the love conquers all discourse applies only to hetero-sexual love. Nowhere in the messages these young women encountered did they hear of the promises of love with other women. Those participants who described themselves as lesbian or bisexual, and who sought positive images of same-sex relationships, found no such images available throughout their adolescence. Cynthia, who grew up in a fairly conservative midwestern town, found that messages about lesbian relationships were either nonexistent or very negative.

> It wasn't until I came to college that I ever read a book where there was a lesbian relationship, or read a poem about a gay person or by a gay person. I didn't know anywhere I could see normal gay relationships. I didn't even have an image of it. All I got was that lesbians are unhappy, and they just need to find the right man. (Cynthia, 22, "bisexual," "white")

As Cynthia's comments suggest, the love conquers all discourse rests on the sexist and hetero-sexist premise that a woman is not complete until she has attached to a male partner. This discourse simultaneously rests on and fuels the presumption that lesbian women or bisexual women in same-sex relationships simply have not found the "right" man. Similarly, it promotes the negative characterization of single hetero-sexual women as unsuccessful, unfulfilled, or "old maids." By advocating not just love, but specifically hetero-sexual love, as central to women's happiness, the love conquers all discourse essentially blames women for any unhappiness they may experience, since all their problems would presumably be solved if they were attractive, pleasing, and worthy enough to attract the right man.

## Implications

> I think it was maybe Freud, from my psychology class? I remember he asked something like, "What do women want?" And I remember being insulted by that. But then I was thinking, I don't know, what do I want? Because I'm not even sure I know what I'm *supposed* to want. (Darla, 19, "heterosexual," "white")

Throughout this chapter we have seen powerful and contradictory messages woven through young women's early hetero-relational educations. The participants have encountered these sets of discourses through a wide range of sources, from families, teachers, and peers to pornography, television, and women's magazines. Perhaps what is most compelling about these early lessons, however, is that these young women were not exposed to one discourse from each set. Rather, all these women were exposed to each of the discourses, often simultaneously, throughout their early developmental experiences. Following Britzman's (1988) notion that subjectivities are the site of multiple and competing discourses, we can see that these eight discourses, and the tensions among them, weave through and help constitute the participants' developing hetero-relational subjectivities. Whether young women accept or try to reject their messages, these discourses have become the raw materials available to them as they attempt to make sense of, and respond within, their hetero-relational experiences.

As important as the discourses made available to young women, however, are those that were absent or denied. We have witnessed a number of discourses that in various ways hold young women responsible for their own exploitation or that cast women's inequality, objectification, or victimization as inevitable. Yet we must also note a compelling *absence* of discourses promoting *male accountability*. The available discourses suggest that if only a woman were more pleasing, more "together" (or both), if only she were better able to perceive the presumably clear lines between normal and dangerous encounters/men, if only she were not sexual, if only she attached to the right man, she would be safe and secure. But each of these messages holds women accountable as the gatekeepers of men's behaviors (White and Niles, 1990), and thus blames women when men exploit or abuse them. A "discourse of male accountability" (Fine, Genovese, et al., 1996), on the other hand, would help ensure that men are held responsible for their own behaviors. Such a discourse would provide young women and the adults around them a framework for understanding hetero-relations in which girls and young women are not automatically presumed responsible for their own victimization. Yet none of the participants could recall hearing such messages throughout her childhood or adolescence.

Further absent from the young women's stories is what might be termed a "discourse of female pleasure without penalties." While we have seen that the together woman discourse allows for young women's sexual desires, it does not address the very real structural, ideological, and interpersonal barriers that often prevent women from expressing those desires, and that punish them if and when they do. The onus is put on women simply to transcend these constraints, presumably through their own acts of will. On the other hand, while the normal/danger dichotomy discourse suggests that abuse and exploitation of women are abhorrent, it does not recognize the abuse and exploitation involved in many "normal" hetero-relational encounters. The young women in this study do not currently have available to them a discourse that both acknowledges their entitlement to express their full sexualities *and* makes clear that they are entitled to do so without losing social respect, being victimized, or being held accountable for their own exploitation.

In the chapters ahead, I explore further the implications of these missing discourses, as well as the implications of the available discourses regarding "good womanhood," "normal" male sexuality, "real" victimization, and "typical" hetero-relationships, for young women's developing hetero-relational subjectivities. We will see that the available discourses, coupled with the absence of a discourse of male accountability or female pleasure without penalties, inform young women's hetero-relational understandings and decision making, and pose complex social and developmental challenges as they construct their adult gendered and sexual identities.

4

∎ ∎ ∎ ∎ ∎ ∎ ∎ ∎ ∎

## Mirror, Mirror, on the Wall

*Deciding How/Who to Be in*
*Hetero-Relationships*

It's just never not there. If I want to go ahead with having sex or expressing what I want, I'm thinking, "Wow, what will he think of the fact
that I know what I want, or know that I want it at all?" I wonder if he'll
lose respect for me, if he'll think I'm too experienced and sort of slutty
or something. But then I'm also thinking at the same time, "What if I act
like I'm unsure of myself, like if I'm not acting sexual enough? Then he's
going to think I'm inexperienced or frigid or a baby or something. Or
maybe he'll feel like I'm letting him down, like I'll hurt his feelings." I
mean, sometimes I know I want it, sometimes I know I don't, and sometimes I'm not sure. But I never know how to act, because I never know
what he's going to think of me. It's like either way, I can't win, so I'm
constantly monitoring how I should be, and either way, I feel like I lose.
I mean, I can either be seen as a baby or a whore. That's not a very comfortable decision.

—Louise, 21, "hetero," "white"

I feel like a baby that I'm confused a lot of the time, but there's
nowhere for me to go to talk about it. If I talked to my family, they'd

be so disappointed and worried that I was even thinking about these things. And if I talked to my boyfriend, he'd think I was unhappy with him or hung up or something. And if I talked with my friends, they'd probably think I was just weird or immature, because everybody else seems to have it all worked out. So I don't know what to think. I don't know who to be, really, because I'm damned if I do and damned if I don't, sort of thing. I can't sort out what I want, because it's hard to separate from what's expected of me. But the thing is, all those things that different people expect of me, they're all a part of me. I just don't know which one to choose.

—Darla, 19, "heterosexual," "white"

THESE WOMEN'S DILEMMAS are not unique. Though Louise and Darla state their cases particularly vividly, they describe a struggle shared by their peers in this study—the struggle to make sense of their hetero-relations within a multitude of contradictory expectations and potentially harsh judgments about their status as young adults and their character as women. Attempting to find or create an appropriate stance in their relationships with men, they "monitor" themselves and try to figure out who they are, or "who to be," as though gazing into a psychological mirror to find an image of themselves that is both personally satisfying and acceptable to those around them. Staring into the mirror, however, each finds her own image composed of a collage of other faces, each with competing messages as to who she should be and how she must present herself. There are her friends, family, and educators. The Religious Right and her *Cosmo* magazine both stare back at her. Her women's studies class sits in the mirror, as do all the partners with whom she has been involved. Each image speaks loudly and with great urgency, and each has conflicting formulae for how she must be. Looking for her "self" in the mirror, she is inseparable from the audiences that both watch and advise from within her head.

Derived from the participants' early lessons in hetero-relations, this collage of faces in the mirror reflects and gives compelling voice to the eight cultural discourses teased out in the previous chapter. Absent from the mirror (or, at best, hovering at the margins) are any whispers of a discourse of male accountability and a discourse of female pleasure without penalties. While these two discourses may have begun to find their way into other cultural spaces (such as feminist theory and politics), they have yet to make it into these women's early hetero-relational experiences. Denied any socially sanctioned discourses for sharing the burden of sexual responsibility with men, these women see many expectant faces in the mirror, but the onus is on them, alone, to maneuver among competing expectations and to shoulder the blame when all these expectations (inevitably) cannot be met.

If we look closely in the mirror, or in Louise's and Darla's quotes above, we can see not only young women's struggle to maneuver among competing hetero-relational discourses, but also an overlapping developmental struggle to present and experience themselves, through their sexualities, as adults. Unfortunately, studies of adult perceptions often pose individuals' understandings as something at which they have simply "arrived," leading us to interpret their voiced perspectives as static representations of what they think about a particular set of issues. A social constructivist position reminds us that individuals are culturally positioned subjects whose narrations must be understood as situated within the larger social and historical circumstances of their lives (Gergen, 1985). But we must take this analysis one step further. In addition to understanding how these young women are positioned *socially and historically*, we also must consider how and where they are positioned *developmentally*.[1] Without a deep consideration of how the culturally constructed developmental challenges of adolescence and early adulthood fold into young women's meaning-making processes, we miss an important dimension of their hetero-relational experiences.

An understanding of women's past lessons does not, in itself, offer sufficient insight into the developmental aspects of their present grapplings. These hetero-relational lessons are not discrete events of the past that simply gave birth to their current perspectives. A closer examination of the participants' stories makes clear that young women's developmental processes involve much more than merely building on past experience to form their current hetero-relational identities. Rather, they are continually constructing and reconstructing themselves as gendered "subjects in progress" within dynamic social contexts, while simultaneously engaged in an ongoing struggle to negotiate the transition from adolescence to adulthood.

In this chapter I explore how the overlapping processes of development into adulthood and development as a gendered subject intertwine in the hetero-relational lives of the young women I interviewed. I examine here three interrelated social and developmental challenges that permeate the participants' sexual understandings and decision making as young women coming of age in a sexist and adult-centered Western culture. Along with the cultural discourses examined in chapter 3, these challenges provide the context from which we may explore women's current perceptions and responses in their hetero-relations.

## Coming of Age as a Sexual Subject: Social and Developmental Challenges

The convergent quests for maturity and gendered identity pose intricate challenges for adolescent girls and young women. As feminist scholars have long noted, mainstream cultural norms and psychology's concepts of healthy adult personhood often clash with dominant expectations for appropriate female gender identity, as well as with certain non-Western cultural values (Bordo, 1989; Collins, 1991; Espin, 1984; Gilligan, 1982; Miller, 1986; Robinson and Ward, 1991; Steiner-Adair, 1990; Taylor, 1996; Vazquez-Nuttal, Romero-Garcia, and DeLeon, 1987; Ward, 1996). While Western cultures often associate healthy adulthood with self-actualization, independence, and action, dominant expectations for female identity include passivity, dependence, and the development of characteristics that are pleasing to men (Miller, 1986; Lykes, 1989; Steiner-Adair, 1990). Coming of age at a point in history when women are increasingly encouraged to strive for adult independence, yet still persuaded to embody classic notions of femininity, these young women develop their hetero-relational subjectivities along the fault line between the together woman discourse and the pleasing woman discourse, outlined in the previous chapter. In a society where sexuality represents both freedom and the possibility of female victimization, this fault line is intersected by the tensions among the normal/danger dichotomy discourse, the male sexual drive discourse, the (hetero)sex as female victimization discourse, and the true victim discourse. Complicating things even further, the entire meaning-making process is contextualized by the contradictory love hurts and love conquers all discourses.

In a culture that so emphasizes but is so conflicted about sex, and particularly about adolescent female desire (Fine, 1988; Thompson,

1995; Tolman, 1996; Tolman and Higgins, 1996), it makes sense that sexuality would emerge as a primary vehicle for negotiating among these discourses as young women struggle with gendered power and adult identity. The participants' stories suggest that for these young women, hetero-relational encounters are not isolated incidents, separable from larger social and developmental contexts. Rather, they represent arenas of struggle with the constructed concepts of adulthood, agency, danger, and desire. Hetero-relations challenge young women to negotiate continuously across multiple dimensions of power—to experience themselves as both actor and acted upon, as potential adult subject and possible gendered object. This plays out through three interrelated social and developmental challenges that pervade young women's understandings and experiences as they grapple with the tensions between adult identity and gendered identity.

### "Big Girls" Do—"Good Girls" Don't

The first social and developmental challenge arises from a tension between two competing messages about gender and sexual entitlement. These are encountered in the larger culture and then reflected back to young women in their metaphorical mirrors. On the one hand, young women are compelled by the together woman discourse to attain an adult status and sense of freedom through hetero-sexual relationships. On the other hand, various elements of the pleasing woman discourse, the true victim discourse, the love conquers all discourse, and the love hurts discourse—often voiced by religion, families, educators, and popular media—urge young women to be passive, nurturant, sexually "pure," "good girls."

Recounting their earlier adolescent and current hetero-relational experiences, participants referred repeatedly to a strong, internalized pressure to appear, to themselves and others, "grown-up."[2] Often expressed in the negative, women described an overwhelming motivation to feel and present themselves as "not like a baby anymore," "not childish," or "not immature." Moving into adulthood in an adult-centered culture, the young women in this study often viewed hetero-sexual involvement as a potential path toward liberation, an opportunity to distinguish themselves from "childishness," "babies," or "little girls." Swayed by the together woman discourse, hearing about the joys of sex, and bombarded by images of sexual women in popular culture, participants were eager to present and experience themselves as sexually mature.

For many of the participants, an important indicator or rite of passage into adult identity involved a first kiss. Chloe, for instance, described her first kiss as a magical transformation, bringing her across a threshold into "real womanhood." Interestingly, she used the passive voice to describe her experience. Rather than kissing a boy, she described herself as having "just been kissed."

> It was so magical. I was thirteen. I remember thinking, "God, wow, I'm like a real woman. I've just been kissed." It seems pretty lame now, but I just really felt like I was finally a grown-up woman. (Chloe, 22, "heterosexual/bisexual," "Caucasian")

For other young women, "losing" virginity represented a shedding of their childhood identities. For some, sexual intercourse was not associated with desire, but virginity was seen as a burden, as something to get rid of. Describing her decision to have intercourse, Tonya reported that it had never occurred to her that she would find it pleasurable (and, indeed, she did not). Instead, she described it as a "rite of passage, kind of like getting Bat Mitzvahed." Even Laura, who had been having sexual relationships with other girls for two years, felt that she would not be an adult woman until she "lost" her virginity by having intercourse with a male.

> I was already totally like a baby dyke. I couldn't imagine wanting to have sex with a man. In most ways, I had lost my virginity a long time ago, but because you're still a virgin until you've had a penis inside you, I wanted to do it. I wanted to know I was an adult woman, no longer a virgin. Then I could go happily back to loving girls, which is what I did, or at least being bisexual. (Laura, 22, "bisexual," "bi-racial/West Black Indian, white American")

Gloria, too, wanted to "lose" her virginity, and so at thirteen she set out to find a young man with whom to have intercourse. Still, she felt she needed an "excuse" for doing so. She told herself that since she wanted to be an author, she would have to know what it felt like to have sex so that she could write about it. Despite being the initiator of this sexual interaction, like many young women, Gloria experienced very mixed feelings in the encounter. She realized that she did not, in fact, want to have intercourse at this time and told her partner she was uncomfortable.

So he finally just said, "Either you finish doing this or you give me a blow job." So it was like "I'll give you a blow job," [*laughing*] which was pretty mean when I think about it, but that's when it happened. It was just very clinical. I wasn't ready. I just wasn't into it. I wasn't all hot and heavy like before when I was really horny. I didn't reach that point. It was fun. You know, I wouldn't have it any other way. I don't know if it was romantic, but it was pretty fun, you know? (Gloria, 20, "heterosexual," "African-American")

Although Gloria initiated this encounter to "lose" her virginity, and although she wrapped up her statement neatly, saying that it was "pretty fun" and that she "wouldn't have it any other way," her description of the actual encounter suggests a less pleasant experience. Her statements that "it was just very clinical," "I wasn't ready," and "I just wasn't into it," along with the young man's insistence that she either "finish doing this or you give me a blow job," suggest that Gloria experienced neither tenderness nor sexual pleasure from her experience. Interestingly, lacking a discourse of male accountability, she decided that she was "mean" for stopping during intercourse, rather than considering *him* mean or inappropriate for giving her an ultimatum instead of simply stopping when she indicated that she "wasn't into it."[3]

For other participants, "losing" virginity was much welcomed, both in terms of sexual desire and as a symbol of passage into adulthood. For Darla, having intercourse for the first time was simultaneously an expression of intimacy with her boyfriend, a physically painful and emotionally frightening experience, and a stepping stone into adult womanhood.

We totally talked about it and we planned it out, because it was on Valentine's Day. He was a virgin too, and it was like, oh, we're so in love and everything. But it was painful for me for like the first five times, but I remember afterward, it was so emotional that we both cried. It was really scary. I remember sitting in school being like, "God, I can't believe I'm so grown-up. I wonder if any of my friends have done this." It definitely made me feel different about myself. It was just too much. (Darla, 19, "heterosexual," "white")

A further marker of womanhood for many adolescent girls involved receiving general sexualized attention from males, often in the form of comments about appearance, sexual invitations, or flirtatious looks and gestures. Many women took what some might call street harassment as an indication that they were being taken seriously as women. Experiencing a sense of excitement and power from being desired by men, Heidi recalled feeling flattered by men's whistles on the street.

> I actually used to like it. I walked to my boyfriend's house one day, and I said, "I got six whistles," and I was happy. That is so sick, because I was like, "Wow, I am actually a woman," you know? "I am actually a woman and guys desire me. This is really weird. This is really fun." (Heidi, 21, "bisexual," "white")

For many participants, sexualized hetero-relations represented a door-way to the supposed power and status of adult female identity. And yet girls' and young women's sexual expression takes on larger meanings in a Western culture that is not only adult-centered but androcentric as well. In such a context, the proud badge of adulthood, which the together woman discourse promises to those who are "sexually active," is tainted by the stigma associated with young women's sexualities (Tolman and Higgins, 1996). These women have learned that sexuality is the key to "together" womanhood—that "big girls do." Yet they have learned just as powerfully from the pleasing woman discourse and the true victim discourse that sexual women are "loose," "easy," or lacking in self-respect—in other words, that "good girls don't."

For many young women, then, the very behaviors that promised a re-markable transition into adulthood also stirred considerable misgivings. Heidi's experience provides a clear example. Unlike the girls who looked forward to "losing" their virginity simply to "get it over with" or to gain status as "a real woman," Heidi wanted very much to "go all the way," but she felt a need to put it off until a certain point so that she could re-main a "good girl." Describing herself as madly in love with her boyfriend, and feeling strong desires at age fifteen to have intercourse with him, she felt an intense and conflicting need to wait until she was sixteen before doing so.

> [I was with my] boyfriend, who I had been going out with for nine months, and just wanted, "please, please, let's just wait until I'm sixteen. I want to be sweet sixteen." (Heidi, 21, "bisexual;" "white")

In Heidi's eyes (at least when she was fifteen), being "sweet sixteen" meant being a virgin. While she had stated that being seen as sexually desirable meant being "actually a woman," she also was aware that, for females, being "sexually active" and being "sweet" are deemed mutually exclusive.

The tension between being a "big girl" and being a "good girl" did not begin and end during such obvious developmental shifts as deciding when and if to have intercourse for the first time. This tension was visible in women's hetero-relational decision-making processes at the time of their interviews as well. The participants did not leave the desire to be seen as a "together" adult behind in adolescence. They carried it through into young adulthood as a seemingly constant need to prove themselves as sexually mature. Similarly, young women's wish to avoid being seen as "loose" or a "slut" remained a powerful influence well past the point when they made the initial decision to "lose" their virginity (or had that "decision" imposed on them). For most of these young women, this tension continued to operate powerfully in every sexual interaction they encountered. Like Louise and Darla, quoted at the beginning of this chapter, Sara saw herself as performing "a constant balancing act" as she decided how to position herself in her sexual encounters with men. She was also well aware of a gendered double standard that put women, but not men, on the spot.

> It's a constant balancing act. It seems guys don't really have to worry so much about this sort of thing, but for women it's really different. It's just always like, you have to be sure of yourself and not hung up and like you know what you want and what you're doing. But on the other hand, you can't look too willing or experienced, like you can't be more experienced than the guy is, and you can't come off looking like a slut, because then you'll look really bad. (Sara, 20, "mostly heterosexual, with a healthy bisexual curiosity, but with no experience," "white")

In many cases the need to be "sexually together" (in order to feel or appear grown-up) and the need to be "not too sexual" (in order to avoid feeling or appearing like a "whore") were overlapped by a third imperative: the need to be sexually accommodating in order to please men. Melissa, for instance, said she sometimes felt unable to avoid sexual encounters with men in whom she had no sexual interest in the first place, for fear of hurting their feelings.

> It's kind of sickening and sad, but when I feel sorry for them, I feel like, you know, you should give them what they need, even if it's not necessarily what

I want. I was socialized, I mean, I thought that self-sacrificing, selfless, sometimes maternal, sometimes a little girl, always willing and ready to accommodate everybody else's needs—that's what makes femininity, I think. Then
if you're not that, you're a bitch. Or not even anything as powerful or desirable as a bitch. But I'd be seen as, what is my fucking problem? A prude, you
know? (Melissa, 21, "heterosexual," "Eastern European-American Jew")

Melissa found herself pulled simultaneously by the pleasing woman discourse, which equates femininity with understanding and self-sacrifice, and
the together woman discourse, which reminds women that those who hes-
itate to have sex with a man are seen as having hang-ups—a notion that
threatened Melissa's desired image of herself as a well-adjusted adult
woman. She "resolved" her dilemma by agreeing to the wishes of men and
sublimating her own, allowing her to fulfill her role as a pleasing woman
without being seen as a "prude" for saying no. Unfortunately, Melissa's
analysis left little room for seeing the refusal of a man's desires, when they
conflicted with her own, as an empowered or "together" choice.

Many women found the developmental tension between being a
"good girl" and being a "big girl" compounded by an interplay of gendered struggles with powerful race, class, and cultural expectations. For
these women, the general ambivalence of the dominant culture was exacerbated by the cultural prescriptions for females associated with their
race, class, and/or ethnic backgrounds. The most prominent such tension expressed in the interviews involved a need to straddle both the
dominant "American culture" and the culture of one's community and
family of origin. Particularly common among women whose parents im-
migrated from non-Western cultures, this tension played out most often
as a tug-of-war between a "traditional" upbringing and a desire to become an "Americanized" adult woman. While women grappled with
contradictory expectations in many areas of their lives, this tension was
expressed particularly powerfully in their sense of hetero-relational entitlement and obligations.

Robin, a young woman who described her mother as "the typical, traditional Dominican woman" and her father as "the even more typical, traditional Latin man," reflected on her struggle to find a reasonable position
in her own hetero-relational experiences. Having had sexual relationships
with men since she was thirteen, she expressed great ambivalence about

her role as a sexual woman, and particularly as a sexually "experienced" Latina from a Catholic family.

> It's the whole madonna/whore thing. I'm supposed to be the chaste, madonna virgin, but who in their right mind is going to be that? My parents would die if they knew. It would be like a shame cast over our whole family. And yet everybody in my neighborhood has been having sex since they were, like, twelve years old. But nobody will admit it, because of this whole mentality. My parents are so, like, Catholic and everything. But it's not just my parents' generation, it's my generation, too. If a girl won't give a guy sex when he wants it, she's, like, not taking care of his needs. And that's supposed to be a woman's role, to take care of a man's sexual needs. But if she does do it, then she's like branded. Because then she's not the good Latina virgin, and she's going to pay the price in the eyes of everybody in her community. There's so much pressure to establish yourself as sexually grown-up and mature by having sex, but then there's just as much pressure to not be like that so you won't be discarded as just another slut. (Robin, 21, "heterosexual"; asked to describe her race(s), she wrote, "I cannot")

Henna described being caught in a double bind that she considered particular to her need to straddle her Korean and American cultures. Although she had misgivings about her first sexual encounter, she felt she owed it to her partner because she had "let it go too far." Like many of the women in this study, she also felt a strong internalized pressure to rid herself of her virginity in order to feel grown-up. The pressures to avoid guilt about not pleasing a man and to avoid feeling like "a young, stupid kid with a dumb, stupid hang-up" (at least temporarily) outweighed Henna's doubts about having sex with this young man. Perceived by her family and culture as "a child" because she is a Korean female, and wanting desperately to be "Americanized" and taken seriously as an adult, she felt that having intercourse would help her feel more like a "real woman."

> I don't have much confidence in terms of being attractive or desirable to men. So, when someone wants to have sex with me, to me that was a big thing, especially because I always feel like I'm not a real woman. I feel like no one would see me as a woman or even as an adult, that I'm just a girl, so for them to want me sexually was something I was a little bit unsure of. (Henna, 21, "heterosexual," "Korean")

While not expressing her sexuality involved seeing herself as childlike, deciding to have intercourse carried a significant cost as well. When I asked what her parents would think if they knew she was not a virgin, Henna replied,

> That's my biggest fear, that they would ever find out. They would be very disgusted with me. I can just picture the look on their faces. Also, the age I lost my virginity, I was sixteen and to them I was a child. I was a baby, and now I regret it. They just make me feel dirty. . . . It's funny, when you hear the words "good" and "bad," they just sound like such simple terms. But it can mean such a huge thing in Korean language. Most of my life I've been trying to prove I was good, and that I wasn't bad, and that I'm not an awful person, and that I'm not all those things they constantly told me. There are terms that are equivalent, I guess, to "stupid," maybe "bitch" even, but somehow it feels a lot harsher hearing it in Korean. I just felt so small, and just so awful, and I just wasn't worthy of a lot of things, and that I was a bad person and that my parents were right, especially my mother. I'd picture the way she'd look at me after she found out. Even now, once in a while I have those little attacks, but I think I'm a lot stronger. But about once a month I really get kind of upset and start remembering everything bad I've done that they wouldn't approve of and just feel really, really awful about myself.

Henna remained caught in what seems to be a no-win situation. In order to escape the stereotype of a childlike Korean girl, she felt she must "lose" her virginity. Yet her decision to do so has left her internalizing her parents' and her culture's judgment that she is now "dirty and small," certainly not descriptions one might associate with either "pleasing" or "together" adult womanhood. This double bind can be seen not only in her initial decision whether or not to have intercourse, but throughout all the sexual encounters in which Henna has chosen to participate. Torn between the desire to express her sexuality and the cultural prohibition against doing so, Henna felt she must censor herself and forfeit her needs in order not to be perceived as a bad Korean woman. Describing her second relationship, which was with a Korean man, she noted that she never felt entitled to ask for things that would bring her pleasure.

> I was always on the verge of saying, "This is what would make me feel good." But I was afraid to show or to enjoy anything because of how he might look at me, because I'm not supposed to enjoy it. A lot of my girl-

friends are Korean who have Korean boyfriends, and a lot of them have never had an orgasm and they don't enjoy it. And I realized all these Korean guys are getting these ideas from their fathers and since they're all in the same social circle and they don't go outside of that circle, they're not going to know the girl is supposed to enjoy it too, that she can. It's strange, but, that summer my boyfriend was Korean, and I was afraid to say anything because we had sex pretty frequently, and I felt like I shouldn't have wanted to have sex as frequently. I should have been saying, "oh, no," you know, because that's the way it's supposed to be. There would be times when we were so close to something that would make me feel really good, and then I just couldn't come out and say it. I was kind of embarrassed, and I kept thinking, "What kind of girl would he see me as, to even to know?" I was afraid it would make him look at me in this light that I didn't want to be seen in.

Women's sense of entitlement to sexual pleasure was also undermined by stereotypes based on social class. Diana, for example, expressed a need to negotiate her desire to be sexual around the need to avoid being perceived as "cheap." Understanding, and frustrated by, the cultural association of "lower-class" females with promiscuity, she felt she had to censor her sexual behavior in order to avoid fueling other people's stereotypes.

I'm like, from the lower class, okay? And people expect lower-class girls to be like sluts or whores, you know? So for me to have sex with more than one guy, it would be seen as, "She's just one more lower-class tramp." Whereas if someone from an upper class did the exact same behavior, she might be seen just as normal or cool or liberated, or whatever. But you have to be very careful when you're from a poor background, because men, and women, too, are all too willing to see you as a piece of white trash. You know, they say there are girls you have fun with and girls you marry. And guys think that lower-class girls are the ones you just have fun with, the ones you fuck around with until you find a nice classy girl to really care about. So I feel like I have to be really careful to act coy and innocent, even when that's not how I feel, so I won't be seen as the cheap, easy tramp stereotype people expect me to be. (Diana, 21, "bisexual," "white")

While Diana was concerned with race and class stereotypes of "white trash," Sondra experienced the weight of social perceptions based on gender, race, and class through her hetero-relational encounters as an African American young woman from a working-class family. Like all the participants in this study, she wanted to feel like a "grown woman" and was drawn to the expression of her gendered maturity through her hetero-relational competence. But she was also painfully aware of the dominant culture's racist perceptions of sexual African American women. As bell hooks (1981) explains, African American women have historically been perceived by the dominant white culture as "sexual savages," possessing an inherent, wanton sexuality, and thus have been treated as "fair game" for men's sexual conquests. Sondra was confronted with this stereotype not only in her sexual encounters, but in such daily decisions as what to wear to school or to work.

> I like to look sexually attractive and all, but I've also learned I can't just go around looking sexy, because people will see that as promiscuous. Whereas you might be able to wear something low-cut or tight or whatever, and people would say, you know, "She looks really fine," for me to do the same thing would be altogether different. And so in my [earlier] teenage years, I wanted to wear all those sexy clothes, but my mother made me wear things that covered me up, because she knew I was more likely to be called a slut than white girls wearing the same thing. And now I know she was right. At the time, I'd be like, "Oh Mom, you're making me look like a little girl. You just want me to look like your little baby." I wanted to look like a grown woman with the makeup and sexy clothes so bad, I just couldn't stand it. But that's the trade-off, because while you'd be thinking you were looking like a sophisticated woman, everybody else would be like, "See, I'm gonna get me a piece of that whore." (Sondra, 19, "heterosexual," "Afro-American/Native American")

Throughout the dilemma between being a "big girl" and a "good girl" we see the powerful interlacings of the pleasing woman discourse and the together woman discourse. Compelled to experience and portray themselves as "together" adult women, the participants in this study were, nonetheless, never far from reminders that they must not present themselves as *too* sexual, or too sure of themselves and their desires in their hetero-relations. Whether they chose to position themselves as sexual agents or as coy and innocent girls, their decisions exacted a significant price in terms of their sense of self.

Developing into womanhood in an era when "together" adults are presumed to be sexually sophisticated, the together woman discourse makes it appear intolerable for young women to be less than completely sexually entitled and knowing. Furthermore, while in many ways the together and pleasing woman discourses contradict one another, the pleasing woman discourse itself subtly fuels the pressure to be sexually involved and competent; young women are told through women's magazines, pornography, and their own interactions that experienced, sexually "skilled" women are pleasing to men. Yet the pleasing woman discourse also contradicts both itself and the together woman discourse. It reminds women that they are to be feminine, and thus shy, passive, and innocent, encouraging them to doubt their entitlement to sexual expression and satisfaction. Aware of the social and personal costs of not being a "good girl," young women are left to struggle with the dilemma of being good adults or being good females. Whatever position they take, there are faces awaiting them in the psychological mirror—parts of themselves—eager to admonish them for making the wrong choice. And when "wrong" choices or confusion lead to feelings of pain, shame, or alienation, the love hurts discourse stands ready to normalize this experience and remind women that such feelings are inevitable (and thus should be seen as tolerable) aspects of hetero-relations.

## The "Together" Woman and Potential Danger

A second social and developmental challenge overlaps but goes beyond the tension young women experience between being a "big girl" and being a "good girl." This second challenge stems from the fact that sexuality represents simultaneously a transition into adulthood and a transition into a complex arena of potential danger and female victimization.[4] As discussed above, for many young women, being a competent and desirable sexual agent represents (however problematically) a departure from the subordinate status of childhood. And yet the together woman discourse's messages about the wonders of sexuality are juxtaposed with warnings, not only about labels of promiscuity and lack of femininity by the pleasing woman discourse and the true victim discourse, but also about the very real possibilities of exploitation and violence against women by the (hetero)sex as female victimization discourse and the male sexual drive discourse. Compounding parental and societal warnings, many young women reached an awareness of potential hetero-relational dangers through their own direct experience with male domination and violence.

Unfortunately, many of the same participants who anticipated the "loss" of their virginity as a much-welcomed marker of adult status also experienced it as frightening, physically or emotionally painful, or exploitive. Cynthia, for instance, was delighted to have the opportunity to have intercourse for the first time. Thinking this would make her feel like "a grown woman," she instead experienced a great deal of pain and disillusionment.

> I thought, "I'm ready to just do it." I just wanted to lose it to get on with things. I was sure this was what I wanted and that it would make me be a grown-up. This guy I had been seeing, we were making out at a party, and he was like, "Come on, now's the time, you've been holding out on me long enough." So I figured, here's my chance, he's initiating and he wants me, so this is my shot and I'm going to just go for it. It was scary, but an excited kind of scary. I thought it was going to be great and I would come out of it a real woman. But we went out behind the house, and he was putting his hand down my pants and it was really exciting, but we took our clothes off, most of them anyway, and it was like he just turned different. He was, like, totally unaware of me, and we weren't making out anymore [*weeping*]. He was just pushing his prick inside of me, and he had his hand over my mouth, so I couldn't say anything. It was like he was in his own little world and unaware that there was another human being there. I was scared and confused. I wasn't excited at all, so I was really dry, and I was a virgin. All I can say is I have never felt so much pain in my life. He just kept shoving his dick into me and keeping his hand over my mouth. He was laying on top of me, so I couldn't get up. It was painful and scary, and not like anything I had ever been led to expect. After he came, which wasn't very long, thank God, he just rolled over, looking so proud of himself. He said, "Do you want me to walk you home?" I just got up and my whole body was shaking, trying to put my clothes back on, and I just said, "No thanks." I went home and took a shower and went to bed. I just cried a lot. (Cynthia, 22, "bisexual," "white")

Frances, too, had looked forward to having intercourse for the first time. But persuaded by the normal/danger dichotomy and the love conquers all discourses, she wanted to be sure that she waited until she met the "right man." Thinking she had found him, she decided to begin a sexual relationship with her boyfriend, only to find out that she was being used as a pawn in this young man's prank.

> I wanted very much for it to happen, to make that final decision that would make me a woman. But it had to be right. I had this idea of, like, the right

man. So when I met this guy and he seemed so sweet and tender, and we really hit it off, I thought, maybe he's the one. We went out a few times and then, for whatever reason, we just knew we were going to do it the next time we got together. I was real nervous, but really excited too. I wanted everything to be perfect, romantic, you know? We knew his parents wouldn't be home, so we went into his parents' bedroom and had sex. It wasn't as great as I had imagined because it hurt a lot. But I was thinking, "Well, this is just how it goes the first time, just try to enjoy it." When we finished, or I guess he finished, because I didn't come, we got up and I was feeling like we had just done something special together. But then I heard laughing, like someone under his breath. It turns out that his brother was home, and they had set up the whole thing on a bet or something. His brother had been watching us through the crack in the door, and this guy who I thought was my boyfriend had like, set up the whole thing to show off to his older brother. I was so humiliated, and he just said, "Geez, I didn't think it was such a big deal. Loosen up why don't you?" I was really crushed, really devastated. I couldn't believe I'd fallen for something so low. And it really made me doubt myself, more so even than him, because I had thought he liked me and found me attractive, and come to find out, he was really just playing a game with me. (Frances, 21, "heterosexual," "American Indian/French")

Both Cynthia and Frances were left hurt and humiliated by what had promised to be a wonderful experience that would bring them pleasure and liberate them from their childhood identities. And yet, when I asked them whether they felt victimized or abused, each woman responded vehemently that she did not. For Frances, acknowledging herself as victimized would have meant that she was a "dumb little girl."

If I thought of myself as victimized, then it would be like I was just a dumb little girl who got in over her head. At the time, I wanted to prove to myself how grown-up I was, so I didn't want to even consider that I might have been taken advantage of. I mean, I knew he was really mean to do what he did, it's not like I denied what happened, but it was just that feeling like, I can't say I was really taken advantage of, because then I'd be naive and stupid. (Frances, 21, "heterosexual," "American Indian/French")

For Cynthia, too, labeling her experience abuse or victimization would entail a forfeiture of her status as a "together" adult. Thus, she drew from the love hurts and the true victim discourses and reasoned that the physical force and profound insensitivity she experienced simply "came with the territory" of being sexual and trying to be "grown-up."

> No, I don't think of it as abuse or victimization or anything, because even though it may have looked that way with his hand over my mouth and his hurting me and all, I just don't think I could ever call myself a victim, because I like to think I have it too much together to ever let myself be victimized like that. I went into the whole thing willingly, and even though I got hurt, I figured, well, I wanted to be a grown-up, so this just comes with the territory I guess. (Cynthia, 22, "bisexual," "white")

For Frances, Cynthia, and others, ideas about victimization were woven deeply with their thoughts about their own maturity and efforts to become adults. Indeed, these young women seemed to see maturity and victimization as mutually exclusive. Their senses of themselves as mature, "together" adults were contingent on not experiencing themselves, or appearing to others, to fit in the category "victim." Informed by the together woman discourse that mature women create their own destinies and should always find sexual satisfaction, acknowledging themselves as victimized seemed to be an admission of failure, requiring them to see themselves as naive, taken advantage of, or "just a dumb little girl who got in over her head." Thus, despite the pain and degradation they experienced, they needed to exclude themselves from the category "victim" in order to be included in the category "adult." Further, having been exposed through schooling, media, and sometimes families to the true victim discourse's contention that victimization is clear-cut and always involves complete physical resistance on the part of the victim, these young women may also have excluded themselves from the category "victim" because they chose to be in the situations in which their exploitation occurred (although, of course, they did not "choose" to be hurt or exploited).

The tangles of together womanhood and pleasing womanhood with potential danger were apparent in other aspects of young women's heterorelational encounters as well. Like Heidi, who understood men's whistles as an indication that she was "actually a woman," many of the participants found pleasure in the attention they received through flirting and sexualized comments or behaviors from unknown men on the street. They often interpreted the attention as a sign of their success as pleasing, sexually desirable women. Most of the participants revealed that they continued to find such experiences exciting, flattering, and reassuring, at least some of the time. Indeed, Tonya acknowledged that if she felt she looked good but men on the street did not make comments, "it makes me feel really bad about myself for that day, at least until I get another catcall." Jeanne noted that men's comments may be "really gross," but they also made her feel sexy and powerful.

> I like it when men whistle or "Hey baby" or "Can I have some of that" or whatever. It's really gross, but I do respond when men respond to me like that. I may just smile, or if they're ugly, I may roll my eyes and give them a look like, "Yeah, you wish!" But it makes me feel like I'm not some flat-chested, boring little kid. Like I'm a sexy, powerful woman who's wanted. (Jeanne, 18, "heterosexual," "Black, Indian, white")

Through these types of interactions, young women experienced a taste of the excitement and sexual power promised by the together woman discourse, along with the satisfaction of being regarded by men as pleasing. However, they also reported that they often experienced those same male behaviors as simultaneously frightening, threatening, or demeaning. For instance, although Jeanne stated above that men's comments made her feel sexy, adult, and powerful, she acknowledged that they could also make her feel vulnerable and, ironically, young.

> When I was younger I got in situations where I probably was way in over my head. I would make lots of direct eye contact, or stare at a guy's crotch or something, I guess to show how advanced I was, and to tease them, to make them want me and then just walk by. There was a thrill to the danger of it, but when I look at it now, I really could have gotten myself in trouble. It's not a very smart way to get your kicks, because there's a lot of guys who are serious. I still worry because it's hard to know what to do when that happens. I like to think of myself as all grown up now, a woman who can flirt if she wants or not flirt if she doesn't. But those interactions can take you right back to high school where you're just over your head, not knowing how to react. (Jeanne, 18, "heterosexual," "Black, Indian, white")

Women also reported mixed feelings about sexual attention from males they knew, particularly those who supervised them at work or at school. Across the study, one in five women described situations in which they had been invited or coerced to enter into sexualized interactions with male bosses, high school teachers, or coaches (none of the women reported initiating these interactions). Like those who experienced sexualized attention from strangers, the women who received such attention from male supervisors typically found themselves simultaneously flattered and frightened. For Evelyn, a sexual relationship with her high school coach represented both an affirmation that she was more mature and desirable than her peers and the threat of getting into trouble if she did not participate in this relationship.

> At first I really liked it. It was like, "Oh, he's chosen me because I'm so mature and he's so attracted to me." And I really liked the extra attention I got from him. It made me feel like I had something more than the other girls on the team. It was exciting that we were both, like, playing with fire, because he was married, and I was only fifteen. It's like we were both forbidden fruit. But as time went on, it became clear that if I didn't go along with his game, I could be cut from the team and I could maybe be reported or something. I thought I could get in a lot of trouble. Plus, this man was like a god to us, and here I was sharing in this intimate, peer-like relationship with him. That's what I thought anyway, because he treated me like a peer, and that made me feel really special and like a woman, not like all those other silly girls in my class. But when I realized just how much power this man had over me, it was really frightening. I don't know if he was using me, exactly, but I do know that I figured out I'd better not say no. (Evelyn, 21, "heterosexual," "Caucasian")

Like Evelyn, Andrea had mixed feelings about sexualized attention from an adult authority figure. While she did not have a physical relationship with her social studies teacher, she found herself excited by his attention to her body. Yet she also worried that his focus on her sexuality meant he was dismissing the quality of her work.

> My teacher always looked at me right in the chest, or right in the crotch, basically. It was kind of exciting having that kind of attention from an older man, but it also made me wonder if he even saw my work or if he was just interested in my body. Some people talk about it as like, harassment, but back then, I mean, it wasn't actually that long ago, but I didn't have any analysis of it. I didn't know how to feel, flattered or disappointed and insulted. It really worried me. (Andrea, 20, "mixed—Lebanese/Chinese/Swedish/American"; asked how she described her sexuality, she wrote, "—")

While not fearing for their physical safety, these women realized that they had reason to fear serious repercussions, both from their "participation" in sexualized contact with more powerful men and from attempts they might make to sever or report such contact. Whether being cut from a sports team (and, as Evelyn later indicated, perhaps losing a sports scholarship), facing disciplinary action, being fired, or having their sense of the quality of their minds or their work undermined, the costs of both participating and refusing to participate in sexualized interactions with supervisors were braided quite clearly with any sense of pleasure.

It is important to recognize throughout this discussion that while participants sometimes described an incident as entirely frightening or entirely fun, in most of their descriptions the elements of danger and excitement were interwoven. That is, they often experienced simultaneously a sense of pleasure and potential danger, power and powerlessness, flattery and humiliation. As Olivia put it, "it lifts you up, but it also puts you in your place." Whereas feminist analyses typically cast harassment as unsolicited and demeaning, these women felt the degradation of men's sexualized attention in contexts of unequal power, but they also experienced it as an affirmation of their adult womanhood. Indeed, women like Evelyn and Andrea interpreted sexual attention from more powerful men as welcomed evidence that they were more mature and desirable than their peers. And women like Tonya acknowledged that their whole day could be ruined if men did not comment on their sexualized appearance. For these participants, sitting on the cusp between girlhood and adult womanhood, such interactions represented both confirmation of young women's sexual maturity *and* an introduction into the domination and exploitation of women that too often accompany adult hetero-relations.

Even more compelling than the coexistence of pleasure and danger is the way these elements sometimes enhanced one another in the participants' subjective experiences. That is, while some found pleasure *despite* potential danger, others found themselves attracted to men or situations *because* of the potential danger. As Jeanne noted, "there was a thrill to the danger" of arousing unknown men and then feeling the power of walking away. As Evelyn suggested in recounting her daring enjoyment of "forbidden fruit," excitement can come from "playing with fire." In such cases, power is not simply externally imposed on an unwilling woman by a dominating male presence. Indeed, young women's own senses of power and pleasure may be fueled by their ability (however tentative) to stare down the normal/danger dichotomy and the (hetero)sex as female victimization discourses and, instead, to flirt with danger. The catch, of course, is that Evelyn, Jeanne, and others needed to rethink the wisdom of flirting with danger once they realized the more concrete forms of power that men could exercise over them (such as undermining academic or athletic pursuits, or chasing after and violating women who dare to walk away). The challenge, then, becomes how to deal with potentially dangerous or objectifying sexualized encounters (whether planned or spontaneous, chosen or imposed) in ways that preserve or enhance one's sense of mature and "together" sexual identity—but without getting hurt. As we will see in chapters 5 and 6, this challenge continues to pull at these women in their current hetero-relational understandings and decision making.

## Sexual Sophistication and Managing Ambivalence

As we have seen from the preceding challenges, the pressure to represent oneself as a "together" adult woman plays a central role in forming how the participants understand and grapple with their hetero-relations. This pressure, both externally imposed and internally felt, gives shape to a third social and developmental challenge that underlies and is incorporated into the two discussed above. The third challenge involves a tension between the enormous ambivalence most young women felt about their hetero-relations and a strong sense that if they were truly mature, sexually sophisticated women, they would experience no confusion, misgivings, or sexual "hang-ups" at all.

Running throughout the interviews was a sense that well-adjusted women should not feel, or at least should not demonstrate, any conflicts or doubts about their own sexual behaviors and decisions. As we can see from the women's narrations throughout this and the preceding chapter, the competing cultural messages young women received—about femininity and sexuality, danger and desire, entitlement and responsibility—left them feeling tremendous ambivalence about how to position themselves in their sexual encounters with men. And yet, despite an awareness of the double binds in which they were placed, women repeatedly expressed a sense that they were not allowed to demonstrate any evidence that they were not completely sure of themselves and their decisions. While they were not supposed to appear "too forward," neither were they supposed to appear "uncool."

For many women, mixed feelings or a change of mind during a sexual encounter not only meant losing face in front of a partner, it also indicated to the women themselves that they were not as mature as they wanted to be. Like Gloria, who described herself as "mean" for deciding to give a young man oral sex rather than having intercourse, participants often expressed embarrassment or a sense of failure when changing their minds during a sexual experience. For instance, instead of seeing her decision to stop a sexual encounter as an empowered choice reflecting her own state of mind, Melissa worried that her confusion and desire to stop signaled that she was "dumb," "uncool," and "immature."

> I just copped out, right in the middle of it. I guess I wasn't as ready as I'd claimed to be. I really thought I could go through with it, but as things progressed, I just started to feel real uncomfortable. He was pretty cool about it, but I felt really dumb. I'm sure I looked totally uncool, you know, acted really immature. I felt like I'd failed him, but more so myself. (Melissa, 21, "heterosexual," "Eastern European-American Jew")

While Gloria and Melissa experienced a change of mind *during* an encounter they had originally chosen, other women reported that the pressure to appear confident and unambivalent was a key factor in their decision to *enter into* sexual situations about which they felt conflicted. More than a quarter of the participants described "losing" their virginity when they did not feel ready, because they feared appearing frigid, uptight, or "uncool" to a partner or to friends. Claudia, for instance, felt a sense of internalized pressure to have intercourse because she worried that the boy she was with would tell their friends and that they would make fun of her for being afraid to have sex. Although she knew about safer sex practices and thought she would never have sex without a condom, she decided to do so at this time, because she could not think of a good reason to give the boy for wanting to stop. Afraid of looking "uptight" and facing ridicule, she "let him do it."

> A bunch of us at camp were out at night and we went into the woods. Everybody was pairing off and going their separate ways. This guy nods at me and gestures to come over to him. He starts kissing me and takes my

hand and leads me over behind this big rock. It was really exciting, because I was afraid I wasn't going to be chosen. We got to the point of,
like, he wanted to be inside me. I didn't have any condoms, and he didn't
say anything about them either. I know about safe sex and I never thought
I'd do anything stupid. But I felt like if I didn't have sex with him, it
would get around like I was some kind of uptight little kid. I felt like I
should wait till I could get a condom. But even though my head was
telling me to just say no, I let him do it because at the time, things were
moving fast and I couldn't think of a reason I could tell him no without
looking like, I don't know, without him and his friends making fun of me.
(Claudia, 21, "heterosexual," "Caucasian")

Whereas Claudia feared losing face in front of her friends, Jocelyn had
intercourse for the first time because she felt guilty for letting things go too
far. Although she had always planned to wait until she was engaged before
having intercourse, she found herself pressured to "go all the way" by a
boy who appealed to the male sexual drive discourse, persuading her that
he had a right to expect intercourse once things had progressed to a certain point. Feeling she had forfeited her right to say no once thing got "hot
and heavy," and fearing he would see her as a "squeamish kid," she said she
"caved" despite her own misgivings.

I guess I just let it go too far. We were making out and we were both
pretty hot and heavy, but I didn't feel ready to go all the way. This definitely wasn't going to be the boy I was going to marry. I was only sixteen.
But he was like, "Come on, I need to. You can't hold out on me. Why'd
you let me get this far? You're just uptight. Relax." I didn't know what to
do. I wanted to just fool around and then stop before, you know, intercourse. I never planned to go all the way with him. He was so persistent,
and I just sort of caved. It's not like I gave into passion or anything, but it
seemed like, "All right, I guess you must be right, I shouldn't have let it
get this far, and now I don't really have any choice." I maybe could have
been persistent and kept saying no, but it seemed like it was my fault for
being wishy-washy, and I didn't want to seem like I was freaking out and
have him think I was some kind of a nut or a squeamish little kid. (Jocelyn, 19, "hetero," "mutt")

A similar fear led some women who had already had hetero-sexual intercourse to become sexually involved with a person or a situation about

which they felt uncomfortable. Robin shared an experience in which she agreed to have sex with a man she met at a party to avoid "losing face and pissing him off."

> This guy was a lot older than me, and I didn't know him. He seemed kind of tough and slick, which was pretty sexy, but kind of like, this isn't somebody I should get too close to. I didn't have any intentions of sleeping with him. He has an apartment, and we went there, which was maybe stupid, but I wanted to hang out with him and maybe fool around a little, and I didn't want to look like I was a prude, because I'm not. I had slept with guys before, and I didn't want to look like I was naive or insult him. Things progressed farther than I expected, and this guy was making me really uncomfortable because he was moving too fast. We were alone in his apartment, and I figured it would be pretty weird if I just got up and left after it had gone so far. I can't really explain what my thinking was, because technically, I could have left. I got so weighed down not wanting to show him how uncomfortable I was. I don't even know why, because it's not like I even cared about him. But I felt like stopping would mean losing face and pissing him off. I was scared, I guess. Like he'd think I was a fuck-up or a tease. (Robin, 21, "heterosexual"; asked to describe her race(s), she wrote, "I cannot")

While Robin stated that she would have been able to end the interaction by leaving the apartment, and that, indeed, she wanted to, she was weighed down by the pressure to act like an adult. The intensity of this pressure was such that even though she did not care about him, she found it preferable to have intercourse with a man who made her uncomfortable rather than risk angering him or showing him how uncomfortable she actually felt.

For many of the participants, the need to seem "together" resulted in a constant monitoring of themselves during their sexual interactions with men. Like Louise and Darla, quoted at the beginning of this chapter, women felt compelled to present themselves as both "pleasing" and "together" throughout their encounters. Endeavoring to look grown-up, sophisticated, and not uptight, they tried to anticipate their partners' judgments of their every move. Wendy spoke of a sort of disembodiment as she monitored herself and scrutinized her behavior for any indications that she might seem inhibited or like "a little child." Indeed, she acknowledged that she is typically so preoccupied with "acting right" that, as she put it, "I don't even feel what I'm feeling."

I always feel like I'm there but not there. Like I'm up on the ceiling looking down on the whole thing, making sure I'm acting the right way and trying to figure out what the right way even is. It gets so that I'm so busy observing myself that I don't even feel what I'm feeling. I'm always checking everything out, making sure I'm making the right noises and pretending I like everything because I don't want him to think I'm frigid or inhibited or I don't know what I'm doing. So when the guy is all hot, I pretend I am too, even if I don't like what he's doing, because I don't want to seem like a cold fish or a little child. It's important to me, I guess, to present myself like I know what I want, even though I really just go along with whatever the guy is doing. (Wendy, 22, "heterosexual," Puerto Rican/Italian")

The women in this study generally felt tremendous pressure to demonstrate complete comfort, sophistication, and lack of ambivalence in their hetero-relational encounters. And yet, given the impossibly mixed messages they had internalized and the various audiences they felt compelled to please (such as families, friends, religion, and male partners), it was very rare, indeed, for women to describe a sexual situation with men in which they *did not* experience some degree of ambivalence. Like the preceding two social and developmental challenges, the need to demonstrate adulthood by appearing clear and unwavering in the midst of such confusion underlies much of the women's current hetero-relational decision making, as we will see in chapters 5 and 6.

## Some Common Themes

Looking across young women's narratives, we can see some common themes underlying their hetero-relational thinking and behaviors amid the social and developmental challenges explored above. As we have witnessed, each challenge incorporates multiple discourses identified in chapter 3 and sets the stage for considerable struggle as women attempt to define and communicate their hetero-relational desires. Whether by compelling them to participate in encounters in which they felt uncomfortable or dissuading them from exploring and asserting their own needs in encounters they had chosen, the pressures to balance a sense of sexual adulthood with other needs—to be a "good girl," to avoid (or eroticize) potential danger, and to manage ambivalence—exacted a considerable toll on the minds and bodies of these young women. For any one voice shouting to them from their psychological mirrors, there were countless others, equally compelling, each sending them conflicting messages. And for each constituent—each part of themselves—they chose to please, others were waiting to express warnings and negative judgment.

The need to present oneself as sexually sophisticated and yet not too "worldly," along with the need to manage danger and to suppress feelings of ambivalence, poses important and problematic challenges for young women's developing hetero-relational subjectivities. The overall challenge, however, is not for young women to somehow escape or transcend the cultural discourses that surround them; trying to step outside discourse would be, as Gee (1987) so aptly puts it, like trying to repair a jet in flight from outside the jet itself. It is simply not possible. As Frye (1983) reminds us,

> None of us obeys all the rules, even if we want to. But the stereotypes, the rules, the common expectations of us surround us all in a steady barrage of verbal and visual images in popular, elite, religious and underground vehicles of culture. Virtually every individual is immersed most of the time in a cultural medium which provides sexist and misogynist images of what we are and what we think we are doing. Our conceiving cannot be independent of culture, though it can be critical, resistant or rebellious. . . . [A woman] is not independent of the power of those images but in tension with it. Her practice is affected by that tension. (p.xiii)

The overall challenge, then, is not to strive to be unaffected by the power of these discourses and dilemmas, but rather to manage the tensions of living within them. As we can see from the participants' stories, their hetero-relational encounters represent ongoing struggles to do just that. A closer look at these struggles reveals at least three important themes that wind through young women's efforts to deal with the overlapping social and developmental challenges they face: an extraordinary focus on audiences, a splitting of mind from body, and a tendency to lose their voices in the face of unpleasant hetero-relational encounters.

## The Centrality of Audiences

Throughout these three social and developmental challenges, we witness a consistent and troubling subordination of women's search for their own desires to the expectations of outside, and often internalized, audiences. Since we are socially and historically constructed beings, our desires are never simply internal, individually derived phenomena; they necessarily incorporate the cultural images and expectations that surround us. Yet the young women in this study appeared extraordinarily focused on the perceptions of others as they negotiated their paths into hetero-relational adulthood. Often women became so consumed with the conflicting expectations of various outside audiences (families versus boyfriends; college friends versus neighborhood friends) about gender-appropriate and developmentally appropriate behavior, that the notion of their own needs and sexual desires was all but erased from consideration.

The significance of the role of audiences in young women's hetero-relations may be analyzed in a variety of ways. A more traditional psychological view might contend that, as adolescents and young adults, these young women are simply more heavily focused on outside confirmation than they might be at earlier or later stages in their lives. Adolescents in Western culture are often thought to be more preoccupied than either children or adults with struggles between the desire to conform to the social standards of their peers and the need to stake their claim in the world as unique and independent individuals (Cole and Cole, 1993). Similarly, sitting on the threshold between childhood and adulthood in a Western culture that lacks clear rituals or rites of passage into adulthood, they may rely more heavily on others' perceptions of them as indicators of their developmental appropriateness as emerging young adults. In an arena such as sexuality, which is so socially charged, but about which this culture remains so ambivalent, adolescents and young adults might be particularly compelled to give more weight to the responses they receive from external audiences.

Yet a simple life stage explanation does not account sufficiently for the intensity of these young women's struggles with the expectations of outside (and internalized) audiences. Rather, it is likely that a developmentally linked emphasis on external confirmation is overlapped and exacerbated by the expectations young women face as members of the "Other" or "marked" gender category, "female." These participants are not gender-neutral individuals at a particular life stage; rather, they are *embodied* adolescent and young adult *women*. Whereas maleness (like whiteness) is taken as the standard, unmarked category, women (like all people of color) are charged as the "carriers" of gender (or race).[5] As such, their hetero-relational behaviors are scrutinized in ways that men's are not. Young women develop their hetero-relational subjectivities with an awareness that it is they who are held responsible for representing morality and sexual "purity"; that it is they who are held accountable for controlling men's sexual behaviors; that it is they who are expected to be pleasing caretakers and desirable objects for the other gender; and that it is they who are criticized whether they attract the wrong men, too many men, or no man at all.

It follows, then, that the participants' preoccupation with the judgment of outside audiences is attributable not only to development but to gender relations, and that it is further entwined with issues involving race, class, and sexuality. As Frye (1983) points out, women are bombarded with a series of "double bind[s]—situations in which options are reduced to a very few and all of them expose one to penalty, censure or deprivation" (2). As we have seen from the participants' narratives thus far, the very experience of deciding how, when, if, and with whom to express their sexualities presents adolescent and young adult women with particular double binds that young men may not face, forcing them to choose between successful adulthood and womanhood, sexual pleasure and safety, and sophistication and the erasure of their own misgivings. It makes sense that young women, anticipating repercussions for any choice made, would be particularly watchful for the responses of those around them. For those whose actions are further scrutinized due to racism, classism, and homophobia, it follows that both the potential repercussions and the need to monitor themselves and others' responses would be magnified. But while the experience may vary in tone and magnitude within and across race, class, and sexuality, the pressures to balance conflicting expectations, to please men and other peers, and to avoid repercussions leave each of these young women looking over her shoulder, waiting for the other shoe to drop.

## Mind/Body Split

Stemming from the importance of audiences is a compelling tendency for young women, both in their encounters and in their narratives, to experience their minds and their bodies as rather separate entities. Of course, they are physically present in their interactions. Yet participants often described a splitting of mind from body so that they could observe and attempt to control their bodies' experiences. In some cases, they inter-preted male attention to their bodies as an indication that something was lacking about their minds.

Monitoring themselves during their hetero-relations to avoid disap-proval, many young women echoed Wendy's sense of being "up on the ceiling . . . looking down on the whole thing . . . so busy observing myself that I don't even feel what I'm feeling." Like Wendy, women such as Louise, Darla, Henna, Sara, and others noted that they spent a great deal of energy "watching" themselves having sex with men, mentally stepping outside their experiences to determine whether they were acting appropri-ately. Participants reported repeatedly that their decisions about how to present themselves physically, how and when to make noises, and how to move their bodies were determined far less by their own bodily sensations than by their mental calculations of what men would want them to do. Preoccupied with their partners' assessments, and sometimes concerned about the judgment of others (families, friends, teachers) who might find out, the young women seemed, at least metaphorically, to leave their bod-ies, trading physical pleasure for mental control.

A splitting of mind from body is further seen in the experiences of those such as Andrea, whose teacher's sexual gestures made her doubt her intel-lectual work and her competence. Consistent with Brodkey and Fine's (1988) findings of university women's responses to sexual harassment, par-ticipants who were harassed by and/or in relationships with male teachers and supervisors voiced concerns that men's focus on their bodies meant a dismissal of the quality of their minds. Unlike Brodkey and Fine's respon-dents, the young women in this study often felt flattered (at least initially) by such attention, believing that being "selected" indicated that they were particularly desirable, special, and mature. Yet each of the women who de-scribed sexualized interactions with a teacher, coach, or boss reported that, at some point, she was made to question the skills she brought to her work situation. For these young women, being seen as a body ultimately meant being diminished as a mind.

## Losing One's Voice

Related to the participants' focus on audience and their splitting of mind from body was the absence from many women's stories of a sense of entitlement to explore their own needs or desires, and to express them when they differed from their male partners' or from cultural scripts for adult, pleasing, or "together" women. While most women described having strong sexual desires and finding pleasure in the sensations of their own bodies, too often these desires became subordinated to men's in their actual hetero-relations. Clearly, some women were coerced into sexual interactions they did not want, and clearly some women voiced their objections but were forced to act against their wishes. But often women spoke of being excited, albeit nervous, to engage in sexualized relations with men, only to find the actual encounters disturbing, exploitive, or displeasurable. And once in those interactions, they experienced great reluctance to voice their pain or misgivings, to tell partners what would give them pleasure, or to end an encounter before a man was "finished."

Although few of the participants expressed an abstract belief in the premises of the male sexual drive discourse, many seemed influenced quite strongly by this discourse in their actual encounters. Often persuaded that male desire was of the utmost importance, many of the women in this study expressed a sense of responsibility to go along with, and even fake being excited by, whatever a male partner was doing, so as not to interfere with his arousal. Further persuaded by the together woman discourse that only immature women express discomfort in sexual interactions, by the pleasing woman discourse that desirable women must give men pleasure, and by the true victim discourse that sexual women deserve what they get, the participants were often unable to find a place for their own needs or pleasure in their sexual interactions with men.[6]

Losing one's voice occurred not only during an encounter, so that men were not told that young women were hurt or dissatisfied; it also continued after encounters were over, through women's inability or unwillingness to express to men their pain, anger, and/or confusion about hurtful interactions. Whether due to fear of reprisals, anticipation of ridicule, self-blame, or inadequate language to name their experiences, participants typically privatized their very mixed feelings about unpleasant encounters.

These women are charged with situating themselves and their experiences in a set of discourses that privilege male pleasure, excuse male aggression, and hold women responsible for pleasing men and acting as gatekeepers for male (mis)behavior (White and Niles, 1990). Further, they must do so in a cultural and developmental context that typically blames female victims, denies young women's sexual subjectivities, and yet equates "togetherness" and maturity with a lack of sexual ambiguity. In such a climate, the young women in this study are left to devise individual strategies for managing their hetero-relations, as well as their ambivalence. As we shall see in the upcoming chapters, these strategies, while sometimes effective on an immediate, personal level, often reproduce the silencing of women's voices and the privatization of the experiences of their bodies.

For the women in this study, the process of positioning themselves as adult sexual subjects is embedded in a strongly felt need to appease a range of constituents with discrepant beliefs and expectations. Returning to the image at the beginning of this chapter, we can see that the participants' senses of how/who to be are not independent of the faces staring back at them from their psychological mirrors—whether from the back of their heads or next to them in bed. Their narrations reveal the translation of pervasive and contradictory hetero-relational discourses into a series of social and developmental challenges for young women transitioning from childhood to adulthood.[7] These discourses and challenges live on in the participants' current hetero-relational subjectivities and are reflected and reproduced in their perceptions, management, and attributions about their hetero-relationships. As we step into an examination of the participants' current hetero-relational strategies, then, it is important to bring with us the psychological and cultural contexts established here, and to appreciate that these young women are embodied subjects-in-progress—drawing from, resisting, and reshaping their prior lessons and experiences—as they attempt to negotiate power and meaning in their various relationships with men.

5

■　　■　　■　　■　　■　　■　　■　　■　　■

# Managing Contradictions

*Getting in, out, and around*
*Hetero-Relations*

Not only was I scared about having sex with him, but I was also sort of scared about not doing it. I felt like it was time to put up or shut up and prove to myself I could do it, and to give him what he wanted. I knew he didn't care about me as much as he wanted what he could get out of me. I felt like if I just said yes I would be cheap or something, so I needed to create in my head what it really wasn't in reality, like I was being swept off my feet and not directly saying yes, like we were swept away by something bigger than both of us. I mean, I chose to do it, but I couldn't quite let myself know that. It had to feel like something that just happened, beyond my control. Then it would be all right. But it wasn't a good experience at all. He was really rough and he was moving me around like I was some sort of prop. Like I was just something for him to act out his pleasure on, not a real human being he was interacting with. It was humiliating, but I just kept thinking, "He really does care, he just doesn't know how to be gentle yet." Or, "He's just so excited by me that he can't help what his body's doing." So many things racing through my head all at once. I didn't feel any pleasure at all. But I just kept pretending like, "Oh, this is so great," so he would get it over with and not get mad at me for being a disappointment. Afterward I felt awful, but also glad I managed to get out of the situation as easily as I did. I never told anyone about it until now, because I felt really dumb that I let this happen to me, and sort of weird for not liking it.

—Claudia, 21, "heterosexual," "Caucasian"

CLAUDIA'S WORDS SPEAK to the many contradictory feelings possible in any one encounter. They also speak to the psychological strategies young women call on to manage moments of pain, anticipation, and ambivalence. Experiencing mixed emotions about entering into this sexual encounter, Claudia first constructs a private fantasy, creating in her mind "what it wasn't in reality." By trying to convince herself that she is swept away with passion and letting it "just happen," she allows herself permission to step into an interaction she wants (albeit for multiple reasons and with very mixed feelings) but feels unentitled to choose actively. Once in the sexual encounter, feeling hurt and objectified, she attempts to lessen the humiliation of being reduced to a mere "prop" for a man to "act out his pleasure on." Here, she turns to cognitive strategies to manage her emotional and physical pain, constructing rationales for his behavior (he didn't know any better; she was so sexy he couldn't help himself) that allow her to preserve her own integrity, even as she is feeling exploited. Finally, we see Claudia developing a third strategy "so he would get it over with," without risking the possible consequences of this man's anger, and without losing face as "a disappointment" to him. By pretending to him (and possibly to herself) that she loved it, she is perhaps able to shorten the encounter and to end it without letting him know that anything was wrong. Even as she reflects afterward on the situation, she feels "awful," and yet "glad" that her strategies worked as well as they did. While her attempts worked to preserve some physical and emotional safety during the encounter, she is left with feelings of self-blame and a sense of being "weird" for having felt bad in the first place.

Claudia's reflections offer a compelling window on young women's complex subjective experiences—before, during, and after their hetero-relational encounters. Although each woman experienced her encounters as private and unique, I heard echoes of Claudia's struggles across countless stories shared by other participants. As I pondered these stories I came to see that, like Claudia, each woman had devised her own strategies to negotiate her way through and around encounters marked by ambiguity and mixed emotions. While these strategies were not necessarily conscious, calculated, or completely effective, they represented efforts to maintain somewhat tentative, but nonetheless important, feelings of control in situations that threatened women's sense of agency.

As young women attempted to assess their hetero-relational experiences and maneuver within them, they often felt vulnerable and profoundly alone. Yet in many ways, they were never alone, for they brought with them a host of other voices that informed their decisions and shaped their options. They spoke of the pressure to please partners, the weight of external audiences who might think less of them, and the need to position themselves as "together," desiring agents, yet still pleasing women, in contexts that could undermine their sense of control. Even as they devised what appear to be personal strategies for protecting their minds, their bodies, and their reputations, those strategies were informed by the cultural discourses and social and developmental challenges discussed in previous chapters. As we can see from Claudia's reflections, their assessments and decisions were often as entwined and contradictory as the discourses that infused them. These young women did not simply face a discrete task of deciding how to handle a particular encounter, nor were their choices straightforward. Rather, they were involved in an ongoing social and developmental process, constructing intricate strategies for making their way through conflicting ideas and provocative dilemmas about maturity, gender, power, and women's and men's entitlement and responsibility to themselves and each other.

It is no coincidence that the participants developed *individualized* strategies to manage their hetero-relations. Turning to the interpretive categories available to them, and navigating the gendered power relations inherited from their societal contexts, these women were left to devise strategies in a culture that privileges discourses promoting women's personal accountability, and withholds or marginalizes discourses that might shift responsibility for men's behaviors onto men themselves. Coming of age in an individualistic society, and encouraged to shoulder full responsibility for preventing or tolerating abuse and exploitation, it is not surprising that participants would privatize their experiences and try, on their own, to develop strategies for making the best of bad situations. Unfortunately, these very strategies also prevented women from seeing the many similarities across their stories, and thus from voicing collective outrage and strategizing together on societal, rather than just individual, levels.

Young women's overlapping attempts to assess their hetero-relations and to position themselves in them wound through at least three facets of their experiences: finding a sense of entitlement to enter into sexual encounters; managing power in those encounters; and ending or diminishing pain and disappointment when encounters failed to unfold the way they had hoped. At each of these points in their hetero-relations, young women developed and used individual strategies as they grappled, both psychologically and behaviorally, with the contradictory messages they had received. For the sake of clarity, I have teased apart women's points of entry, management within, and ways of ending their encounters. However, it is important to note that these facets of their experiences were often merged (e.g., entering into a sexual encounter could be simultaneously a way of "ending" harassment; agreeing to have oral sex could be a way of ending the threat of forced intercourse). Thus, I do not mean to imply that women's attempts to enter, manage, and end their encounters represent parts of a linear process. Instead, we may better understand them as "snapshots" of various points in an ongoing and entangled set of experiences.

Examining the strategies women used at these various points in their hetero-relations, we will find women making sometimes ironic use of the cultural constraints placed on their sexualities in order to experience feelings of personal power and entitlement. As we look closely at young women's hetero-relational strategies, we can see that each strategy in some way defies the dualisms (consent/coercion, agency/victimization, subjectivity/objectification) often presumed in scholarly and activist literature and in popular debate. Indeed, in each of these strategies we will see young women synthesizing what appear to be dichotomous notions, so that supposed opposites seem to merge and become nested within one another.

## Making an Entrance: Initiating (or Justifying) Sexual Encounters

In the midst of cultural messages telling young women that sexuality is the path to adulthood and freedom, but that "good girls" are not sexual initiators, many of the women found entering into sexualized hetero-relations a tremendous psychological challenge. Even in this progressive college setting, the participants expressed a great deal of difficulty feeling entitled to simply choose, in a straightforward manner, to express their sexualities in relationships with men. When discussing relationships in the abstract, they spoke with great conviction about women's right to sexual fulfillment. But in their actual encounters, when things got "hot and heavy," their own experiences often felt much more complicated. As Sara put it, deciding how, when, and if to engage in hetero-relational encounters could be "more than just a little tricky."

The young women in this study clearly felt strong sexual desires on which they wished to act. Throughout the interviews, I heard wild and steamy stories filled with passion, excitement, and intrigue. While many spoke of the nervous delights of seduction, flirtation, and titillation, other women cut right to the chase. As Martha put it, "I'm very sexual—horny is horny, and there's nothing wrong with that." A few women, like Natalie, reported occasions where they openly and unapologetically initiated or accepted men's invitations to have sexual encounters.

> I was so hot. I wanted this man really bad. We were flirting all night long and I was so aroused I thought I'd die. We danced really sexually and I was going out of my mind. We were both really hot and I knew he wanted me because I could feel his erection through his jeans. And he knew I could feel it, too. We went out to the parking lot and made out in the car. Then he asked if I wanted to go somewhere and I said, like, "God, yes!" We got this hotel room, which I had never done before, and we had sex all night and it was really wild. I had never experienced anything like that, and I don't know if I ever will again. Even if I never do, it was so totally worth it. (Natalie, 19, "bisexual"; asked to describe her race(s), she wrote, "unimportant")

Clearly, these women are not lacking a desire for sexual enjoyment. Yet despite the palpable presence of sexual desire, each of the participants (even Martha and Natalie) relied on psychological strategies at some point in her hetero-relations to express or justify her entitlement to sexual pleasure. They were so caught up in a web of conflicting messages and expectations that it was, unfortunately, quite rare for a young woman to describe an encounter like Natalie's, where she felt able to choose, without apology or regret, to experience pleasure and act on her own desires. Across the interviews, young women spoke of three main strategies for making an entrance into hetero-relations they desired. These strategies allowed them to create a sense of entitlement to, or justification for, their sexual activities, in light of the conflicting messages and gendered power asymmetries woven through their lives.

### Letting It (Making It) "Just Happen"

Although we saw in chapter 4 that the participants felt considerable pressure to appear "sexually sophisticated," many also described a simultaneous pressure to avoid feeling or seeming too "forward" or "knowing." Compelled by the message that "good girls don't," many women felt they needed to find seemingly passive ways to assert their sexual desires. Wanting to express their sexualities, and yet feeling unentitled to do so directly, many women chose to put themselves in situations where sex could "just happen." *Letting* it just happen became a strategy for *making* it happen without facing the psychological and social consequences of appearing "too willing." I was struck by the frequency with which young women used such expressions as "it was totally innocent," "things just happened," or "one thing just led to another, and before I knew it. . . ." Although many of the women who used this strategy said they wanted very much to engage in the sexual relationships they were describing, they felt unable, or unwilling, to describe themselves as active agents initiating, or even willingly consenting to, sexual encounters with men.

Sondra, for instance, was torn between her desire to express her sexuality and her simultaneous belief that "good girls don't." Feeling pulled by the pleasing woman discourse she had so internalized, she was unable to enjoy the sex she desired if she felt she had consented too willingly.

> It doesn't look good if I say I want it. I'd feel so self-conscious that I wouldn't be able to enjoy myself anyway, and I'd lose the mood. The only way I can really feel okay about enjoying myself is if he really coerces me into it. Which is kind of funny, because if I act on what I want, I can't let myself want it. But if I'm forced to act, not violently forced but kind of coerced into it, then I can feel like I was seduced, so then it's okay because it kind of just happens. (Sondra, 19, "heterosexual," "Afro-American/Native American")

Although Sondra's concern stemmed from a fear of not looking good to someone else if she consented to sex, that concern actually became incorporated into her own sense of desire. Experiencing a loss of passion as soon as it was expressed, she constructed her sexual encounters so that she could be "coerced" into doing what she actually wanted. More than "playing hard to get" or being a "tease," she was genuinely unable to experience pleasure unless she felt that she was forced. Not wanting to feel violently forced, she then transformed coercion into seduction so "then it's okay." Although Sondra's phrase "it kind of just happens" implies a passivity she needed to preserve, her psychological grapplings were anything but passive. Disturbed by the pleasure she felt initially, she needed to transform desire into coercion, and coercion into seduction, in order to experience that pleasure as acceptable. Of course Sondra's strategy, while active and complex, is potentially very volatile. While she may distinguish between force and *violent* force, the men she is with (not to mention the legal system) may draw different lines, subjecting her to physical abuse. Indeed, she said later in her interview, "It's gotten a little weird sometimes. I don't necessarily recommend it, but it's, like, the only way I really know."

For Melissa, letting it just happen involved the fantasy of being "taken" by a man who is bigger and stronger than she. Ironically, she found that playing a more passive role allowed her to diminish her feelings of vulnerability. Interpreting being "in control sexually" as having responsibility for pleasing her partner (rather than as an opportunity to please herself), she found pleasure in "passivity" and letting someone else "take over."

> That is such an amazing feeling, like a childhood feeling, like you're just this tiny little thing and somebody comes and picks you up and takes you wherever they want. It's really hard for me to be in control sexually. To me, you're really vulnerable when you're really trying to please somebody. Yet, with me, I think it has to do with passivity. I mean this might be kind of fucked up, but my fantasies are always like, I'm lying there and he just takes me, my whole body, he sort of takes over. (Melissa, 21, "heterosexual," "Eastern European-American Jew")

Other women, like Rachel, have found they are only able to express their sexualities directly with new partners when they are drunk or high on drugs. For Rachel, consenting while sober meant that she was making a conscious decision to have sex, something she was uncomfortable doing. Only by "loosening up" first with drugs or alcohol could she feel uninhibited enough to act on her sexual desires. Significantly, being drunk or high also allowed her to feel that she was "less conscious about the decision" so that she had an "excuse" and could feel less guilty about having had sex after an encounter was over.

> I always have to be pretty drunk or stoned to feel like I'm uninhibited enough to say yes. Not like fall-down drunk, but buzzed, at least. That way I can be less conscious about the decision. It can act as an excuse, "Oh, I got too drunk and I was all over him." Like things I would want to do when I am sober, but that I couldn't give myself permission to do without loosening up first. If I know I want to go home with someone, I have to get buzzed, not just so I can get up the nerve, but more like so I'll have an excuse or something. (Rachel, 21, "heterosexual," "white")

Paula took this strategy one step further. Although she said she often drank to allow herself to have sex, she acknowledged that she sometimes *pretended* to be drunk or high when she was not, so that others would not know that she was actively and consciously initiating a sexual encounter. She spoke of two identities: "the person I am" and "who I am inside." Paula needed to somehow suppress her everyday identity in order to allow her sense of inner self to act on her desires. Feigning intoxication allowed her permission to act in ways she otherwise could not.

> I've sometimes pretended to be more drunk or stoned than I am, because it's sort of like stepping into a role. It's like, the person I am can't really go up and start seducing a guy. But who I am inside would really like to. So I put on this role, like I'm kind of tipsy, and then it's okay for me to be really forward. It's like everybody knows people do things drunk that they aren't totally responsible for. So that way I feel less judged, so I feel less inhibited, almost like I really am drunk, even though I'm really sober. I suppose it's really just a way of being able to do what I want without being so self-conscious about the costs. (Paula, 20, "Spanish-America"; asked to describe her sexuality, she wrote, "?")

These women expressed difficulty feeling entitled to sexual pleasure unless they could convince themselves or others that a sexual situation was "totally innocent" or not "premeditated," language implying that deciding consciously to have sex, and acting on that decision, would somehow be criminal. Peggy Sanday (1990) has found in her important study of fraternity gang rape that young men often try to "work a yes out" by giving a woman too much alcohol or otherwise coercing her to retract her initial refusal of their sexual overtures. Feminists such as Sanday have appropriately pointed out that this practice is exploitive and encourages men to find forced sex with a woman acceptable, as long as she did not "technically" refuse them. While women's strategy of becoming (or pretending to become) intoxicated might appear, on the surface, to be an endorsement of men's practice of "working a yes out," it is important to note that letting/making it just happen represents a way for women to enter into encounters they *already want*; it does not represent a desire to be forced or manipulated into an encounter they have not chosen. Indeed, all the women in this study stated emphatically that they never wanted to be forced to have sex against their will. But those who adopted the strategy of letting/making it just happen did indicate that they needed a man to take the lead in order to feel comfortable agreeing to have sex with him. Paradoxically, for these women, finding a way to let sex happen *to* them became one way (perhaps the only perceived way) to be sexual subjects and yet still be pleasing women.

This strategy poses a compelling challenge to the presumed consent/coercion dichotomy underlying legal, social science, popular, and often feminist thinking. While consent and coercion are typically posed as mutually exclusive, some young women find they can allow themselves to "consent" to sexual relations only by appearing to be "coerced." Rather than experiencing consent and coercion as opposites, these young women merge the two to allow themselves pleasure without being weighed down by guilt and self-consciousness. This merging must not be misconstrued to suggest that young women wish to have men demand that they take part in unwanted sexual encounters. These women invoke the strategy of letting/making it just happen to facilitate interactions in which they very much wish to participate. This strategy does, however, demonstrate that apparent dichotomies are often less than straightforward in young women's lived experiences. In a culture that censors young women's sexual expression and threatens forfeiture of "pleasing woman" status for initiating sexual encounters, these women make efforts to carve out spaces as sexual subjects while attempting to preserve their image as "good girls." As such, some women find that action requires passivity, consent requires an appearance of coercion, and agency requires seeming to give up control.

### Doing "Everything But"

A second strategy gives young women a way to experience and act on their sexual desires without "technically" having sex. For most women, doing "everything but" meant engaging in any type of sexualized behavior other than heterosexual intercourse. I first became aware of this strategy in an interview with Jocelyn, as she described the difference between "being sexual" and "fooling around."

> I would do oral, like giving blow jobs or letting guys give me oral sex. You know, just about everything but. But I wasn't sexual until I was much older. That's when I lost my virginity. I did a lot of fooling around and we came and everything from oral sex and masturbating each other when I was younger, but I wanted to wait until I was a little older before I had sex. (Jocelyn, 19, "hetero," "mutt")

While I had interpreted "being sexual" as including a wide range of sexualized behaviors with men, with other women, or with oneself, Jocelyn pointed out that "being sexual," for many women, is reserved for having hetero-sexual intercourse, or "going all the way."

> Being sexual is when you go all the way. You know, like having sex. Intercourse, all the way. Everything up to that is just like fooling around or hooking up with somebody. Even if it's completely clothes-off, hot and heavy, orgasms and everything, I don't count it as having sex unless it's, well, actual fucking. I don't know if it's a good way to think about it, but that's the way I've always separated it.

The distinction between fooling around (oral sex, "outercourse," sex with other women, and so forth) and having sex (hetero-sexual intercourse) was no small matter for many young women. In fact, doing "everything but" served at least three important purposes for the women I interviewed. In their early experiences, it allowed many participants to take part in sexualized behavior with both males and females without forfeiting their "status" as virgins. In the minds of these young women (as in the ideologies of Western and other cultures), "loss" of virginity was seen as an official event associated specifically with penile/vaginal penetration. Since many women had clear ideas about the appropriate age or circumstances for "losing" virginity, they placed great stock in the distinction between intercourse and "everything but."

> I wanted to be a virgin until I was at least sixteen, like sweet sixteen. So I fooled around with my boyfriend up to that point, but never beyond, so we could be together, but I could still be a virgin. As much as I loved him and wanted so badly to have sex with him, I needed to be a virgin until I was sixteen. So we did everything except actual intercourse. (Heidi, 21, "bisexual," "white")

This strategy served a second purpose by allowing young women who had already had intercourse to distinguish various levels of intimacy across their encounters. Women often reported that they reserved intercourse for sexual encounters with men they loved or for whom they felt something "more than just sexual." Each of the women who used the "everything but" strategy for this purpose indicated that intercourse was one of the less *physically* pleasurable sexual activities in which she engaged. Yet for many women, it was tied symbolically to greater levels of *emotional* intimacy than any other behavior. For instance, when I asked Andrea the number of men with whom she had been sexual, her numbers differed, depending on whether she was talking about "sex" or simply being "really physical." Although she had done "everything but" with several men, she had had intercourse with only a few because she experienced more emotional intimacy and vulnerability (although less physical pleasure) from this form of sexual expression.

> Sex for me is something special, something I've only shared with a few guys. So when I think of how many guys I've had sex with, I'd say it was only four. But when I think of how many guys I've been really physical with, that's a lot more, like maybe twelve or fourteen. But I wouldn't count those as sex, because sex is really special. I wouldn't let someone inside me unless I really cared about them. It's not that it even feels so much better physically, because that's not how I tend to have orgasms. It's more like an intimate thing. Having a guy inside you makes you potentially very vulnerable, so you don't want to share that with just anybody. (Andrea, 20, "mixed—Lebanese/Chinese/Swedish/American"; asked to describe her sexuality, she wrote, "—")

Finally, in the minds of some young women, a willingness to have het-ero-sexual intercourse was tied to promiscuity or "sluttiness" in ways that "fooling around" was not. By doing "everything but" in most of their het-ero-relational encounters, and reserving intercourse for a few select men, participants were able to enter into sexualized interactions with a range of partners without looking, to themselves or others, promiscuous for having had sex with too many people. For instance, by counting sex partners as only those with whom she had had intercourse, Paula found that she felt less guilty about being "too sexual."

> I've slept with a lot of guys if you count all the guys I've ever gotten naked with. But I count the number of guys I've had actual sex with, just the num-ber I've had intercourse. Friends compare, like, "How many guys have you been with?" I have this rule that I only count guys I've gone all the way with, which is ten. Because if I went all the way with everybody, I'd feel like I looked like a slut. So I decide when I'm with somebody whether I want to go all the way, like, "Let's see, is he worth adding to my list?" The guys I've done it with, I really, really wanted to. But if I'm not so sure about them, I do everything but actual sex, so then I don't feel so guilty afterwards about being too sexual. (Paula, 20, "Spanish-American"; asked to describe her sex-uality, she wrote, "?")

By "doing everything but," these women were able to straddle the good girl versus big girl dilemma and to be sexually "together" without losing their status in the pleasing woman discourse. Yet this strategy some-times posed problems as well. Although "doing everything but" allowed participants to preserve their sense of both "pleasing" and "together" womanhood while engaging in sexualized experiences, it has also put some young women in a position to face strong male pressure and disappoint-ment. Invoking the male sexual drive discourse, these women's male part-ners have sometimes pushed them to go from "everything but" to "sex" when they did not wish to do so. Although Paula indicated in the quote above that doing "everything but" has allowed her to have actual "sex" only with men when she "really, really wanted to," she later said that she has had intercourse with more men than she wanted to, because she has felt pressure to "give in."

> Sometimes it gets kind of sticky when I don't want to go all the way with a guy but he puts the pressure on, or the guilt trip. It's really awkward and it's

not clear what to do. Sometimes a guy will accuse you of being a tease. Why can't I just do as much as I want? But guys think if you cross a certain line they deserve to go all the way. It's really weird sometimes, because I'll doubt myself, like, am I just being a prude or am I being unfair to him? Sometimes I've given in. That's why the number of guys I've slept with is ten and not a little lower. The pressure can really put you on the spot if guys don't understand, and sometimes you do what you don't want to do. (Paula, 20, "Spanish-American"; asked to describe her sexuality, she wrote, "?")

In the face of the male sexual drive, discourse which suggests that men's sexual urges must always be satisfied, as well as the pleasing woman discourse, which tells women that it is their responsibility to fulfill men's desires, participants sometimes found it difficult to do "everything but," because this strategy depends on men's willingness to comply with young women's wishes. Unfortunately, as we will see in chapter 6, men do not always uphold their end of the presumed arrangement.

## Choosing to Be a "Bad Girl"

Finally, a small number of the young women I interviewed elected to deal with the conflicting demands of being both sexual and "innocent" by choosing consciously to turn their backs on the faces in the mirror that stressed the cultural requirement to be pleasing women or good girls. Three of the women made a clear decision at some point to be, as Laura put it, "a Bad Girl: capital *B*, capital *G*." By her definition, a Bad Girl is a girl or woman who is openly and unapologetically sexual, and who derives a sense of pleasure from refusing to comply with social prescriptions for being a "good girl." This strategy stands in rather sharp contrast to letting/making it "just happen." Laura explained the thinking that prompted her decision, early in adolescence, to become a Bad Girl.

I grew up with all that madonna/whore stuff. It was all around me growing up. It was real strong in my community and my family. The whole madonna/whore thing is supposed to be like a threat. For girls, it's supposed to make you want to be the virgin. But I realized when I was around fourteen that madonnas were good girls, but whores had fun. I decided enough with that madonna crap, I wanted to have fun. I decided right there that I was going to just go for broke. Be a bad girl and just have a good old time, even if somebody wanted to call me a whore. In fact, it was like a point of

pride with me. If somebody had come up and called me a whore or something, I would have said, "Thank you" or something crazy like that. (Laura,
22, "bisexual," "bi-racial/West Black Indian, white American")

Theresa, too, decided to become a bad girl at an early age. Realizing at
age thirteen that she felt strong sexual desires and wanted to act on them,
she was simultaneously aware that "good girls don't." It quickly became
clear to Theresa that her desire to have sex outweighed her desire to be
seen as a nice girl, and so, she said, she decided to become "a slut."

Basically, I just decided to become a slut. Really, I mean, that's what I decided to do. I decided I wanted to have sex and I wasn't going to be like the
passive, demure little lady about it and try to pretend I was a nice girl, because I knew that once you decided to have sex you were never going to be
a nice girl anymore in anyone's eyes anyway, so why not just accept the fact
and be a slut? I knew exactly what I was doing, and I basically felt really empowered by it. (Theresa, 19, "heterosexual," "bi-racial")

While Theresa described a sense of empowerment gained through her
choice to become "a slut," she went on to say that her decision did entail
a certain loss.

I felt mostly really good about deciding to be a slut. But there are other
things you miss out on. I never got to feel like I could just be feminine. First
of all, you get alienated from girlfriends because they think you're conta-
gious or something. And second of all, if you go to do things other girls do,
like makeup or doing your hair pretty or clothes and that, it's like you're
never seen as doing it because you're a girl. It's only seen as you're doing it
because you're a slut.

While the women who used this strategy felt they were making a clear
and empowered choice, it is important to note that they were compelled
to make that choice within a framework that was not necessarily their
own. That is, while choosing to be a bad girl was, for these young
women, the more attractive of two options (being a good woman or a
sexual woman), the fact that they found only two options, and that they
experienced those options as mutually exclusive, reveals the constraints
placed on them by a deeply androcentric, hetero-sexist, and sex-con-
flicted culture.

## Vying for Position: Strategies for Managing Power in Hetero-Relations

Whether young women experienced a particular encounter as voluntary and pleasurable (as in the decision to engage in a sexual interaction that was wanted), coerced (as in acquaintance rape or street harassment), or both, they appeared to expend considerable energy finding ways to "vie for position" in their sexual experiences. In light of their expressed need to feel strong, self-determined, and sexually sophisticated, the participants voiced a powerful motivation to perceive themselves as in control of even their most unwanted circumstances. Interestingly, even those women who used the strategy of "letting/making it just happen" to *enter into* their encounters spoke of the need to manage power *in* their hetero-relations in ways that allowed them to interpret themselves as ultimately in control (although sometimes while not wanting others to perceive them as in control). Yet, given the dominant power structures that frame men as actors and women as recipients, this was often difficult to do even in encounters that women had explicitly chosen.

Once involved in hetero-relational encounters, the young women relied on three main strategies to find meaning and claim an empowered space in interactions that could otherwise threaten their sense of safety, agency, or personal integrity. With each strategy, women took elements of hetero-relations that might be frightening or demeaning (objectification, danger, or exploitation) and attempted to transform them into something chosen and desirable.

### Becoming a Desired Object

A particularly common strategy for expressing sexual subjectivity was, ironically, to endeavor to become a good sexual object. In a culture where young women have so little access to "legitimate" gendered and hetero-relational power, many attempted to capitalize on one of the few areas where they were perceived as powerful—the ability to attract and arouse men. Having learned from the pleasing woman discourse that a woman's desirability to men defines her social worth, many of the participants expended incredible energy trying to position themselves as desirable objects. Evelyn, for instance, was aware that women possess few avenues to power in their hetero-relations, and so she concentrated on using her physical attractiveness to right the balance.

> I think women really don't have as much power as I used to believe. But one thing that makes me feel powerful is the feeling that I'm desirable to a man, because if a man is really wanting me, it's like I've got him eating out of the palm of my hand. If I've turned some guy on, that makes me feel strong and powerful because now he's the one who's vulnerable. He's all horny and I can either give him what he wants or I can reject him. And he doesn't really know which one it's going to be. I spend a lot of time thinking about this stuff and trying to make sure I come out on top. (Evelyn, 21, "heterosexual," "Caucasian")

Tonya attempted to cultivate a sense of personal power and self-worth by accumulating evidence that men found her attractive. Tonya has considered herself overweight, unattractive, and unpopular throughout most of her development. She described the summer when she was sixteen as the best time of her life. Away at summer camp, and having just lost thirty pounds, she became involved with a boy for the first time, describing him as the first boy who ever found her attractive. Although she did not find herself attracted to him, she decided to become involved with him anyway, "because I wanted to lose my virginity, and having a boyfriend is really helpful when it comes to losing your virginity." When I asked Tonya why she wanted to "lose" her virginity with a man to whom she was not particularly attracted, she responded that she saw this as her last chance. She attributed her opportunity to have sex to the "magic" of camp and felt that once she got home, "that magic will wear off and no one will ever give me a chance again." Seeing her attractiveness as fleeting and her everyday self as undesirable, Tonya felt she must grab her chance while opportunity presented itself. It turned out that this was not her last opportunity. Since that time, Tonya has had intercourse with other men. Describing her second sexual experience, she said,

> I was excited [but] not for him. Just because I could list in my notebook that I slept with someone else. I still count how many times and how many people, hoping for this number by year's end and by the anniversary [of the first time]. It's the numbers that are more important than anything else, because I wasn't greatly attracted to him. I mean, it wasn't anything. I didn't particularly enjoy it. I didn't particularly think I would. Whether or not I have any

desire to, I'll usually initiate, just so I can get the numbers down. Whenever I have sex I put down the number. Under January 1, which will also be under the next January 1, I have a little "h" for height and a little "w" for lowest and highest weight, and sex numbers, so I can compare it to next year. (Tonya, 18, "straight," "Jewish/white by race and religion")

Tonya acknowledged that she is so concerned with being desirable that it matters little whether she is feeling sexual desire herself. Indeed, she has devised a system to quantify her attractiveness, giving her a basis for comparing her desirability from year to year. She is focused so heavily on outside affirmation that collecting evidence to report in her notebook has become more important than experiencing sexual or romantic pleasure. In her quest for greater numbers, she has not only had sex with men she did not find attractive, she also has had unprotected intercourse, even though she believes in the importance of safe sex. Although she said she worries to this day about the ramifications of not having used a condom, she confessed that she would probably do it again, "because to me, it's more important to get that number down."

Later in her interview, Tonya expanded on her lack of pleasure with her first sexual partner, and on the fact that it had never even occurred to her that she would experience pleasure. When asked what the experience meant to her, she responded,

Well, first, that I existed. Second of all, that you were something that could be had sex with, like, did that make any sense?

I found Tonya's statement quite provocative. Describing herself in the passive voice as an object, as "something that could be had sex with," she both finds and loses her position as a person. Indeed, it is by being seen as a desirable sexual thing, an object, that she finds a way to be a subject. First by "losing" her virginity, and then by counting sex partners and sexual encounters, she now somehow knows she "exists."

Alicia, on the other hand, has learned to become a desired object by adopting the image of what she called "the perfect Asian femme fatale." Whereas Tonya affirmed her desirability by having sex whenever she got an opportunity, Alicia felt she must "give off vibes of complete sexuality" while also remaining aloof and off limits to men. It was by tempting men and then refusing them that she derived a sense of power.

I learned from a very young age, from my mother and the other Filipinas in my community, that Asian women are supposed to possess these mysterious, magical powers over men by being the perfectly sexual, perfectly delicate, but totally aloof china dolls. We're supposed to suggest a totally desirable object of adoration. There is supposed to be such a power in the ability to drive men wild with a simple, well-calculated glance. And it does feel powerful. But the problem is, you're supposed to be such a good object that you never get to have any fun. It's like you're supposed to give off vibes of complete sexuality, but in reality, you have to remain chaste and pure. The vibes you give off are, "I'm too good for you to have sex with, or to even approach." But the upshot is, I'm really not allowed to have sex with you, even if I want to. And these poor men, who are pining after us, they still get to have sex whenever they want, but we can't, or else we lose our worth as a powerful sexual object of desire. It's really pretty messed up, but it's also a really hard mentality for me to get out of. I really do get a lot of pleasure out of it. But if I'm not the to-die-for, Asian femme fatale, I don't know how to be. There's no way for me to just be Alicia, because it's never safe for me to see who that might be. (Alicia, 22, "heterosexual," "Asian")

Alicia's experience speaks clearly to the irony of "being a desired object." Women using this strategy are, arguably, aspiring to their own sexual commodification and personal erasure. As Alicia put it, "there's no way for me to just be Alicia." Both Tonya and Alicia experienced a subjective sense of power through their ability to master the rules of hetero-sexual attractiveness and through their ability, however illusory, to navigate or control men's desires. Yet they also described a subordination of their own sexual pleasure to the need for outside (male) confirmation.

As Frigga Haug (1987) argues so skillfully in her book *Female Sexualization*, women are socialized to find pleasure in "slavegirl behaviors"—the very behaviors and practices that support women's own objectification. In such a context, it makes sense that young women would use these skills, however problematic in the broader hegemonic scheme of things, to foster a sense of power and value in their own hetero-relational encounters. In a social climate where many young women feel they have little access to other forms of hetero-relational power, "being a desired object" seems to offer these participants a sense, albeit often temporary and fragile, that they are in control of their encounters—that they are the ones who set the agenda.

Young women often described a sense of fun and excitement from being a desired object. Yet they also alluded to at least two problems with this strategy. First, while many women derive feelings of power and pleasure from their ability to attract men, that power is still contingent on men's judgments of their desirability. With this strategy, if a man does not judge a woman to be pleasing, she derives no power from this strategy at all. Therefore, her strategy works only if she spends her time and energy figuring out what men will find attractive, and then molding herself to fit that image.

This strategy also poses a second problem. Having learned from the male sexual drive discourse that men are essentially at the mercy of their hormones, these women reason that their ability to arouse men (and their ability to withhold sexual gratification) is the one thing that can make men vulnerable to them. But this strategy apparently overlooks the fact that the male sexual drive discourse also sanctions men's use of sexual force by contending that men, once aroused, are unable to control their desires and are therefore justified in using coercion. Indeed, being a desirable object is effective only if men do not exercise their socially sanctioned power to insist on women's sexual "cooperation." Thus, this strategy may make women feel quite powerful when all goes well, but that "power" is very fragile indeed.

## Playing with Fire

Attempting to vie for position in their hetero-relations, some women derived a feeling of power and excitement through their ability to face sexualized danger and overcome the odds. Rather than stepping away in fear of the warnings of the (hetero)sex as female victimization discourse, some women took this discourse on as an exciting personal challenge. In no case did women eroticize *victimization* in this study. But interestingly, many did eroticize *danger*. Not unlike the thrill of skydiving or tackling a dangerous mountain, the satisfaction of "playing with fire" comes from standing up to and outwitting a powerful obstacle, in this case, male sexual danger. Louise, for example, sometimes found pleasure in seducing what she called "dangerous men."

> It's really titillating to play with the odds. If I can hold my own in a situation where it's semidangerous, there's such a thrill in that. I like to see if I

can seduce dangerous men. Men who are a lot older than me or like heavy leather, tattoos, motorcycle types. Wild guys who are kind of rough. They're not at all the kinds of men I would get involved with for a relationship, but there's something really sexy about turning them on. So if I'm out at a bar, I'll try to pick them up and just see what happens. I like that feeling of semi-powerlessness, like what's going to happen next kind of feeling. I would never do it in a place where I was completely over my head, because it's not like I want to get hurt. Definitely, definitely not. But kind of flirting with danger. That's what I like to do. Push the limits and see how far I can go. (Louise, 21, "hetero," "white")

Laura recalled hitchhiking with friends during her adolescence. Wearing "provocative" clothing and standing in "sexy poses," they would wait to be picked up by men in cars. Although Laura looked back and saw that she and her friends could easily have been hurt, she described the ability to play with fire as exciting and fun. Central to their sense of power was the ability to arouse men and then choose whether to accept or reject their offers of rides and sex.

We would get all made up and wear really provocative clothes, like really short skirts or shorts cut off really high with our asses half sticking out, and halter tops or T-shirts ripped off around our shoulders. Usually three or four of us would stand on the strip downtown in these sexy poses and hitchhike. Guys would always pick us up. Sometimes guys would look nerdy or freaky or something, and we'd be like, "no way." That was fun too, because we could reject them. And when some guys stopped by that looked cool, maybe a little bit dangerous, but not really freaks, we would get in. It was really wild, just like letters in *Penthouse* or something. We would fool around or give them blow jobs, not really sex so much. Nothing ever happened where we got really, really hurt, but it was close a couple of times. When I look back, we were so stupid, like we could have gotten in so much trouble. But we thought we were these hot grown-up chicks who were so sexy we were invincible. It was stupid, but it was a lot of fun. (Laura, 22, "bisexual," "biracial/West Black Indian, white American")

Melissa, on the other hand, described herself as "sexually naive" and "fairly inexperienced." For her, playing with fire was linked with fantasies about "being taken" by a man who was stronger and more experienced than she was. She found herself attracted to men who were "macho," "wild," or "assholes" because they could lead her to do things sexually that she was reluctant to try herself. Playing with fire allowed her to be swept away by a man who was wild and experienced. She described her attraction as a teenager to a man she met while on a class trip. Excited by the fact that he seemed "dangerous" and "raunchy," she hoped that he would "break" her.

> That was like the end of innocence. . . . These four guys were really like gods. They were really rough and kind of wild. They gave me a lot of shit and a lot of kind of sexist, verbal abuse. They were really obnoxious to women. I never had anyone call me a slimy cunt before. Being called a slimy cunt, you know, hits you in the face. But I went, "Oh, this is the new kind of assholes, but it's sort of more." I liked Mike. I really wanted him. I wanted him to kind of break me, and he knew I was really innocent. He came to me in the night and I was all turned on. But oh my God, it was all happening so fast. He wanted me to touch his penis. I just didn't want to. He grabbed my hand and he was pulling my hand toward his crotch and I was pulling my hand away and he just like, "bye." He was really pissed off and he left. I just felt like, "Oh God, I really fucked up," and I was so scared. It was that feeling of like, I fucked up, but also, fuck that. He was an asshole. (Melissa, 21, "heterosexual," "Eastern European-American Jew")

While Louise and Laura used playing with fire to experience and demonstrate their sexual sophistication, Melissa used this strategy to overcome what she saw as her relative sexual inexperience or "innocence." But in each case, men who were perceived as wild or dangerous posed a challenge to these women, representing excitement and mystery. While Melissa's experience with Mike turned out to be a disappointment, and while Laura reported coming close to being hurt while hitchhiking, their attractions to "wild" men and to potentially dangerous situations demonstrates the thrill that can come from playing with fire.

In these women's experiences we see danger and desire not as dichotomous, but as intimately entwined. This strategy becomes a way of managing the potential for hetero-relational danger by incorporating it into their desires, rather than fearing and seeking ways to avoid it. In examining this strategy, however, we must not confuse playing with fire with masochism. Traditional notions of female masochism imply that women derive physical and/or psychological excitement from the experience of sexual pain and abuse. Playing with fire, on the other hand, involves an excitement in confronting danger, but with the assumption that one is ultimately in control and is not going to be hurt. Thus, while these young women are playing with fire or flirting with danger in their sexual lives, it should be clear that they are not motivated by masochism. Rather, they are simultaneously drawn to and attempting to diffuse male domination, acting on their desire to experience a sense of power and accomplishment in overcoming a challenge.

The potential costs of this strategy are obviously great. While young women may achieve a sense of *psychological* empowerment by playing with fire, this feeling does not, unfortunately, translate into physical or social forms of power. Indeed, psychological empowerment, that is, personal feelings of strength and autonomy, may actually mask a lack of sociocultural empowerment or access to the resources and status necessary to fulfill one's needs (LeCompte and Bennet, 1988). Although the young women who play with fire wish to believe that it is they who are in control, men still have the power to call their bluff or "make them pay" by overpowering them physically and by appealing to the male sexual drive and true victim discourses if women attempt to hold them legally responsible for rape. Indeed, in a legal system that continues to view women's claims of victimization as suspect, men may offer women's willingness to play with fire as "proof" that they "asked for it." Thus, as in the case of "being a desired object" and "doing everything but," the participants' sense of power rests on men's willingness not to "pull rank" by exploiting the physical and/or societal power they can exercise over women.

### Being the One Who Can Change Him

In a third strategy to vie for position, several women described finding a sense of personal power, hope, and purpose by trying to change an aloof, selfish, or abusive man into a sensitive partner. For some women, this strategy involved attempts to change a man entirely, by helping him become a more contented individual who was more comfortable with himself and his world. These women described their efforts to help a man over what they perceived to be his shyness, emotional wounds, or self-centeredness, by waiting patiently and being a selfless, supportive woman offering him complete positive regard. For these participants, changing men was framed rather like a social service project, a way of applying their skills as women to the project of nurturing and transforming a man who was seen as lack-

ing the sensitivity and emotional security needed to form a mutually satisfying relationship. Taking on the love hurts discourse as a challenge, becoming involved with angry or insensitive men provided a means of experiencing their own strength, and often making sense of their own mistreatment, through martyrdom or the ability to make a positive impact on
their partners and their relationships.

Sondra used this strategy as a way of making sense of her current relationship with a man she described as "cold and aloof," "not very tender,"
and "just generally angry at the world." Interestingly, she recalled that she
chose this man because his insensitivity posed a challenge for her.

> If you met him, you'd think he's not a very nice guy. But I've always seen
> potential in him. He doesn't always treat me, well, let's just say he's not very
> tender. He's sort of rough and just generally angry at the world, and I get
> sort of caught up in that. He has a warm side, but it doesn't come out very
> often. He's just really cold and aloof. God, it must sound like, "Why is she
> hanging out with this creep?" But I was attracted to him because he was so
> cold. He was like a challenge to me. Sometimes it gets a little old, like we've
> been together about seven months now. But I feel like if I can just pull him
> out of his shell, be patient and supportive and show him how warm I can be,
> maybe he needs one person to turn things around in his life. Because he's
> gone through a lot in his life. A lot of abuse in his family and what have you.
> I want to be maybe a role model for him, like the one person in his life he
> knows he can depend on, and maybe then he'll open up. I just want so much
> for him. If I could just break through, then I know he could get so much
> more enjoyment out of life. (Sondra, 19, "heterosexual," "Afro-Ameri-
> can/Native American")

Women tended to view waiting patiently as a selfless act while they were
involved in the task of trying to change a man and help him feel better
about his life. On later reflection, however, several women recognized
other agendas. Buying into the love conquers all discourse, some women
spoke of using their unwavering strength and love to change a man to fit
their own fantasies of a perfect mate (whether or not this fit with his visions
for himself). Some also described experiencing power over a man through
the belief that they knew his true nature better than he knew himself. They
acknowledged feeling both a sense of superiority and security in a relationship by making a man indebted to them. Sondra, for instance, noted

that her patience with her partner served her own purposes as well as her boyfriend's.

> Maybe it's a little arrogant, but it's like a challenge for me, wanting to show him the error of his ways. Guys don't really know their own inner emotions as much as women do. So maybe this is my area of expertise. Emotions, that's the area where I know a lot more than him. So I get to be like the martyr or something, and that gives me a little more power than him in that aspect of the relationship. It's sort of like I'm training him or something, too [*laughing*]. It's like, once I'm through with him, I'll have him just the way I want him, so that's what makes it worth the work. (Sondra, 19, "heterosexual," "Afro-American/Native American")

Like Sondra, who derived a sense of power in her relationship from her role as emotional expert, Stephanie saw herself in a "one up" position because her boyfriend needed her. Feeling that she was the only person in the world to whom he could turn for support, she looked past his domineering behavior and instead saw him as the less secure one in the relationship.

> I would never say this to him, but I think it puts me in the one up position. I take care of him, like I'm the person he can come to who'll accept him in the world. Even though he seems cold and domineering, it's really that he's insecure, I think. So I sort of take care of him emotionally. I read in my gender class that puts women in a one down position, but I really think it puts me one up, too, because we both know he needs me. That makes him vulnerable to me, and that gives me a sense that I'm doing something good in the world, but I'm also a little superior. (Stephanie, 21, "heterosexual," "white")

For other women, the desire was not to change a man's personality entirely, but to be the one and only person with whom he dared to be intimate. These women envisioned occupying a special place in the life of a man who was otherwise "obnoxious." For instance, Cynthia discussed her attraction to men she considered "freaks" or "assholes." Although she described herself as a feminist and as looking for equality in a relationship, she also found herself drawn to men she described as "flippant, cold, have an attitude." Pondering what she saw as a discrepancy between her abstract desires for a mate and the men to whom she was actually attracted, she said,

I think there's a draw to that cold, "I don't really give a shit about anyone."
For me and friends I've talked to, there's this idea that you're going be the
right woman, you're going to draw him out, and he's going to respond to
just you. And underneath it all, he's really great, and he really cares a lot, but
just about you. But it ends up generally that you don't find anything, no
matter how hard you dig. There's like some illusion that that's what you're
supposed to do. (Cynthia, 22, "bisexual," "white")

While Cynthia wanted the sense of power that came from being "the
right woman to draw him out," she recognized a second motivation for
seeking domineering men that was interwoven with but seemingly quite
different from the need to be needed.

I know that idea is coming from somewhere, because everybody seems to
have it. I'm not sure where it comes from. It seems like it's both of them. I
can like tame him. But like I need a man to keep me in my place. Like I want
equality, and I want all these things, but I also want to be treated maybe like
a little girl or something.

Cynthia derived two perceived benefits from becoming involved with
someone who did not currently possess the traits she said she valued. By
being the one who could change him, she experienced a sense of power
and the opportunity to occupy a special position in a man's life. At the
same time, she found a way to be "kept in her place," thus avoiding the
potential discomforts of being an independent subject. By feeling simultaneously indispensable and "like a little girl," she was able to experience
both sides of a complex power dynamic in her relationship.

This strategy allows young women to position themselves in the pleasing woman discourse in a way that highlights the selflessness and other
"virtues" associated with good womanhood. Being the only one who can
change an otherwise wild or selfish man implies that a woman is so pleasing, so valuable, so desirable, that a man will find it preferable to change
himself rather than lose her. Thus, even though these young women often
endured mistreatment and disappointment, they hoped to find in this
strategy a way to feel powerful and indispensable in what they might otherwise consider alienating hetero-relations. While the women's stories suggest that this strategy is seldom effective in actually changing men, it does
allow young women to feel needed, and thus to experience a sense of
higher purpose in their relationships.

## Getting It Over With: Strategies for Controlling Hurtful Encounters

Women went beyond developing strategies to find acceptable ways of stepping into and negotiating power in their hetero-relational encounters. They also constructed strategies for "getting it over with" when those encounters became unpleasant. While they were not always able to avoid situations in which they were abused or exploited, these young women developed compelling strategies for shortening their encounters and finding ways out. As participants described their struggles to preserve their own physical and psychological integrity in painful encounters, four main strategies emerged for getting it over with. These strategies have much in common with those discussed in the previous sections: they focus on striking a balance among competing discourses, encourage individualistic, psychological solutions, and provide ways for young women to "control" their circumstances without appearing ambivalent, immature, or unsavvy. They differ, however, in their purpose: whereas the strategies discussed previously are employed to allow young women *access into* and a sense of *power in* their hetero-relations, the strategies examined here are used to help *get them out* of situations that have become painful, abusive, or exploitive.

On the one hand, we will see that these strategies often encourage young women to accept individual responsibility for their own victimization. As such, the very strategies that help them cope also tend to shut down possibilities for critique and serve to divert attention from male responsibility. On the other hand, it is important to remember that in relying on these strategies, young women are making understandable use of the cultural tools available to them in a social and interpersonal context that sends very mixed and problematic messages about entitlement and victimization. In each of the following strategies we will see a continuation of women's paradoxical relationships to gendered power. These experiences are not reflected in such unidimensional notions as "no means no" and "rape isn't about sex, it's about violence," or, on the other hand, "women must like abuse, or else they would just leave." Instead, we will see women drawing on seemingly incompatible discourses and personal stances in order to create a reality that, for them, is at least psychologically tolerable.

## Stroking Egos

For some young women, getting it over with entailed, as Cynthia put it, "stroking men's egos," by telling their partners that they were enjoying painful or even abusive encounters, when in fact they were not. Stroking male egos was a way for participants to remain "pleasing women" by not complaining or disrupting men's pleasure with an acknowledgment of their own pain. Accepting the terms of the male sexual drive discourse, as well as the love hurts discourse and the notion that sexually sophisticated women always find (or at least feign) pleasure in sex, some women indicated that they had never seriously considered the idea that they were entitled to interrupt a man's sexual pleasure or to risk hurting his feelings during an unpleasant sexual interaction. Other women were able to contemplate such entitlement when thinking about hetero-relations in abstract terms, but were unable to feel or access that entitlement when actually in a painful or unwanted encounter.

Darla described her own and other women's reluctance to tell male partners when they felt pain during sexual encounters. She was clearly uncomfortable with assigning women responsibility as caretakers of men's sexual egos. Nonetheless, she felt compelled to fill that role. Although she said she stopped faking orgasms, she noted that her friends still did, and that she continued to assume responsibility for putting male sexual pleasure ahead of her own. Describing her decision not to tell a partner that intercourse was painful for her, she said,

> He was nervous enough as it was, and, you know, women fake orgasms and feel they have to. Even now, with my last boyfriend, I think I'm just particularly small or tight, and sometimes we would have problems, and I'm always the one that's like, "Just relax, it's okay," and it's always me. I always take on that role, and I think women just do, you know? That's why women fake orgasms and men are allowed to just get all excited and get crazy, and I always feel like, I don't know. I don't want to think it's like this, but it almost seems that we put them before us. I don't know if I do, but ever since I was fifteen, I've always taken on that role. I don't know why. I know my friends do it. I just talked to a friend of mine and she had an experience like this where it was painful to her, but she wanted him to be happy, so she totally didn't say anything. And I yelled at her for that. I was like, "don't," you know? But two or three years ago, I would have done the same thing. (Darla, 19, "heterosexual," "white")

Similarly, Heidi described a sense of responsibility both for men's physical pleasure and for their feelings of adequacy. She said she sometimes had sex when she did not want to because she felt sorry for a man who was aroused and then not brought to orgasm.

> It's usually that I'm not really into it, but I might do it anyway because I feel like I have to get him off, you know, I have this responsibility. Or I'm just in it for the physical feeling, and I just want it to be over, you know? I don't want to have to deal with it. I want the person out of my bed. . . . I just felt really bad, you know, this poor guy, he's suffering [but] I didn't do anything I didn't want to do. . . . [I faked orgasms] all the time, because I wanted him to stop. I'd be like, I wish he would just hurry up already. And I kind of had to do it because I loved him and I wanted to make him happy. (Heidi, 21, "bisexual," "white")

Heidi and Darla stroked male egos to shorten the duration of, or manage their ambivalence about, sex in which the pain inflicted was presumably unintentional and unknown to the men involved. While one might argue that men have a responsibility to find out whether an encounter is pleasant or painful for their partners, few would consider such situations victimization. However, for some women, encounters involved violence or humiliation that was deliberately inflicted by their partners. Even in such situations, many women attempted to stroke men's egos to end the encounter as safely and gracefully as possible. Rachel, for instance, described using this strategy in situations where a partner was intentionally demeaning and causing her physical pain. Reluctant to hurt her boyfriend's feelings, and fearful that he might turn on her if she complained, she dealt with his mistreatment by getting it over with as best she could.

> My boyfriend would like to hit me and call me a slut and other mean names during sex. He would pretend he was raping me and that I was loving it and just couldn't get enough of him. He wanted to tie me up and stuff, and he liked to dominate me during sex. I didn't know how to handle it, so I thought I should just pretend I enjoyed it too, you know, so we wouldn't get into a hassle. I guess it was partly because I was afraid of him turning on me, but it was also because he was my boyfriend and I thought I should just try to grin and bear it. This was my first really sexual experience, and I thought that was just what I had to do. The sex didn't last that long, so I always thought, "Well, if I can just wait it out and act like I like it. . . ." I don't

know, I just never thought I could say something, because he needed to think he was so great in bed. I never told him I was humiliated and hurt. I just didn't dare to hurt him. (Rachel, 21, "heterosexual," "white")

Cynthia also spoke to the potential physical and emotional consequences of failing to please a man by appearing to be pleased herself. She found that the "hassle" of stroking egos was less distasteful than dealing with being considered a "domineering bitch" or having a man "go ballistic." Apparently seeing these as her only two choices, Cynthia was willing to stroke egos when feeling hurt rather than risk getting "in even more trouble."

> I guess it's a hassle always stroking their egos, like you know, "Oh, you're so great," and "Oh, I really love what you're doing," you know, even when you don't. But believe me, it's more of a hassle not to. Because then you have to feel guilty and everything. Because then it's like you have to take care of the fact that he might feel bad, or inadequate, or something. And it's just easier to keep them feeling good about themselves. I think maybe the main thing is that I don't want him to see me as a cold bitch. And if I don't act like, "Oh, this is really good for me," then I think men see you as a domineering bitch. So I guess it's like, men get their needs met directly, but women need to get their needs met indirectly. I guess it sort of sucks, but it's better than taking the chance of pissing them off. If you piss them off, even if you're the one who's getting hurt, you could be in even more trouble. So he could take it out on you that you're implying he's a bad lover, and then he could make the pain you were feeling during sex seem like nothing. Some guys just really go ballistic when their male sexual egos are bruised. I just can't be about taking that chance. (Cynthia, 22, "bisexual," "white")

Cynthia felt that in order for her to be honest about her lack of pleasure, she would have to face being perceived as a "cold bitch" by her partner and take a chance of "pissing him off," consequences she was not willing to risk. Since she was well aware of the potential for volatility in hetero-relational encounters, it seemed worth it, to Cynthia, to fake her own pleasure, even when she was in pain, in order not to experience the potential wrath or abuse of an angry male partner.

For these women and others, stroking male egos was not simply a goal in itself, it was also a means to an end. That is, it seemed to them more expedient, as well as psychologically and/or physically safer, to fake their own pleasure than to tell a man that they wanted to end an encounter or preferred to do something else. Stroking egos also allowed women a way to navigate the tension between the pleasing woman discourse and the male sexual drive discourse and to meet the social and developmental pressure to avoid seeming ambivalent in hetero-relational encounters. As Sara put it, "this way everybody wins." Unfortunately, "winning" for these women needed to happen indirectly, and it was equated with enduring an encounter rather than enjoying it.

While perhaps providing some short-term benefits, this strategy reproduces the privileging of men's emotional and sexual needs over those of women. As Sandra Bartky (1990) points out in her provocative essay "Feeding Egos, Tending Wounds," by encouraging deference to men's wants and needs, feeding egos fuels inequality in hetero-sexual relationships:

> Insofar as the emotional exchanges in question are contained within a gendered division of emotional labor that does not require of men what it requires of women, our caregiving, in effect, is a collective genuflection by women to men, an affirmation of male importance that is unreciprocated. The consistent giving of what we don't get in return is a performative acknowledgment of male supremacy and thus a contribution to our own social demotion. (109)

By prioritizing men's egos and sexual desires at the expense of women's right to determine the conditions of their hetero-relational encounters, stroking egos subordinates young women's desires and discourages hetero-relational reciprocity. While this strategy may feel useful in the moment, it also helps to reproduce power asymmetries in young women's relationships.

## Mastering the Male Body

A related strategy involved "mastering the male body." Here, women learned how to manipulate men's bodies to make them ejaculate quickly, so that they could end unpleasant sexual experiences as soon as possible. As with "stroking egos," this strategy allowed young women to get it over with without men ever knowing that their partners were displeased or in pain. Feeling unable or unentitled to assert their needs verbally, many young women instead learned to capitalize on the knowledge that heterosexual sex often ends when the man ejaculates (a phenomenon women might resent in other circumstances). By mastering the male body, they were able to limit the duration of a troublesome encounter without having to deal with a man's anger, judgment, or disappointment.

Describing herself, rather proudly, as having "mastered the art of making men come," Robin explained, "I figure the sooner I get him off, the sooner I get him off me."

> I made it my business at an early age, around thirteen I guess, to learn how to give the perfect blow job. I can also give the perfect hand job, so that I can get men off to just get it over with. That way, I'm totally in control. Because once they come, then you're off the hook. Or at least it buys you some time to get out of the situation gracefully. Hopefully, if you play your cards right, they'll just fall asleep. Men are such suckers. They're so easy to manipulate. The only thing is, sometimes they get pissed off if you make them come too early, like it's your fault, their lack of self-control. Then you just say, "No, I love it when you come. It's so exciting to me." Barf! (Robin, 21, "heterosexual"; asked to describe her race(s), she wrote, "I cannot")

Some women used mastering the male body to avoid having intercourse in situations where they felt uncomfortable "going all the way." Many women felt unentitled to tell a man that they were uninterested or ambivalent about having intercourse, and so they used their ability to bring a man to orgasm through oral sex or masturbation in order to end a sexual encounter before intercourse could begin. Some women had already had intercourse, but wished to avoid it in a particular situation or with a particular person, usually because they did not feel safe. Chloe described such a situation with a man she met while alone on vacation, waiting for her friends to join her the next day. Afraid that the man might rape her if she did not "give him something," she decided to have oral sex in order to avoid having intercourse, and avoid his anger.

> I hooked up with this guy and he took me out to dinner and then we sat around talking. And I mean we hadn't even kissed yet or anything, but he says, "Is this really all you want to do?" like I was a little kid or something. I wasn't really too sure how I felt about him. I mean, I had just met him that afternoon, but he had taken me to dinner and everything. So I was thinking, "What must he be thinking?" And then I got thinking, "Here I am all alone in my hotel room with this guy and I don't know a soul in this town, and if

I say no and he rapes me because he thinks I led him on, well then, who's going to believe me, and who's even going to hear me if I dare to scream?" So I just basically gave him a blow job to satisfy him so that I wouldn't have to have actual sex with him. I really didn't want to have sex with him, but I felt like I had to give him something, and that just seemed like the least offensive way to go. Least offensive to me without offending him. (Chloe, 22, "heterosexual/bisexual," "Caucasian")

Mastering the male body affords young women a sense of control amid their voicelessness, by at least allowing them to shorten a painful, frightening, or otherwise undesirable experience. It also becomes a source of pride for some women, as they delight in their covert ability to manipulate men. Unfortunately, like stroking egos, this strategy leaves uninterrupted the dominant assumptions and practices that compel women to be both sexually pleasing and emotionally nurturant, and that dissuade them from voicing their sexual needs and entitlement to their own pleasure. Accepting the male sexual drive discourse's claim that men, once aroused, must be brought to orgasm, this strategy tries to make the best of a bad situation. Yet, while it allows young women some control over the length of a sexual encounter and may allow them to escape negative judgment or abuse, it reinforces, rather than challenges, these women's inability to state explicitly that they wish for an encounter to end (or never begin).

### Trying to Like It

Whereas women used the previous two strategies to try to control *men's* behavior, some developed a different type of strategy through which they tried to manipulate their *own* subjective experiences of an oppressive sexual situation. Fearing reprisals, young women often felt they could not control the material circumstances of their unpleasant or victimizing hetero-relational encounters. However, they could attempt to control how they felt about that encounter at the time that it was occurring. While they often did not feel able to end an encounter physically, they felt they could, in a sense, end it psychologically by trying to turn the encounter into something positive. In an effort to avoid feeling victimized, some young women reported trying to feel excited in the midst of forced sex, so that they could at least lessen the emotional pain they were feeling. Women also used this strategy in an attempt to prevent an experience from "qualifying"

as a case of rape. In a peculiar synthesis of the popularized feminist assertion that "rape is not about sex, it's about violence," and the conservative
notion that "women do not get raped unless they ask for it," these young
women attempted to use mind over matter by trying to like it—or trying
to make it be "about sex"—so that they could avoid the psychologically
threatening acknowledgment that they were being raped.

Robin's first experience of sexual intercourse was violent and unwanted.
Aware that she could not win a physical struggle with the man involved,
she tried, instead, to control her subjective experience of the encounter by
trying to find the man attractive. Interestingly, her main concern was to
avoid being beaten up so that her mother would not know she had been
in this situation (yet another example of how these young women carry
outside audiences into their encounters).

> I got into this situation where I went up to this guy's apartment, and we
> were making out and things, and I didn't want to have sex, but he did, and
> it was a long struggle and everything. And he did hit me and stuff, and then
> I was like, "Okay, fine." I just, you know, because if I really try to fight him
> and then I get beat up, what am I going to say to my mother? That was like
> the main thing in my mind, was like, "Oh no, what if he punches me or cuts
> me or something? What am I going to say to my mother?" I kept seeing me
> really feeling different if it would have been another guy. I really wasn't at-
> tracted to him, and I was trying to get attracted to him or like, get turned
> on, but I couldn't. (Robin, 21, "heterosexual"; asked to describe her race(s),
> she wrote, "I cannot")

When I asked Robin why she tried to make herself attracted to him, she
explained,

> I was thinking that if I can get turned on, then this will be consensual, like,
> a good experience. It was like I was trying to manipulate my own mind or
> something, so that this wouldn't seem as bad as it really was. I mean, espe-
> cially for my first experience, I wanted it to be something I wanted, not
> something that was forced on me. So I tried really hard to make it into some-
> thing that I wanted, but I couldn't. I just really couldn't.

Although she knew the situation was "bad," Robin still hoped that by
manipulating her own desires, she might be able to transform a violent
encounter into a consensual one. Like Robin, Jocelyn tried to convince
herself that she was excited while being forced to have sex, so that her

experience would not really be rape. For both women, trying to like it represented an attempt to feel some sense of choice and control, even as they were being forced and hit.

> I kept telling myself, just relax and try to like it. Try to think of something exciting, try to think of someone you would like to be having sex with so you can get aroused and then this won't really be what it is. If I could just find some way to be turned on, at all, then I would know I was in it and then this wouldn't be really like rape. (Jocelyn, 19, "hetero," "mutt")

It should be noted that none of the women who attempted to use this strategy succeeded in becoming aroused while being hit or forced. It is also important to note that although Robin and Jocelyn tried to like it in the hopes that their own arousal would prevent their experiences from qualifying as acquaintance rape, this strategy did not operate in reverse. That is, their inability to like it did not result in their naming these forced encounters cases of rape. In fact, in Jocelyn's case, the very effort to use this strategy left her dealing with a haunting double bind.

> For years afterward, I felt caught in a catch-22. First of all, how could I have been so messed up as to think I could ever find what he did to me exciting? But second of all, I still thought, how could I have let myself down by failing to pull it off? (Jocelyn, 19, "hetero," "mutt")

Feeling either unable or unentitled to change the physical circumstances with which they were faced, these young women tried as best they could to alter their subjective experiences. By attempting to control their minds' interpretations of their bodies' experiences, they struggled (albeit unsuccessfully) to harness what little power was available to them to preserve their own integrity during demeaning or victimizing encounters.

### Hoping He'll Notice

In a final strategy for getting it over with, young women relied on nonverbal cues to indicate their displeasure to a man during a sexual encounter. While women often felt unable to articulate their feelings of pain, objectification, or disinterest directly to a male partner, many tried indirectly to communicate a desire to end an encounter by changing their posture, pretending to fall asleep, or crying. Wendy, for instance, had difficulty expressing her lack of desire for her boyfriend because she did not wish to hurt his feelings. Instead of telling him that he was hurting her during sex, she would cry and hope that he would notice and stop.

> We would be having sex, again, and I wouldn't want it, but he was my boyfriend, you know, so I never really felt like I could let him down by saying no. But a lot of the times it hurt me. He wasn't the most considerate lover. So I would lie there underneath him, crying, while he was doing it. I didn't feel like I could exactly say no, but I hoped that he would see me crying and just stop, I don't know, out of guilt or concern or something, even pity. Of course he never did. He'd just keep going, and then afterward, he'd say, "Didn't you like it?" And I would say, "Yeah, it was good." (Wendy, 22, "heterosexual," "Puerto Rican/Italian")

When I asked Wendy if she kept her pain to herself because she was afraid of him, she responded,

> I was never afraid of him, but I was afraid of letting him down, for me, I guess, as much as for him. I like to please him, I mean, I love him, I want him to be happy, right? It gives me a sense of pleasure.

Although Wendy described herself crying in pain, she said she derived a sense of pleasure in pleasing her boyfriend. Not wanting to be responsible for letting him down, she put up with the pain of their sexual encounters and hoped, in vain, that he would notice her tears. She explained that when he did not, she would tell him "it was good" so that he, at least, would be happy.

Tonya, on the other hand, used her body posture in order to communicate to men that she had "had enough." Eager to be a "desirable object" so that she could accumulate as many sexual experiences as possible, Tonya felt uncomfortable telling men that she was not aroused during sexual interactions. In order to get out of a previously chosen encounter as quickly as possible, she consciously shifted her body to signal her annoyance.

> I need to have as many lovers as possible. Like I said, I keep track and I need to know that I've had sex with a lot of people. But I don't enjoy the sex itself. It's more that I need to know I've had it. So when I'm with somebody, I just want to get it done with. I would never, never say anything, because then I would feel like a freak. But I just move away, or twist my body or something, like I'm annoyed by what he's doing. That way it can look like

it's not me who's disinterested in sex, but like it's him who's just doing it wrong. And, you know, usually a guy will notice, and then you're off the hook. I'd rather have them just think they're a bad lover who can't really turn me on than to have them think that I'm just frigid or let them know that I led them on to get the numbers, but that I'm really not into the experience. (Tonya, 18, "straight," "Jewish/white by race and religion")

Whereas Wendy used this strategy to end physically painful encounters while preserving her partner's ego and her appearance as a "pleasing" woman, Tonya used nonverbal communication to shorten undesirable encounters by making men think it was they who were inadequate to please her, rather than thinking that she was "frigid" or a "freak." In both cases, however, the goal was to get it over with without having to articulate their wishes explicitly.

Gloria reported that she sometimes pretended to fall asleep when she was "stuck" in a sexual situation she would prefer to be over. Like Wendy, she did not wish to hurt her partners' feelings, and, like Tonya, she worried that she would look "frigid" or "fucked up" if she told a partner she would like to stop or to do something different.

Sometimes it just goes on way too long. Guys have this thing that, like, they're real studs if they can last all night. I'm like, "Come on, already, enough. This is just not fun for me." But rather than hurt their feelings, I've just pretended that I'm just too tired. That seems to be an acceptable excuse. I mean, sure, he's disappointed, but it's not like I'm telling him he's a boring lover. That would just be too much. I could never just tell him I wanted to stop. So I'll be yawning, not like I'm bored, but like I'm so exhausted that I just have to sleep. If he asks if I want to stop, I'll usually just be like [yawning], "No, that's okay." But I'll say it in a tone like I really am so tired, and I hope he'll pick up on the tone in my voice and suggest we stop. Actually, that usually doesn't happen. He'll usually just be like, "Oh, okay, good," and keep going. So I'll eventually pretend I just can't keep my eyes open, and that I wish that I could because I'm loving it so much. That way it doesn't really hurt his feelings, and even though I know he's disappointed, it's not like he thinks I'm deliberately cutting him off. That way I don't look frigid or seem too fucked up. (Gloria, 20, "heterosexual," "African-American")

Lacking a sense of entitlement to begin and end sexual situations when they choose, these young women are left hoping men will notice their pain or dissatisfaction and end an encounter for them. On the one hand, they want to be seen as pleasing and avoid appearing ambivalent. On the other hand, they wish to get out of situations that are painful or unpleasant. Caught between these competing desires, these women find they must create indirect, seemingly "passive" ways of making their needs known. As we saw in the discussion of "losing one's voice" in chapter 4, these women feel they cannot risk appearing unsophisticated or unpleasing by voicing their desires (or lack of desire). They must therefore count on their partners' perceptiveness and willingness to stop. Yet, as many of the participants' experiences demonstrate, young women's male partners often fail even to heed their *explicit* requests or expressions of displeasure. Thus, relying on a partner's compassion by silently hoping he'll notice may be a very tenuous strategy.

In each of these strategies for entering, managing, or exiting hetero-relations, young women struggle to find agency and entitlement in a larger cultural context that presents them with pervasive and constraining messages regarding women's pleasure and desire and male domination. These young women do not simply elect to adapt their behavior to one or another of the cultural discourses discussed in chapter 3, nor do they necessarily experience their sexualities on one side or another of a set of dichotomies such as consent/coercion or pleasure/danger. Rather, in the midst of overlapping social and developmental challenges, they grapple continuously (although perhaps not always consciously or explicitly) with the tensions among competing discourses, both internalizing and resisting their messages.

Similarly, these women do not adopt one type of strategy to use in every circumstance. Rather, most of the participants rely on a range of strategies, depending on the situation they face and their goals for the interaction. Thus it is not the case, for example, that certain women rely exclusively on being a desirable object while others use playing with fire to vie for position in their hetero-relations. Instead, the participants often use multiple strategies in any one encounter, and they may use different strategies at different times, depending on their particular wants and needs.

With these understandings, then, we must resist the temptation (however politically compelling) to reduce young women's hetero-relational experiences to such dualistic characterizations as consent *or* coercion, agency *or* objectification, pleasure *or* danger. Rather, we must view their hetero-relations as ongoing, gendered, and developmental struggles with complex and constructed relationships to danger, power, agency, and desire. Indeed, we have seen that young women may make ironic use of their own objectification to foster a sense of agency. They may use the potential for danger as a way of experiencing sexual power. They may privilege men's emotional and sexual desires in order to feel indispensable and in control. And they may find they need to feel or appear coerced in their sexual relationships in order to feel entitled to consent.

Rather than maintaining such dichotomies as "no means no and yes means yes," these stories force us to acknowledge that young women have often internalized many powerful, androcentric cultural notions, such as the following: once men are aroused, they cannot stop until they ejaculate; women who lead men on must follow through; "good women" must honor men's egos by always appearing pleased; or women who feel ambivalence or discomfort during sexual encounters are frigid, disappointing, or sexually unsophisticated. As such, their experiences of their own sexualities are shaped by these notions (even as they may resist them) as well as by their desires to be entitled and pleasured sexual subjects.

Constructing their hetero-relational subjectivities amid a confluence of cultural discourses that deny their positions as entitled sexual subjects, these young women rely on individualized, often indirect strategies to express their own needs. Indeed, those strategies often attempt to transform their own desires into those of men, as in trying to like it and being the one who can change him. Working from the schemas available to them in their larger culture(s), the participants devise strategies that may be functional for them in an isolated encounter (although often they are unsuccessful even on an individual level), but that tend to simultaneously reproduce dominant power imbalances. Lacking a discourse of female pleasure without penalties and a discourse of male accountability, the young women in this study must try to accommodate and reshape the problematic discourses available to them. Pressured, at the same time, to appear grown-up and sexually sophisticated, they typically experience difficulty voicing the ambivalence that so often stirs inside them. Thus, they are left trying to negotiate among the contradictions by using their individual strategies as best they can.

## 6

■　■　■　■　■　■　■　■　■

# Controlling the Damage

## *Making Meaning When "Things Go Badly"*

It was violent and hurtful and really scary. But I don't think I could ever call it rape. Let's just say that things went badly.

　　　　　　　　　　　—Olivia, 22, "heterosexual," "Caucasian"

There are lots of times when women can't control the shit that men do to them. I mean, come on, men are really the ones with all the real power. But I figure, as long as I'm already going to get screwed, at least maybe I can set the terms of the abuse or humiliation. At least I can try to control the damage.

　　　　　　　　　　　—Elaina, 22, "lesbian/bi," "white"

DESPITE WOMEN'S BEST EFFORTS to manage power in their het-ero-relationships, all too often "things go badly." And when they do, young women, like Elaina, are motivated to "control the damage." As with their strategies for managing contradictions *in* their encounters, women's strategies for controlling the damage tended to rely on individual, psychological maneuvering, rather than on expressions of outrage or collective work toward prevention and redress. These strategies typically involved rewriting painful experiences to make them seem less frightening or alienating—somehow less overwhelming than "victimization" or "abuse." Women formed attributions that allowed them to feel that their victimizing circumstances were somehow under their own control—that, in fact, they could not have been victimized because they were complicit in making things go badly. Contrary to right-wing claims that women are eager to go public and "cry victimization," these women went to great psychological lengths to privatize their experiences and to "disqualify" themselves as victims. Indeed, only two women in this study ever referred to a personal experience as victimization, even though the vast majority (90 percent) reported at least one instance of violence or coercive sexual contact. Young women recounted many detailed stories of pain, humiliation, manipulation, violence, and force in their hetero-relations, and they were willing to concede that "things went badly." Yet they were largely unwilling to use such labels as "rape," "acquaintance rape," "battering," or "abuse" to describe those experiences to me or to themselves.[1] Interestingly, while they rejected terms like "victimization" to define their own encounters, they were quite willing to apply such terms to the experiences of others.

In this chapter I attempt to shed greater light on this phenomenon by examining the psychological strategies young women develop for controlling the damage of their abusive hetero-relational encounters, and by exploring the cultural and situational forces that motivate them to avoid naming their experiences victimization. We will see that women often reflect back on the very strategies they relied on to enter, manage, and make an exit from their encounters, and transform them into internalizations of personal responsibility for their own abuse. Although their strategies may appear counterintuitive or even self-defeating, we will also find that the cultural discourses they have internalized and the social and developmental challenges they face *encourage* these women to resist naming their victimization, to devise individualized coping strategies, and to attribute their mistreatment to their own behavior. Finally, we will see that while women may derive certain psychological benefits from their attempts to control the damage, the individualized nature of those attempts tends to squelch collective resistance and thus to leave dominant hetero-relational power asymmetries intact.

## When the Political Turns Personal: Naming and Forming Attributions When "Things Go Badly"

Throughout the interviews I noticed a marked discrepancy between young women's abstract or political assertions about female victimization and their assessments and attributions for their own painful experiences. These participants were well aware that women are victimized and they were consistently sympathetic to their plight. Yet they also tended to distance themselves from others' experiences and often saw themselves as "exceptions" who could not be abused. Uncomfortable seeing themselves as victims, they found (or created) reasons to explain why their own experiences did not "qualify" as abuse. Tonya, for instance, applied a different standard to label her own experiences than to label the experiences of others. Needing to believe that she could not be raped, she interpreted her own experience of forced sex as not "really" rape.

> I know a lot of women, like one in three, get raped in their lifetime. But I know it could never happen to me. Not that it couldn't happen, because it could, I mean, God, it sort of has. But for me, I say it was kind of like rape. For other people, it's rape. But for me it's just like it was kind of like rape. Kind of like acquaintance rape, but not really that. (Tonya, 18, "straight," "Jewish/white by race and religion")

Often women pointed to "flaws" in their own judgment to explain why their encounters did not count as victimization. Yet they did not find such fault with others. While Louise maintained that women never choose to be abused, and while she described her own violent encounter as "horrible," she attributed this to her personal decisions.

> I don't think women ever want to be abused. I wouldn't say I was abused, because I knew this guy might want to have sex. I didn't think he was going to force it so far, but I did decide to go to his apartment. I chose to be in that situation. I didn't like it, it was really horrible, but I just should have made a different decision. (Louise, 21, "hetero," "white")

Tonya's and Louise's statements speak to a gap, seen throughout the interviews, between women's abstract convictions about abuse on the one hand, and their reflections and attributions about their personal experiences on the other. In order to better understand this discrepancy, we need to delve further into these young women's complex constructed and reconstructed understandings of their own and others' experiences.

### Forming Attributions: "I Should Have Known Better"

As I listened to young women's stories of abuse and domination in their hetero-relationships, I sought explanations for the discrepancies in their attributions for their own versus other women's negative experiences. As a social psychologist, I was aware of a phenomenon known as the "fundamental attribution error" (Ross, 1977), and I wondered whether it would shed light on these women's perceptions. The fundamental attribution error suggests that when people attempt to explain their own negative experiences, they tend to overestimate the impact of situational factors. In other words, they attribute their own misfortunes to forces outside themselves rather than to their own decisions. At the same time, people are thought to attribute the misfortunes of others to flaws in their behavior or their character. Basically, the theory states that if something bad happens to me, I assume it was caused by forces beyond my control; but if something bad happens to you, I assume it must have been your fault. Working from this theory, one would assume that women would be more likely to attribute their *own* mistreatment to external factors (such as an abusive man, threats of violence, or a misogynist society) and to attribute the mistreatment of *other* women to character flaws, weakness, or poor judgment on the part of the individual woman.

The reflections of the young women in this study challenge the assumptions of the fundamental attribution error. In fact, these women were far more likely to excuse other women from responsibility for their abuse but to take personal responsibility for their own mistreatment. The participants tended to explain hypothetical descriptions of sexual aggression with statements such as "It was rape, there was nothing she could do." Further, they tended to make clear-cut statements about both the prevalence of women's victimization in general and the importance of not blaming victims for their own abuse. Martha's and Sondra's assertions were quite typical:

> Women are victimized every day. Shit, more like practically every minute. But society just blames women. They think it wasn't really that bad, or they

think she was at fault. But rape is rape. Abuse is abuse. We can't keep denying it or blaming women. There's nothing women can do because there's a
male patriarchy all around us. Abuse isn't something women choose. Abuse
is something beyond their control. (Martha, 19, "white"; asked to describe
her sexuality, she wrote, "Female")

Practically everyone I know has either been raped or beaten or sexually
abused. It's everywhere. Women are victimized and nobody cares. I care,
you care, but society in general doesn't care. Women are blamed for
everything. But I don't believe there's a woman in the world who chooses
to be abused. That kind of thinking is just so ignorant. Of course women
don't want to be abused. They just can't get out of the situation, or he
tells her it's normal. But it's not normal. No way. It's abuse and it's
wrong, and something should be done because women who are raped and
beaten, they want to get out. (Sondra, 19, "heterosexual," "Afro-Ameri-
can/Native American")

Like others in the study, these women maintained that "abuse is abuse"
and that women are victimized through no fault of their own. And yet,
when assessing their own experiences with similar dynamics, participants
were more likely to offer responses such as "It wasn't exactly rape, because
I could/should have said no" or "I chose to go/stay with him, so it
wasn't really abuse." How can we explain this gap in women's responses
to their own and others' victimization? To what can we attribute the discrepancy between this finding and the predictions of the fundamental attribution error?

The fundamental attribution error takes for granted the existence of a
*straightforward, ungendered event* whose causes are to be assessed. It assumes, for example, that a rape has occurred, and that the task at hand involves determining who or what was responsible for its occurrence. However, as we have seen throughout women's stories, hetero-relational encounters are seldom clear and discrete events, and they are never
gender-neutral. Rather, these young women tended to perceive their own
encounters as complex and often murky experiences that defied straightforward description as "normal" or "victimizing," "consensual" or "rape."
Young women brought with them into each encounter a range of complicated discourses and ongoing dilemmas. Each encounter represented an
arena of struggle with interpretation, rather than a clearly definable incident. Thus, with only two exceptions, these young women did not apply

simplified terms such as "rape" or "victimization" to their own experiences. In order to make sense of young women's attributions, then, we must back up and explore the processes by which they *named* (or refused to name) their experiences.

### Naming: "For Her It Was Rape, for Me It Was Just Complicated"

During the interviews, when women described encounters that "went badly," I asked them how they labeled or defined those experiences for themselves. Interestingly, even when women had just recounted experiences of pain, humiliation, force, or coercion, they seldom referred to those incidents with labels suggesting victimization. Cynthia, for example, had just described an encounter with a man who forced himself on her during a date, ripped her clothes, and then left her by the side of the road. When I asked what she called that experience when thinking about it to herself, she replied,

> I mostly think of it as a really bad night. If you're asking do I think I was raped, no, I wouldn't really call it that. I mean, I was forced, yes, and I was hurt, and things didn't go how I wanted, but I was in the car with him. It was all really complicated. I mean, I was there, I could have chosen not to go. So no, I don't really call it rape. (Cynthia, 22, "bisexual," "white")

Intrigued by her response, I then asked Cynthia how she would define that same experience if it had happened to a friend. Laughing, she responded,

> Wow, that is so awesome! If my roommate came home and told me the exact same story had happened to her, I'd tell her, "You call the hotline, you call the police! You're a victim! That guy raped you and you should report it!" Wow! But, I don't know. For her it would be rape. For me is was just so complicated.

For Cynthia, the very fact that she was in the car with her attacker was enough to prevent this experience from qualifying as rape. When assessing her own situation, she focused on herself as a subject who willingly went on a date with this man. However, when the scenario was altered to involve someone else in her place, her focus shifted immediately to the constraints of the situation and the abusive nature of the man's behavior. Only then was she willing to call this encounter "rape."

Robin, too, found it difficult to apply terms like "acquaintance rape" to her own experiences. When I asked if she had labels available to her to name the violent encounter she had just described to me, she indicated that although she felt she *should* be able to use the word "rape," she was reluctant to do so.

> No, not at all. Even now when I talk about it, I just said acquaintance rape because I know that's like, what I should identify it as. But when I talk to people, sometimes I say, "well, kind of rape, but not really rape." And [friends say], "What do you mean? Just because you know him doesn't mean it wasn't rape." I mean, consciously I know, and if I were examining other women's experiences or something, and she said, "I went home with this guy and I didn't want to have sex but he forced me or I was so intimidated that I just did," I would say that's rape. But I feel like I have another standard and I did internalize a lot of ideas that it was sort of my fault, and how can I say it's rape when I went up there? You know, what was I expecting? It's true I was really naive, but I feel that it doesn't really do me any good to explain that to anybody, because it's like nobody can really understand. (Robin, 21, "heterosexual"; asked to describe her race(s), she wrote, "I cannot")

Although Robin's friends would support her in calling her experience "rape," and although she would assign that label to an identical experience if it had happened to someone else, for Robin, her own encounter was, at most, "kind of like rape, but not really rape." For her, the decision to go to the man's apartment overshadowed the significance of her naïveté and desire not to have sex, as well as the power of his physical violence and use of intimidation. Like Cynthia, when assessing the nature of her own situation, Robin focused on the moments where she positioned herself as an active agent. Her own subjectivity outweighed any situational factors, and she was thus precluded from being a "victim."

These findings seem to turn traditional attribution theory on its head. Rather than naming an incident and *then* determining its cause, as the fundamental attribution error would suggest (Ross, 1977), these young women needed to first determine who was at "fault" *before* they were able to name the experience. Significantly, in their assessments of their own encounters, they equated responsibility with taking a subject stance. Other women were given the benefit of the doubt—that is, the coercive conditions of the situation were taken into account. But when they reviewed their own experiences, even the most oppressive situational factors were effectively erased by the slightest expression of their own agency.

From these women's reflections, we can see that in situations that are complicated (which they always are), or in which young women see themselves as active subjects (which they have tried so hard to be), they tend to distance themselves from the "victim" label that they would willingly apply to another woman's experience. If they can attribute their own mistreatment to the slightest misjudgment or expression of choice, they cannot name that mistreatment a case of abuse. But why is this the case? Why would women not want to name victimization? And why would they be motivated to blame themselves? To develop a greater appreciation of the dynamics of naming and attribution, we must reexamine the discourses and social and developmental challenges that inform these young women's interpretations.

## Refusing to Be a Victim: The Transformation of Meanings

Results from earlier studies (Fine, 1982, Kidder and Fine, 1986) suggest that the ability to *name* an injustice is an important factor in victims' ability to *perceive* a particular incident as unjust. Such findings suggest that naming an event victimization might be an empowering step toward making sense of the mistreatment they have endured. Yet there existed, in the minds and circumstances of these young women, compelling reasons *not* to name their experiences victimization. Indeed, women often did a great deal of psychological work to avoid applying victim-associated labels to even their most violent hetero-relational encounters.

When trying to find labels to describe the experiences they had recounted, participants tended to modify or reinterpret their previous accounts and attempted to explain why "things went badly." As we saw in chapter 5, these women often took great pride in the hetero-relational strategies they had developed for carving out a subject stance when entering into, managing, and exiting their encounters. However, they tended to *transform the meanings* of those strategies when forming attributions about those same encounters after they had become abusive. The strategies they had developed to assert or justify their sexual agency quickly became reasons why they were personally responsible for their own abuse. A closer look at young women's thoughts and contexts reveals several interlocking explanations for their tendency to downplay the severity of their experiences and blame themselves for their own abuse.

## *A Context of Zero-Sum Guilt: "If Only I Hadn't . . ."*

One apparent reason for women's reluctance to apply such labels as "rape," "harassment," or "abuse" to their own situations involves a profound lack of fit between their complex lived experiences and dominant definitions of victimization. As Kahn and Mathie's (1999) research on rape scripts has revealed, women who hold images of "real" rape as a violent, isolated act committed by a stranger are unlikely to name themselves victims in cases of acquaintance rape. The young women I interviewed learned, through their early educations and subsequent experience, that the term "victimization" is reserved for supposedly clear-cut cases in which women use "good judgment" in an effort to avoid potential victimization; state a clear and emphatic "no"; attempt to fight off the perpetrator; and, once victimized, run away from the perpetrator, seek help, and never wish to see him again. But few of the women's encounters met such criteria. Because their subjective experiences often blurred the supposed victim/agent dichotomy, young women's heterorelational encounters seldom fit neatly into the narrowly defined category "rape" or "victimization." Forced to work within the binary system imposed by the normal/danger dichotomy discourse and the true victim discourse, the participants had few terms to adequately define situations that failed to conform to the dominant, "ideal" script for victimization. They were left, by default, to place their experiences in the only other available category—"not *really* rape" or "not *really* victimization." Thus, when attempting to name their encounters, they diluted, denied, or delegitimized the severity of their own painful experiences.

Women's inability or reluctance to name their own victimization took various forms across the interviews. Some voiced a lack of entitlement to use such terms as "rape," "acquaintance rape," "abuse," or "harassment" in deference to women they perceived as "true victims." Because their own situations were often profoundly complicated, and therefore not "real victimization," they felt that applying such labels to their own experiences would somehow do a disservice to those women whose cases (they presumed) were straightforward. Describing herself as a feminist, and deeply concerned with issues of violence against women, Evelyn stated,

> I think maybe victimization or rape should be reserved for really bad cases of rape. To say my experience was rape maybe waters down the cases of real victims. It feels, I don't know, kind of unfeminist. There were a lot of factors why he did what he did to me, so it's awfully complicated to talk about. The fact that he forced me, it happened within a whole lot of other things. So I don't think it would be fair to women who are outright attacked to call myself a victim of rape. (Evelyn, 21, "heterosexual," "Caucasian")

Other women's reluctance to name their experiences stemmed less from a lack of entitlement to use such terms than from a desire to separate themselves from "real victims." The category "real victims" allowed them to construct an "Other" against whom to evaluate their own lives, and in comparison to whom their experiences did not seem quite so tragic. Rachel, for instance, compared her own experiences with those of "battered women," enabling her to view her boyfriend's tendency to hit her as not so extreme.

> I just thank God it wasn't so extreme as women who are abused. Battered women, they're in horrible situations that they can't get out of. We've studied that in my feminism classes. I was sometimes hit and sort of humiliated by my boyfriend, but I wasn't battered like a lot of women. Those women I just feel so sorry for, because I know I could have had it a lot worse. (Rachel, 21, "heterosexual," "white")

In these women's cases, entitlement or willingness to name their own victimization appears hampered not only by the conservative normal/danger dichotomy discourse and true victim discourse, but also by a popularized feminist discourse that has taught them that abuse is uncomplicated—that "no means no and yes means yes," and that "rape isn't about sex, it's about violence." Rather than empowering these young women to identify and feel outraged by their own victimization, such statements against male violence may have unwittingly contributed to their inability to claim their own abuse, because their lived experiences are seldom so straightforward.

Both the language of conservatives and the language of popularized feminism may suggest to young women that consent and coercion are mutually exclusive, that abuse is a violent "event" occurring in a particular dyad (or group, in the case of gang rape or group harassment), and that in cases of "real" abuse, the perpetrator is the agent and the victim is a powerless object. But looking back at their own encounters, these young women found evidence that they made conscious choices, or that at least, in Cynthia's words, "I was there." They were not powerless objects. Indeed, participants expended remarkable energy ensuring that they positioned themselves as active subjects, despite their often objectifying circumstances. Conversely, these women did not reflect back on the men involved as "perpetrators," "sex offenders," or "batterers" who had complete power over them. While they described violence or fears of violence during their encounters, in reconstructing their experiences they also found moments when they might have made different choices. And, unfortunately, in a context of zero-sum guilt (Fine, 1990), a moment of female agency is all that is required to focus responsibility on the woman and excuse the man (or men) from accountability.

Similarly, in focusing on an encounter as an individual event (or even a series of events) and attempting to determine whether or not victimization occurred, the available discourses overlook the contexts in which heterorelational dynamics are embedded. As we saw in previous chapters, these young women are not (as they would like to believe) autonomous agents capable of transcending social constraints and exercising free will. Women's choices and possibilities are socially and historically constructed from within a sea of oppressive double binds (Frye, 1983; Valverde, 1987; Sawicki, 1991: Bartky, 1990). Thus, we can see that coercion does not begin and end with a particular encounter, nor is it simply imposed by an individual man. Rather, women's encounters take place in an already present cultural *context* of coercion and power asymmetries, which has been established throughout their gendered developmental histories. By the time a woman gets to the "event" of abuse or exploitation, this context is so firmly in place that totalizing displays of power may not be needed to convince her that she should submit to a man's desires. Such displays *are*, however, needed for her to name that encounter "victimization." Denied both a discourse of male accountability and a discourse of female pleasure without penalties, these women are unable to factor in a context of coercion when assessing their own experiences of abuse. Thus, they consider only the dynamics of the particular encounter and, most often seeing that the individual man did not render them *totally* powerless, they determine that they must not have been truly victimized.

### "Together" Women Aren't Victims: "I'd Like to Think I Had Enough Strength"

As we saw in chapter 4, the young women in this study have internalized a belief that mature, well-adjusted women lack any ambivalence about their hetero-relational behaviors. Incorporated into this notion is the further belief that strength as a woman is inconsistent with victimization. Persuaded by the together woman discourse that women must be strong, "together," and in control of their own lives, many women have integrated into their self-concepts the notion that competent, adult women are too sophisticated in their judgment to be lured into a position where they could be victimized. Whereas a strong woman presumably acts, a victim is acted on. In the minds of these young women, seeing themselves as victims would imply that they were naive, gullible, or desperate. Given the significance attached to seeing themselves as "together" women, acknowledgment of victimization would represent a threat to their already tentative identities as competent and mature hetero-relational subjects.

Although their own lived experiences typically defied the supposed victim/agent dichotomy, we have seen that these women nonetheless incorporated this dichotomy into their thinking about their hetero-relational experiences. Needing to believe in their own sexual agency, and subscribing to the belief that victimization and agency are inherently separate phenomena, the participants were unable to entertain comfortably the notion that they could be simultaneously victims *and* subjects. Thus, the desire to be "together" sexual subjects supported women's tendency to view their painful hetero-relational experiences as resulting from their own active and informed decision making. While such an attribution relies on women taking personal responsibility for their own abuse, in this circumstance, accepting personal responsibility appears more affirming than acknowledging victimization.

Melissa's hesitation to apply the term "rape" to her own frightening experience demonstrates the importance of preserving a "strong woman" self-concept. While she was initially excited to have sex with a man she had met on vacation, the encounter soon became violent and out of her control. The man, who had originally agreed to wear a condom, later refused. The incident left Melissa with a great deal of pain, confusion, and a sexually transmitted infection, revealed by an abnormal pap smear a few months later.

> It was very alienating. It was a very strange situation, and it was this weird combination of feeling turned on, but feeling repulsed and feeling in a lot of physical pain. He was really big. The intercourse was kind of rough and hard. And the other thing is, I said, "All right, fine," because I expected him to put the condom on and then [be] inside me, but he didn't put the condom on. It was before I could even really get back and take the wheel for a minute. But I think that was the point where I really lost control, because all of a sudden he was inside me, and I was like, "Are you going to put the condom on?" And he was like, "Don't worry, don't worry." It was like, shit, you know? It's so hard to say no and push somebody off you, especially when he's really big, and plus, I'm in this thing. I don't want to ruin the magic of this weird moment. So that was the point I remember thinking, "This is not going to be a good day. He's inside me without a condom." (Melissa, 21, "heterosexual," "Eastern European-American Jew")

Although Melissa described the encounter as violent, painful, and alienating, and although she felt unable to say no because of the man's physical strength, she was not comfortable referring to the incident as "rape." Her reluctance to use such a label may stem, in part, from the fact that she felt "turned on" by this man during parts of their encounter. A more powerful factor contributing to this reluctance, however, appears to be a perceived threat to her character if she were to acknowledge herself as having been raped:

> It was like a kind of weird violent kind of thing. I don't feel like I could have really said no. I don't know if I necessarily would call it rape. But I would say that he was so strong and big and on top of me and it was like he was totally in control from the get go. Sometimes I think it was rape and sometimes I don't know if it was rape. You know, when somebody says to you, "I know nice girls like you don't have a condom," but I do, and then having sex with them. I don't know, because "rape" is such a loaded word, it's really hard. It's really scary to think about using it in terms of your own life. I remember times when I felt like I was raped, or I let myself kind of be raped, or kind of taken, but in terms of that incident, I think I was seduced. I don't know

if I'd say I was raped. Number one, because I feel like I want to have enough faith that I have enough strength of character as a person to be able to, if I really didn't want to, to say no. And it wasn't that I said no.

When I asked Melissa to elaborate on those times when she did feel like she was raped, she quickly modified her statement, saying, "Oh no, I don't mean really raped, just more like taken, not really raped, no, I'd never say that." For Melissa, as for many other women, "rape" was "such a loaded word" that it was too frightening to apply to her own experiences. As Melissa indicated in her description of the encounter above, in order to believe that she had "strength of character as a person," she needed to believe that she would have been able to say no, despite the fact that, in her words, the situation was a "weird, violent kind of thing" and "he was totally in control from the get go." And if she believes she was able to say no but did not, then she must not have been raped. Compounding her sense of personal responsibility, this man invoked the pleasing woman discourse to remind her that "nice girls" do not carry condoms. Thus, not fitting the scripts for "pleasing women" or "true victims," she was left without a category in which to place her experience. Unable to see herself as raped, Melissa found it far preferable to consider herself "seduced" or caught in "the magic of this weird moment."

Given the power of the victim/agent dichotomy, it appears nearly impossible for young women to acknowledge the condition of being victimized without also accepting the identity "victim," an apparently monolithic category that precludes agency in the minds of these participants. That is, once she is a victim, a woman is always and *only* a victim, as though other dimensions of her personhood cease to exist. In this dichotomous framework, women are allowed no room to be an active agent *who has also been victimized.* Compelled to choose between a victim or agent identity, and unable to reconcile a lack of agency with the adult self-image they are working so hard to develop, they must rewrite their victimization as seduction, "a weird encounter," or, as Melissa put it, "not a good day."

### The Risk of Not Finding Support: "Why Stick Your Neck Out?"

A third factor contributing to young women's inability or unwillingness to name their own victimization involves the inadequacy of existing social supports. For some women, it was preferable to leave their experiences un-named than to acknowledge themselves as victims and risk not finding sup-port for their plight. Women often expressed a fear that if they came for-ward with claims of victimization, they would lose the respect of those around them. Aware that others might view victims as neither "pleasing" nor "together," these women feared that they would be stigmatized by family or friends. Already feeling alienated by their abusive experiences, they feared even greater alienation if they shared their victimization with others. Henna, for example, remembered fearing that an acknowledgment of rape would lead her friends to see her as "a stupid kid who couldn't even take care of herself."

> I didn't want to tell anybody, especially to tell them I'd been raped. I wanted to tell somebody about it, because I felt really dirty and hurt and scared. But I didn't want to, because my friends were all more experienced than me, and I thought if I told them, they would just think I was a little kid who couldn't handle myself. I was already so self-conscious about my height and feeling like, not a woman. I didn't want to be thought of or talked about as a stupid kid who couldn't even take care of herself. So I just thought, this was a bad experience, but I'm just going to try to put it behind me and try to pretend it never happened. (Henna, 21, "heterosexual," "Korean")

Rather than risk alienation and further doubt about her identity as an adult woman, Henna resolved not to name her painful experience rape, but rather, to think of it as just "a bad experience." Thus she tried (al-though ultimately unsuccessfully) to bury it and simply move on.

Women also expressed a fear that those around them would blame them or fail to support them in a time of need. As we saw in chapter 3, women such as Elaina, Gloria, and Chloe were exposed as children and adolescents to the pain and disillusionment of not finding support. Aware that the adults in their lives were unwilling to confront male sexual aggression but were quick to diminish its significance and to blame girls and women who were victimized, these women concluded that they should not seek advo-cacy for the abuse they endured. As Elaina explained, telling others she had been victimized would have made her feel worse.

> It's just not worth it. It's already bad enough to feel what you've gone through. Why stick your neck out and talk about it if you know what kind of reaction you're going to get? They would never say, "This was rape" or

"This was abuse." They'd say, "What were you doing? Why didn't you stop him? Why do you want to make such a fuss?" It already felt like shit. Why make it worse by sticking your neck out by saying, "I was raped" if you know you're just going to get rejected? And then why even call it that to yourself if you can't talk about it to anyone else? That would just make you feel even worse. (Elaina, 22, "lesbian/bi," "white")

Rather than risk being disappointed or further hurt by those who should offer care and support, Elaina and others kept their pain inside. Aware that, without a context for discussing their feelings, labeling "would just make you feel even worse," they left their experiences unnamed and unspoken, even to themselves.

Even those women who had already found some sources of support still feared rejection if they named abuse. Although earlier in her interview Robin described her women friends' encouragement to name her experience "rape," she was still nagged by a sense that other important people in her life would fail to understand the complexity of her situation. Robin's misgivings were fueled by her boyfriend's lack of support and the negative responses she expected from other male friends.

They wouldn't get it. I know they'd be like, "What'd you do, what'd you do?" to bring it on myself. My boyfriend doesn't understand. He just thinks he would have fought, so I could have fought. So it comes back down on my head. Even though my girlfriends would be supportive, the other people in my life would think I had no right to say "rape" because I should have fought him more. Based on my boyfriend's reaction, I wouldn't expect to get support. Far from it. (Robin, 21, "heterosexual"; asked to describe her race(s), she wrote, "I cannot")

For Robin, naming her experience victimization would have meant not only exposing her pain and vulnerability, but also risking the victim-blaming reactions of friends. To reduce the likelihood of such disappointment, Robin chose not to name her experience rape or abuse.

Naming a bad experience "victimization" literally entails the risk of adding insult to injury. Facing the likelihood of blame, lack of support, and alienation from those closest to them, these women found that the costs of naming outweighed the costs of privatizing their experiences. While it may be painful to hold their feelings inside, these women found it even more stressful to express their emotions and risk learning that their support systems had failed them. As Elaina put it so clearly, "Why even call it that to yourself if you can't talk to anybody else about it? That would just make you feel even worse."

### Diminished Expectations: "I Don't Really Think Men Get It"

Compounding their low expectations of support systems, many young women indicated that they fully expected to be dissatisfied in their romantic and sexual relationships with men. Informed by the love hurts discourse, and thus believing that a certain amount of alienation or exploitation was inevitable in their hetero-relations, these women did not necessarily draw clear lines between simple dissatisfaction and abuse in their own relationships with men. Having been persuaded by the male sexual drive discourse that men's sexuality is inherently aggressive, they often saw coercion or manipulation as typical (even if undesirable) male behavior. And having learned from the normal/danger dichotomy discourse that typical encounters are defined as normal, they did not name their own experiences victimization, even when they were exploitive and hurtful.

Interestingly, most of the women interviewed expressed an *abstract* sense of entitlement to sexual pleasure and respect in their relationships with men. Alicia and Paula, for instance, held strong views about equality and mutuality in women's hetero-relations.

> I think women, not just men, deserve to be treated with love and respect. I want a relationship that's based on equality and honesty and trust. And mutual satisfaction, I think that is very important. (Alicia, 22, "heterosexual," "Asian")

> You have to have both people getting their needs met. Not just one person or the other. That's in any kind of relationship, not just marriage. Even just in sexual relationships. Usually the man just believes his needs should come first. And a lot of times women, they may not consciously believe that, but they put his needs first, too. But I don't think that's how it should be. Sexually, they should both be able to express what they want. And they should share the housework if they live together. I wouldn't want to put up with less than total respect and equality from a man. (Paula, 20, "Spanish-American"; asked to describe her sexuality, she wrote, "?")

Yet when I asked these same women to describe the dynamics of their *personal* relationships, they (and many others) expressed a belief that it was unrealistic to expect men to fully respect or be able to accommodate their needs and desires.

> I don't really think men get it. It's not that they're bad people, necessarily. Maybe it's just how they're socialized, but I don't think a man can ever really give me what I'm looking for. Maybe it just comes with the territory. Maybe I should try to be a lesbian. I mean, I love men, and I'm attracted to men. But I've never had a man who gave me as much as I gave him, and it probably won't ever happen. I want equality and openness, but it seems the man always comes first. I don't even mean to, but, you know, he sets the pace, he sets the tone, when he's finished, you know, sexually, we're finished, even if I haven't come. It's not a good way to be to have his needs always be more important than mine, but I think that's just the way it is with men. I don't think they know any better, and maybe I've just given up trying. (Alicia, 22, "heterosexual," "Asian")

> The guys I know, even the nice ones, they're all really out for what they can get. They're just really selfish. I don't think anyone ever teaches them that the woman's needs are important too. It's all about scoring and their pleasure. Even my guy friends, as lovers I'm sure they're really ignorant. Guys are taught to be selfish, sexually and just in general. My boyfriend now, I care about him, and there are other things I get from the relationship, which I guess is why I'm in it. But I don't expect that much from him. If I want understanding or tenderness, I go to my friends. And if I want to be sure I have an orgasm, I masturbate. Like after we have sex, his needs are met, and I go in the bathroom and masturbate. (Paula, 20, "Spanish-American"; asked to describe her sexuality, she wrote, "?")

Here we see a gap between these women's abstract notions about their hetero-relational entitlement and their actual experiences in their relationships. While they stated that they wanted and deserved to have their desires met, they appeared fairly resigned to dissatisfaction in their actual relationships.

As we saw in chapter 3, many young women learned, most often from their mothers or other adult women, not to expect much from the men in their lives. Often the men they observed growing up did very little to counter such low expectations. Wendy's grandmother, for instance, taught her that men were inevitably lazy and abusive, and that women should keep them as drunk as possible. Henna recalled learning that "men chose and did, and women followed and listened," and that only men were entitled to sexual enjoyment. Theresa's brother stressed that men "only want one thing" and that it was her responsibility to keep them from touching her. Natalie's family told her that "men wanted to take something from me, and I wasn't supposed to give it to them." Melissa learned from her mother, simply, that "men don't come through." It is perhaps not surprising that with such powerful early lessons, and still lacking a discourse of male accountability and a discourse of female pleasure without penalties, these women have diminished expectations of men and hetero-relationships.

Interestingly, the warnings of the (hetero)sex as female victimization discourse, intended to frighten young women away from involvement with men, seem in many women's cases to have backfired. Instead of keeping women from exploring their sexualities, such warnings have led to a sense that mistreatment is inevitable. With such low expectations for hetero-relational fulfillment, young women were unlikely to name abuse in their own relationships, because it appeared so unavoidable and so common.

## Intolerable Dissonance: "He Was So Good to Me, I Could Never Call It Abuse"

While many women were taught that men are aggressive and unreliable, they were also exposed to the normal/danger dichotomy discourse, which told them that there are "good guys" and "bad guys," and that one should not be confused with the other. As we saw in women's recollections of their early educations, most girls were warned about the existence of dangerous men, but few were told that those men might include family members, lovers, teachers, or friends. Since they were encouraged to rely on "good guys" for protection, acknowledging a trusted man as a "bad guy" often evoked considerable dissonance. Rather than entertain such dissonance, some women found it preferable to leave their abusive experiences unnamed as such.

Diana's experience provides a clear example of the potential costs of naming a "good guy" an abuser. After leaving home at fourteen, she moved in with her teacher and began having a physical relationship with him. Indebted to him for providing her shelter and support, she was unable or unwilling to consider her experience with him abuse.

> I left home when I was fourteen. I stayed with my teacher, which was really great, but when I look back at it, it was a little weird. He was so cool, though. I mean he took me in and fed me and took care of me. I love him for what he did for me. I wasn't in love with him. I was more just very grateful. We were like this funny couple, because he was about thirty-five and I was fourteen. He was really sensitive to the fact that I was so young. So we never, I mean, it wasn't sexual. He was cool about that. I would just undress for him and he would masturbate, or I would jerk him off, or sometimes give him head. But he never laid a hand on me. He knew I was just young. We had to be really careful about going out and everything, because we couldn't let anybody at school know. They would just think like it was abuse or something, and they would make me go back to my mom or to a shelter. They would have made it into something abusive or illegal. But it wasn't, because he really protected me. If it wasn't for him, I would have had it a lot worse. (Diana, 21, "bisexual," "white")

When I asked whether she ever thought her relationship with her teacher qualified as statutory rape or sexual abuse, Diana answered,

> No. I wasn't into the sexual part, and he knew that, which is why he never forced intercourse or anything. I think he respected that I was too young. I never really thought of myself as being coerced or anything, I just thought, "This is what I owe him. He takes care of me, and I should do this to make him happy." If it wasn't for him, I'd be on the street. Well, maybe that does make it a little coercive. I mean, it was sort of, do that or find somewhere else. It didn't really occur to me that I had a lot of choice. But he was so good to me, I could never think about it as abuse.

For Diana, the fact of her teacher's kindness erased other considerations: that he was thirty-five, that she was a minor, that he was in a position of authority over her at school, that she "wasn't into the sexual part," or that she had to "do that or find somewhere else" to live. Indeed, even though she undressed for him, masturbated him, and gave him oral sex, she maintained that "it wasn't sexual" because "he never laid a hand on me." Rather than seeing these acts as abusive or exploitative, she interpreted them as evidence of his sensitivity to her young age and lack of sexual feelings for him. While she was willing to entertain the possibility during her interview that her situation was "weird" or "a little coercive," she was unable to reconcile his care with the notion that he abused or molested her. The costs of such a realization would not only have involved being out on the street as a teenager, but even now would induce profound disillusionment about the one person in her life who had taken her in at a difficult time. So Diana chose to understand her experience as a mutual relationship, a give-and-take arrangement between a compassionate adult and a needy adolescent, rather than two years of exploitation or statutory rape.

While women were often eager in their interviews to discuss their dissatisfaction with boyfriends and lovers, only Diana was willing to describe a personal relationship with an intimate as involving victimization.[2]

> I haven't really had many bad experiences where they felt clear, where I felt like I could put my foot down and say, "This was abuse." Only my relationship with Tony. It didn't last very long, because I was like, "I've gotta get out of here." But I was with him for a while before I felt like I could say, "Wait a minute, I'm the victim here. You are not the victim," which is what he was trying to make me believe. But no, I realized it wasn't normal for him to grab me and hit me and try to cause me pain. I've had relationships where pain was erotic, like s/m, but where it was consensual, a mutual type of thing. And I think that's fine, you know? If both people are into it, that's cool. But this guy, Tony, it wasn't about that. It was more about just abuse.
> (Diana, 21, "bisexual," "white")

Women shared stories of forced or coerced sex, physical pain, and humiliation induced by their lovers, as well as outright violence. But because they often loved and/or depended on these men, they resisted naming their relationships abusive. For instance, although Evelyn described physical violence in her current relationship, she was careful to avoid labeling her boyfriend an "abuser."

> I always thought I would never stay with a man who hit me. I was brought up to respect myself and to expect much more. But when you're in the situation, it just becomes different. I still think I would never be in a relationship where I was being really abused, but my boyfriend has slapped me and I'm still with him. He's basically a really good person, and we share a lot together. It's just that he has a really bad temper, and when he gets upset, he sometimes hits me. God, that sounds so bad. But most times he's really decent, so I don't think of the times he hits me as so severe. I mean, it's not

like he hits me every night or something. It's really very seldom, actually. Well, there was this one time that he had me up against the wall and he was holding my hair and punching me in the stomach. But he really apologized after, and I don't think that will ever happen again. I know this might sound like, whatever, but he really is a good person. He's not an abuser. (Evelyn, 21, "heterosexual," "Caucasian")

In light of her love and commitment toward this man, Evelyn was unwilling in her interview to call his violence "abuse." Despite the fact that he had slapped and punched her, she was moved by his apologies and described him as a good person who just happened to take out his bad temper on her. Whereas Evelyn said her boyfriend hit her when he was angry, Sara acknowledged that her boyfriend used physical force during their sexual experiences.

The sex is lots of times pretty rough. Sometimes it just feels like I'm an object that he does things to, rather than somebody that he's really with. He's pretty aggressive sexually, and a lot of times it really hurts. It hurts me physically, because a lot of times I'm not at all ready and he just goes ahead anyway and he's really rough. And it hurts me emotionally, too, like it kind of hurts my feelings. It's kind of degrading to have someone you care about treat you like an object in bed. But when he's all hot and horny, it's like, he needs it, and I'm just sort of beside the point. (Sara, 20, "mostly heterosexual, with a healthy bisexual curiosity, but with no experience," "white")

When I asked if this felt like sexual abuse, Sara immediately defended her boyfriend by noting the love they shared.

Oh, don't get me wrong, I love this guy and he loves me. It's just that sex is one area of our lives that I don't expect to get much pleasure from. If I could get aroused by his style of sex it would be much better. But he's so harsh and, like, wham bam that I can't ever really enjoy it with him. I've had good sexual relationships with other people, so I know what it can be like, but I think he's just not a very considerate lover in bed. That's just the way he is.

Sara could describe her sexual experiences with her boyfriend as painful, humiliating, degrading, and displeasurable, and she could describe him as harsh, aggressive, and inconsiderate. But when asked to consider the possibility that he was sexually abusive, she immediately pointed to their love for each other and explained, "that's just the way he is." Presumably, the fact that she loves this man and he loves her means that she is not sexually abused. It seems impossible that he might simultaneously be the man she loves and a man who victimizes her.

### Needing a Just World: "I Couldn't Imagine That Happening to Me"

A final explanation for these young women's resistance to consider themselves "victims" involves a need to preserve the belief that they are safe in their relationships and their social worlds. Having developed their heterorelational subjectivities with/in the (hetero)sex as female victimization discourse, the male sexual drive discourse, and the love hurts discourse, the participants have been exposed throughout their lives to warnings about the dangers of men and hetero-relations. Yet also influenced by the pleasing woman discourse, the together woman discourse, and the love conquers all discourse, they have been taught that hetero-relations are among the most important realms of their adolescent and adult lives. Assured by the normal/danger dichotomy discourse that dangerous men are identifiably different from those with whom they are intimate, young women may find it particularly difficult to identify victimization as part of their own hetero-relational encounters.

Women's acknowledgment of their own victimization would require an acknowledgment of their vulnerability to danger in the most intimate aspects of their lives. Striving to find a secure place in an arena marked by potential dangers, women needed some way to separate their own relationships from the potential victimization about which they had been warned. By refusing to identify their own encounters as victimization, the participants were able to preserve a sense that their own relationships were somehow impervious to the dangers facing women in their hetero-relations.

Tonya indicated in her interview that she had never been abused, although she stated that she had been in a sexual situation where she was forced or coerced. While she was well versed in feminist issues and quite aware of violence against women, she said she could never picture herself being raped.

> You know, no one is above being raped, but I am. In the back of your mind you think, you know, no one is going to rape me. So, no, I can't picture myself in that situation. But sure, I can picture every one of my friends in that

situation, and I can picture my parents in that situation. (Tonya, 18, "straight," "Jewish/white by race and religion")

Acknowledgment of other women's victimization often elicited the participants' feelings of sympathy or outrage for an abstract "Other," but it did not necessarily invite young women to reflect on their own vulnerability. When focusing on another woman's experience, participants were able to label an encounter "abusive" because they were still able to distance themselves, finding reasons for the victimization that did not require an acknowledgment that the same sort of abuse could happen to them. Alicia, for instance, was both sympathetic and angry on behalf of a friend who had been raped.

My friend was raped by a guy, and I was so angry for her. I still am, you know? It's so unfair what she went through. It makes me mad that women still have to go through this kind of stuff. I think that guy was a total user and a total prick. I could kill him if I ever laid eyes on him. I could never imagine that happening to me. (Alicia, 22, "heterosexual," "Asian")

If these women were to name their own victimization, they would need to ask themselves, "If *someone like me* could be victimized, is anything safe?" And, reflecting on abuse by an intimate or "good guy," they would need to wonder, "If *someone like him* could be a victimizer, is there anyone I can trust?" Further, if women were to allow themselves to believe that they were victimized once, then they might have to acknowledge that it could happen again. Needing to frame themselves as active subjects in control of their worlds, these women had a great psychological investment in not labeling their own experiences abuse (Janoff-Bulman, 1979). As Melissa explained above, "Rape is such a loaded word, it's too scary to think about applying to your own life."

Young women's refusal to name their own victimization may reflect a need to believe not only that their relationships are safe, but also that their world is just. Previous research (Borgida and Brekke, 1985; Carli and Leonard, 1989; Furnham and Gunter, 1984; Gruman and Sloan, 1983; Lerner, 1980; Lerner and Miller, 1978; Summers and Feldman, 1984) suggests that, in an effort to maintain a belief in a just world, individuals are motivated to form individualized, and hence victim-blaming, attributions for others' victimization. These women's stories, however, add a new dimension to these findings. Whereas previous studies suggest that observers hold others personally accountable for their victimizing circumstances, these young women acknowledged and offered non–victim-blaming attributions for the victimization of others, even as they held themselves personally responsible.

To understand the discrepancy between these women's responses and previous findings, we must remember that the young women in this study were, in general, already quite painfully aware of the prevalence of violence against women and had learned—often through their college courses, political involvements, and experiences with other women who had been abused—that women are not individually at fault for their own victimization. They could not, therefore, preserve a belief in a just world by denying the injustices done to women in their hetero-relations. Thus, they might have been less motivated than a casual observer to form victim-blaming attributions about other women's abuse. Indeed, participants were quite willing to acknowledge other women's abuse and to absolve them of responsibility for their mistreatment. However, aware that violence touches the lives of so many women, and needing to preserve a belief that their *own* world was just, they needed somehow to distinguish themselves from "those women" who endured abuse. Unable to escape an acknowledgment of the injustices done to others of their gender, these women were able to maintain a belief that their personal lives remained just and safe by indulging in a slight twist of logic and refusing to accept that their own mistreatment could qualify as victimization. To support this belief, they needed only turn to the true victim discourse and the normal/danger dichotomy discourse to find evidence that their own circumstances defied the definitions of "abuse."

## Changing the Subject: Women's Strategies for "Controlling the Damage"

Operating in a context of zero-sum guilt (Fine, 1990) and amid the dissonance created by a failure of support systems, "good guys" who are also "bad guys," and the lack of predictability of an unsafe and unjust world, young women were challenged to preserve a sense of self after enduring hetero-relational encounters that had "gone badly." Seeing victimization as a threat to their senses of self, and often having diminished expectations for their own hetero-relational encounters, these women were understandably reluctant to name their experiences with such loaded terms as "victimization," "rape," or "abuse." Yet they were still compelled to make sense of why things went badly.

In order to make sense of their painful experiences, women needed to construct explanations for their mistreatment that would both preserve their subjectivities and enable them to avoid the potential costs of labeling their experiences victimization. They most often accomplished this by rewriting their stories in ways that allowed them to explain their abuse without losing themselves. By "changing the subject" of their own encounters, they were able to maintain a sense of personal responsibility, allowing them to prevent their own erasure. While their strategies often appear, at first glance, to simply encourage self-blame, a closer look shows that they are actually attempts to take psychological charge of painful experiences so that young women may appear in their narratives as active subjects, despite their abuse (Janoff-Bulman, 1979).

### Taking Responsibility

Women "changed the subject" most often by reexamining and then reinterpreting the strategies they had used to maintain a sense of agency during their entrance into, management in, and exit from hetero-relational encounters. Looking with hindsight at encounters that "went badly," they often transformed those very strategies into indications that they were personally (and often entirely) responsible for their own abuse.

As we saw in chapter 5, very often young women felt uneasy telling men directly that they were uncomfortable in their encounters. Fearing reprisals, or equating a request to stop with ambivalence and immaturity, they relied on strategies such as "hoping he'll notice," "stroking egos," or "mastering the male body" to end an unpleasant encounter. When examining why things went badly, however, they often reduced these carefully developed and executed strategies to one basic fact: "I didn't exactly say no." Diminishing the significance of the constraining circumstances that rendered them unable to say no in their encounters, these women stressed only the fact that they failed the requirement of the true victim discourse to state and enforce a clear and emphatic "no." Thus, even if they were visibly crying, trying to leave, or sending obvious signals that they were in pain, they assumed full responsibility for failing to be clear about their needs. For instance, rather than holding her partner accountable for failing to stop when she cried and pulled away during sex, Rachel focused on the fact that she did not actually utter the word "no." Thus, she blamed herself for his actions.

> I mean, I was crying and sort of pulling away, and hoping he'd notice I was upset and stop, but I didn't exactly tell him no. I could have said, "Get the hell off me! I want to go home!" But I didn't. I just laid there crying and hoping he'd stop. Maybe if I'd said something, who knows? Maybe things would have been different. But as it happened, I never exactly said no to him, so I really just have myself to blame. (Rachel, 21, "heterosexual," "white")

Even women who did say the word "no" still tended to blame themselves when things went badly. Although Robin said no and asked her partner to wait, and although she acknowledged in her interview that she tried to manage her situation as best she could, she still faulted herself, concluding that perhaps her "no" wasn't "no enough."

> I should have been more assertive. I was trying just to get out of the situation as gracefully as possible. I was just trying to make him feel like, I don't know, like trying to make the best of it by trying to make him come as fast as possible. I sort of told him, like, "Let's wait," but he kept going, so I figured I'd just better try to get him off so he would stop. I don't know, I should have been more assertive when I was trying to tell him I didn't want to. Maybe my no wasn't no enough. (Robin, 21, "heterosexual"; asked to describe her race(s), she wrote, "I cannot")

Reexamining their own victimization, many women blamed themselves for being so naive as to believe they could predict or control men's behaviors in the first place. Women originally used strategies such as "doing everything but" or "letting/making it just happen" as a way to balance their sexual desires with an avoidance of repercussions for appearing too "loose" or "willing." Yet once things went badly, they interpreted those same strategies, often with apparent disgust, as indications of their own stupidity or naïveté. Andrea, for example, was angry about what happened to her. However, she directed her anger not at the man who hurt her, but rather at herself for being so gullible as to believe that she could do "everything but."

I was so stupid to think I could go out there and mess around without getting hurt. I guess I was really naive. I thought I could handle it. I don't know, maybe I just didn't think. It never really occurred to me that I would be hurt. I just trusted guys and thought he would stop if I was uncomfortable. I was just really young and way out of my league. I can't believe I was so gullible. (Andrea, 20, "mixed—Lebanese/Chinese/Swedish/American"; asked to describe her sexuality, she wrote, "—")

Others used more active strategies such as "playing with fire" and "being a bad girl" to experience feelings of power and entitlement in their hetero-relations. Yet when things went badly, they tended to punish themselves for the very agency they had worked so hard to establish. Women like Laura and Jeanne suggested that they had been presumptuous ever to expect that they could express their desires without suffering repercussions. Over and over, I heard young women reflecting on their experiences and criticizing their actions by asking themselves, "What was I thinking?" "What did I expect?" or "Just who did I think I was?"

It was my own fault, in a way, because I was trying to be so grown-up and just assert myself and what I wanted. I played around, I hitchhiked, I picked up men I shouldn't have. I look back at it now, and I think, "Just who the hell did I think I was?" I mean, I had no business getting into half the situations I was in. I just should have known better. I just should have known, you can't play with fire without expecting to get burned. (Laura, 22, "bisexual," "bi-racial/West Black Indian, white American")

I really should have been more careful. You can't go around strutting your stuff without it catching up with you. When I think about it, I mean, really, what did I expect? (Jeanne, 18, "heterosexual," "Black, Indian, white")

In a similar translation of previous strategies, women who had relied on strategies like "doing everything but," "being a desired object," and "playing with fire" tended to take personal responsibility after the fact for sending mixed messages or leading men on. Despite their abstract critiques, these women apparently bought into the male sexual drive discourse and the (hetero)sex as female victimization discourse once abuse had occurred. Indeed, they pointed to any evidence of their own interest in sexual or romantic contact, and then turned it on themselves so that their behavior became a justification for men to force them to have sex.

Trying to understand why things went badly, they blamed their own expressions of sexual desire rather than men's decisions to victimize them. Claudia blamed herself for "making out" with a boy in her room on a class trip. Although she told him she did not want to have sex and "totally tried to stop it," she looked back on the encounter from *his* perspective and concluded that he was justified in forcing her because she sent him "mixed signals."

> I thought it was really cool and I expected we would kind of work up to things and then see what happened. I definitely didn't expect to have sex with him, not then and there. It didn't occur to me that he would try to force anything. It was so exciting, and we were kind of drunk and away from home and the whole thing was just so exciting. I didn't mean to lead him on, but I see it now from his perspective, and I was all over him, and in the beginning I was into it just as much as he was. But I was thinking like, making out, not sex. But I guess I must have been sending out totally mixed signals. I can see how he would have assumed that since I brought him back to my room, and my roommate wasn't there, and we had been fooling around, I mean it's understandable that he would have thought we were going all the way. It went too far for me and I was getting scared. I totally tried to stop it, but he was like, "Come on, who are you kidding? You know you want it just as much as me. You know you wanted it all along." He just didn't take no for an answer, and we, or maybe I should say he had sex with me, because I was just laying there wishing this wasn't happening. I look at it as a failure of communication, really. He was young and I sent him mixed signals, so of course he was going to see that as an invitation to have sex. I just should have chilled out and been much more careful about the kinds of signals I was sending out. I should have realized I might be leading him on. (Claudia, 21, "heterosexual," "Caucasian")

By taking responsibility, these women have changed the subject of their own victimization, replacing male accountability with an assertion of their own personal responsibility for allowing men to misuse them. "He hurt me" becomes "I *let* him hurt me." "He forced me" becomes "I should have stopped him." "He wouldn't take no for an answer" becomes "I can see his point." Excusing men from responsibility for their own actions, they insert themselves as the culpable subjects of statements about their own abuse. Thus, believing themselves responsible for their painful encounters, they need not name those experiences "victimization."

## *Relinquishing Rights*

Some young women seemed to prepare a second strategy *in anticipation* of things going badly. They then referred back to this strategy, both during and after their victimization, to assure themselves that they were not, in fact, victims at all. This strategy involves a rather ironic, and in many ways troubling, psychological decision to give up one's right *not* to be sexually abused, in order to maintain a sense of control and choice in the process and aftermath of being violated. Women who developed this strategy chose to attribute their experiences of (what many would call) acquaintance rape or other abuse to decisions they had made prior to the experience. Each of the women who relinquished rights displayed a bold insistence that she was an active agent who had freely exercised a choice to be sexual and was now therefore not a victim, but rather a stoic individual accepting the unpleasant consequences of her own decision making.

In a paradoxical use of self-blame, these participants found a sense of psychological safety in maintaining that they were not powerless beings who had been unjustly acted on, but that they were instead responsible for their own fate, however damaging. Often accepting the male sexual drive discourse's claim that men possess a natural, aggressive sexual urge that must be satisfied, these women were also quite invested in the together woman discourse. They experienced themselves as having knowingly played the odds by being sexual, and they were now committed to accepting the role of a graceful loser.

Theresa, who discussed her decision to become a "bad girl" at age thirteen, used the strategy of relinquishing rights. Theresa contended that she knew that she was choosing to be a "slut," and that she was therefore relinquishing any right to ever "cry rape," even when it was true. Even though she said her experience would have been rape if it had happened to a "nice girl," she now felt she had no right to complain. Indeed, she maintained that it was "worth the price." However, she did not, at least in her interview, critique the notion that there must be a price—that being a sexual teenager and later being a rape victim/survivor must be deemed mutually exclusive.

> I wasn't stupid. I knew when I decided to become a slut that I would never be able to cry rape, even if I ever did get raped. I basically gave up any right to say rape, but it was worth it to me. I just wanted to be sexual,

and it was worth the price. So when I was seventeen and this guy sort of, well, it would have been rape if it had happened to a "nice girl," but when that happened, you know, I said to myself, "Well, you knew this could happen when you stepped out there. You can't turn back the clock now." I just felt like I was, what is it they say, paying the piper? So I just figured it came with the territory and I couldn't ever really complain. (Theresa, 19, "heterosexual," "bi-racial")

In a similar fashion, Laura decided that she was "not rapeable" because she "always went into things with [her] eyes wide open." Although her descriptions of her experiences contain many contradictions to an outside observer, for Laura, there was an internal consistency that made the events in her life more tolerable.

I always know exactly what I'm getting into. I chose to be sexually active, I mean very active, a long time ago. I help myself to what I want, and there are never any surprises. And so when there are surprises, like something I can't handle, like when I get myself in over my head, I know that this is what I've chosen to do, that I am the one that let it happen, you know? And so, even in the times when I haven't had any control over a situation, you know, like once it starts, I know that I always have control because I'm the one who has chosen this. Well, maybe not chosen this situation exactly, but I've made a choice, and nobody can take that away from me. There's really nothing I can't handle. (Laura, 22, "bisexual," "bi-racial/West Black Indian, white American")

The young women who adopted this strategy were fully aware of the cultural prohibition against women's sexual entitlement, and they both resisted it and incorporated it into their thinking. Initially, they resisted the pleasing woman discourse by choosing to express their sexualities. Then, once victimized, they maintained a belief in their subject position in their negative experiences by reasoning that their mistreatment was simply the predictable cost of violating that very discourse. It must be noted that this strategy did not prevent them from feeling the scars of their victimization, nor did it prevent them from feeling outrage toward their abusers. As Laura continued,

The time when that guy sort of, like, beat me up over the condom thing, I mean, I was furious, you know? I mean nobody treats me that way. But even though it hurt a lot and everything, I mean, I didn't really let it bother me too much. I mean, I figure, I made my bed, and I chose to lie in it [*laughing*]. Wow, how's that for apropos?

While this strategy clearly did not erase women's anger or abstract sense of entitlement to fair treatment, it did seem to keep young women from transforming their outrage into a willingness to name their experience an injustice that deserved to be remedied.

Adamantly opposed to labeling themselves victims in their hetero-relational encounters, these women attempted to make their mistreatment more tolerable by forming attributions that made their abuse seem self-chosen. This strategy involved taking personal responsibility for things going badly as a way to maintain a belief that they were not merely objects, acted maliciously upon by another, but rather that they were active agents in control of their own experience.

## Making Higher Meaning

Women also tried to make sense of their own victimization by attempting to find some higher meaning for their mistreatment. Needing to find some reasonable explanation for why things went badly, they searched for ways to place their experiences in a broader framework that could account for such an apparently unjust and uncontrollable event. Here they drew on a compelling combination of the love hurts and the love conquers all discourses. Most often they attempted to make higher meaning by finding "logical" explanations for men's behaviors, making exceptions, and/or trying to understand their mistreatment as part of a larger, more hopeful picture of a healthy relationship or fulfilling encounter.

Many women attempted to find meaning in their victimization by trying to understand the psychological motivations of the men involved. They searched for underlying psychological imbalances, traumas, or misunderstandings in the men who violated them in order to explain, dilute, and often forgive their abusive behaviors. Stephanie attributed her boyfriend's violence to his own insecurity and presumed history of abuse. Interestingly, while she was able to consider *him* a victim of abuse, she was unable to see *herself* as a victim of his violence. She said she did not take his behavior personally, but neither did she hold him responsible.

I don't think he ever meant to hurt me consciously. He was having problems, I think, like with his own identity. He never said so, but I think he was
probably abused. And so I always felt like he couldn't really control his
anger, and that's why he took it out on me. It seems to make sense to me. I
mean, why else would he act that way? I just tried to understand that it
wasn't about me, or it wasn't about us. It was really coming from somewhere
else inside of him. He wasn't abusive, he was just acting out his frustrations
from his own experience. I don't think he wanted to hurt me. It just sort of
happened. (Stephanie, 21, "heterosexual," "white")

These young women not only attempted to make higher meaning
about violent relationships in which they had some long-term emotional
investment, they also searched for psychological explanations to make
sense of violence and coercion in casual encounters. Diana attributed an
encounter that might otherwise be called date rape to a lack of communication and confusion on the part of the man who forced her to have sex
even after she "pulled back." She cast her pulling back as a reason for him
to force her, rather than as a reason why he should have stopped.

I've always told myself that we really just didn't communicate at all about
what we wanted. I should have told him up front that I wasn't planning to
go home with him. But that felt kind of weird. I mean, you don't exactly
flirt with somebody and also tell them right out, you know, I don't want
to have sex at the end of this, even though I probably should have. What I
think happened is that he misunderstood, or I just wasn't clear like I
should have been. So he probably thought this was just normal and maybe
didn't know I was scared. And maybe being rough and forceful is just his
way of having sex. I mean, who knows, really? For me it was a terrible
night and I was scared and hurt. But for him, he probably didn't mean for
it to be like that, exactly. When I pulled back, that probably hit a nerve
and he just felt he should force it further. I would say that he probably
didn't mean anything by it, it's just that we kind of didn't connect.
(Diana, 21, "bisexual," "white")

Like the women in Brodkey and Fine's (1988) study of sexual harassment on a college campus, these women formed attributions for their
abuse that diverted responsibility away from the men who violated
them. By attributing men's behavior to psychological problems, ignorance, or their own failure to communicate, they were able to make

sense of their experiences without needing to believe that men consciously victimized them.

Women also made higher meaning by trying to understand an abusive encounter as an exception, an unusual phenomenon that they could explain without referring to the incident as victimization. Participants often tried to find psychological or situational reasons why a particularly painful or frightening encounter would not count as an instance of abuse. Gloria recalled an older man who lived in her building when she was a child. Although the man exposed himself and masturbated in front of Gloria and her friends, she described him as an "exhibitionist" rather than a "flasher" or a "child molester," so that she saw him as a harmless, "crazy old man."

> He would come downstairs and take his clothes off, take his dick out of his pants and wave it at all the little girls playing on the sidewalk. It was okay, though, just weird. It wasn't like he was a flasher, he was just an exhibitionist. He didn't touch any of us. He would just stand there looking at us and playing with himself. My mother knew what he did, and she just said, you know, "He's kind of off, just let him be." So I just figured he was not quite normal. I'm trying to think, was I scared of him? Well, kind of. I mean, he was really creepy and we all were too young to be seeing a grown man masturbating while he was looking at little girls. But because my mother knew about it, and because, you know, he was kind of crazy anyway, I think he was on some kind of medication, I just figure he was just one weird guy who probably didn't even know he made us uncomfortable. Looking back, I just have to laugh, because I couldn't really think he was a flasher or a child molester and my mother just said, "let him be." (Gloria, 20, "heterosexual," "African-American")

Knowing that her mother was both aware of this man's behavior and unwilling to intervene on her behalf, Gloria made this man "just this one weird guy" rather than a man who was committing a crime and victimizing children by exposing himself and masturbating in their presence. Recognizing this as a form of sexual abuse would entail acknowledging herself as a victim and her mother as complicit by failing to protect her. Thus, she explained, "I just have to laugh," allowing her to make this man, and his behavior, an exception to "real" sexual abuse.

While many women made exceptions by finding reasons to excuse men for their behaviors, they also made exceptions by writing off an individual man as an evil character or, as Robin explained, "a once in a lifetime kind of jerk." Robin was clearly unwilling to forgive the man who forced her to have sex. Yet she made her case an exception to "rape" by attributing her situation to bad luck and viewing her abuser as simply "an obnoxious character" out to prove his manhood.

> Oh, it wasn't really rape, per se. He was just a real asshole. He was this slick, obnoxious character who was out to prove what a stud he was and how mean he could be. I wouldn't say I was abused. He just really roughed me up to prove he was some kind of man. He was a total jerk. He is just this vicious guy and I just happened to find him attractive for some reason at the time. But I just basically write him off. I don't even count him as someone I had real sex with, because he was just such an idiot. He was mean and obnoxious, just an asshole. Like a once in a lifetime kind of jerk. Just my luck. (Robin, 21, "heterosexual"; asked to describe her race(s), she wrote, "I cannot")

By either rationalizing or pathologizing men's violent or exploitive behaviors, women were able to make their own mistreatment an anomaly, an unfortunate event that would never happen again. As Jeanne stated,

> There are some really fucked up guys out there, and sometimes they pull some weird shit on you. But that doesn't mean you cave into it. You just move on, learn a lesson, and swear it won't ever happen again. (Jeanne, 18, "heterosexual," "Black, Indian, white")

A final way of making higher meaning involved attempting to understand men's behavior as an indication of some other, more desirable hetero-relational dynamic. Unable or unwilling to consider themselves abused or exploited, participants tried to fit their victimization into a larger framework in which the abuse was simply a painful part of romance or friendship. Olivia's experience provides a powerful example. Her first sexual experience was with a young man she had desired for a long time. Although she described the young man as "a total womanizer" and "a Don Juan type," she had hoped to change him, to show him through her loyalty and selflessness that she was really the only woman for him. It was with this man that she "lost" her virginity, after a New Year's Eve party—an experience that brought her floods of contradictory feelings.

> I was in bed, and he [came in and] laid up on top of me, and I mean I must have been half asleep, half intoxicated, and one thing led to another, and he

was done. And he passed out on top of me, and I just cried. I think part of me cried because I was like, this is not the greatest thing that ever happened to you. There was some pain involved, and he was doing it for his own satisfaction, but I think part of this crying was because I just wanted him to wake up and make up for this. I remember wanting him to hear me crying so he would be like "What's wrong?" so I could connect with him again. . . . Unfortunately, we developed a friendship through all of this, since I still, unfortunately, love him as a friend. Just too bad that it keeps running over that line, and I worry about it, and I need to consciously step back from it, and I couldn't do it then. I don't think I was scared, because he had this air of he knew what he was doing. And I was excited because I thought this meant something, and then I was just devastated . . . it's odd. I could simultaneously know that it meant nothing, yet I cried. I thought this meant so much more. I mean my wanting to believe got in the way of what my sort of gut reaction should be to him. That was the first time, and every time after that, whenever he came to me it was like, I would just be excited because every time I thought, you know, this must be it. This was a turn in our relationship. It never was. (Olivia, 22, "heterosexual," "Caucasian")

Throughout her interview, Olivia described her relationship with this man as exploitive, obsessive, and psychologically abusive. In fact, of their first sexual encounter, she said,

It was horrible. I mean, not just like bad sex, but really like violent. It was practically rape, had I not consented. If I hadn't consented to him, it would have been rape.

Although Olivia tried, through her tears, to show her "friend" that she did not want to have sex, she still saw herself as consenting, despite his physical violence. While one might argue that true "consent" loses its meaning in a context of violence, she nonetheless needed to hold on to her sense of agency, believing that otherwise, "it would have been rape." During that first encounter, and for several years afterward, Olivia attempted to make sense of this and similar experiences by making higher meaning, viewing it as a sign of a deepening relationship. Although this young man continued to misuse her, with each encounter she rationalized that this must be "a turn in our relationship." From this perspective, she could convince herself, although never totally, that her experience was not acquaintance rape or sexual exploitation, but rather a symbol of a romantic relationship that was yet to come.

With each of these ways of making higher meaning, young women attempted to view their mistreatment from a more palatable perspective. Whether through finding/creating deeper motivations for a man's behavior, making exceptions, or translating abuse into a prelude to a more meaningful relationship, these women assured themselves that they were not victimized, but rather caught up in a symptom of some larger phenomenon. In so doing, they could make sense of their experiences without naming themselves victims and without forfeiting their belief that their world, in general, was safe and just.

## Turning the Tables

A final strategy for controlling the damage involved "turning the tables," so that young women could, in their minds, reduce men who had exercised sexual power over them to mere sexual conquests or exploited pawns. In an effort to maintain a belief in their own agency, these women mentally reconstructed their own experiences of exploitation, turning them instead into evidence that they, and not their abusers, had had the last laugh.

Frances shared a particularly interesting way of turning the tables. She stated early in her interview that she had had a new hole pierced in her ears every time she "scored" with a man. It became clear later in her interview, however, that she practiced this ritual only after encounters that had gone badly. Explaining the meaning of piercing her ears, she stated,

> You can see that I have a lot of holes. Right now it's at eleven, one for every guy I scored. Well, I've actually slept with more than eleven guys, way more, but these are the guys I feel like I got the best of. That's why I call them a "score." Every time I've been with a guy who was a real fucker, a real asshole to me, I get a new hole put in my ear. It's gotten to be like a ritual with me. It's just my way of saying, "Hey, I did you," you know? Like, you know, "You may have been a fuckhead to me, but I got the last laugh because you were just another notch in my belt, or like, another hole in my ear." (Frances, 21, "heterosexual," American Indian/French")

Whereas in chapter 3 Tonya described keeping count of her sexual encounters in a datebook as visible evidence that she was a desirable object or that men found her "worth having sex with," Frances kept score with her earrings as a way of turning the tables on men with whom she had had unpleasant sexual experiences. Although this practice did nothing to interrupt men's violence or to hold them accountable in any direct way, it did diminish men's power in Frances's mind, allowing her to see herself as prevailing even in violent encounters.

Other women used the receipt of money, gifts, or favors as ways of turning the tables. Elaina's first attempt to turn the tables occurred when she was an early adolescent. Having been raped by her boyfriend with her friends looking on, and having acquired a reputation for promiscuity from the incident (as described in chapter 3), Elaina decided to allow boys to claim they were her boyfriends as long as they would do favors for her, such as doing her homework. By essentially ordering boys to do what she wanted in exchange for allowing them to be (or to say they were) her boyfriends, she was able to feel some sense of control and thus make sense of her painful experience.

> By the time we were thirteen, he was madly in love with me and would do anything I told him, and I just kept telling him to fuck off. It was really funny, because we reached an age where I could order him around. And it's like, I have scars from this boy. He was really powerful for a couple of years, and then everything shifted. I still had this reputation of being a whore because these things happened to me when I was ten, but it was powerful then. Boys were reaching an age where they really wanted something, and you could really do anything. They're like, "If you go steady with me I'll do things for you," and you're like, "Okay, I guess I'll say yes." But I was really uncomfortable with it. Just, "You can tell people I'm your girlfriend, but you have to do what I tell you." (Elaina, 22, "lesbian/bi," "white")

As a young adult, Elaina expanded that strategy into an exchange of money for sex. Although she was aware that this strategy did not give her "real power," it did allow her to control the damage mentally when things went badly. She explained that money tipped the balance of power in her favor, even when men exploited or abused her.

> Sometimes I've just slept with men because I have to. They give me money, and I give them sex. It's totally like prostitution, because I know they really have the power, that I'm being treated like an object to them, a whore that they can do what they want to. But there's something about money that gives me a power. I would never feel okay about it if I did it for free. If they don't give me money, then they're in control of me. If there's money in-

volved, then I have some control, too. It's like, they may fuck me, but I set the terms of how I'm going to get fucked. It may not be real power, because they can still fuck me over, but it's mental power, which helps you control how much damage, or what kind of damage they can do to you.

Theresa took a somewhat more active route to righting the wrongs that were done to her. Rather than marking her own body or equating power with money, Theresa turned the tables by seeking revenge on an ex-boyfriend who had sexually abused her. Not unlike the characters in the movie *Thelma and Louise*, she decided to act out violently, rather than forcing herself to "sit there and take it." Yet she did not feel able to confront him directly or name her experience to others as acquaintance rape; she instead secretly sabotaged his car.

> I wasn't going to sit there and take it. The relationship was over, but I was still mad. He was awful to me, and I was furious. So what I did was, I knew where he parked his car at night, and I knew how much he loved his car. So I went out there in the middle of the night with a friend, and we just slashed the hell out of his car. We kicked it in and slashed the tires and the roof. I felt really great about it. He may have hurt me, but I got the last word in. I wasn't going to take it sitting still. (Theresa, 19, "heterosexual," "bi-racial")

By getting revenge on her ex-boyfriend, Theresa felt vindicated. She was empowered by her anger to fight back, but her victory was nonetheless covert and primarily psychological, for she never confronted him directly about his behavior. Although she felt proud of her ability to cause him distress, she acknowledged that she still felt the pain of the abuse she endured. Turning the tables was her best attempt to wipe the slate clean.

At first glance, turning the tables appears akin to practices feminists have long observed and critiqued among young men—exploiting others for sexual enjoyment, personal gain, and the opportunity to add to the proverbial notches in the bedpost (or in this case, the holes in the earlobe). A closer examination, however, reveals an important distinction. While young women may derive a sense of power and excitement from this strategy, that feeling is still constructed *in opposition to male power*. None of these young women reported deriving any sense of sexual pleasure from their attempts to control men, to reduce them to conquests, or to cause them pain. In fact, they tended to describe these sexual encounters as profoundly dissatisfying and often painful. For these women, the sense of satisfaction came not from exploiting men for their own sexual desire, but rather from turning the tables or having the last laugh—from the ability, if only for the moment, and if only in their minds, to make a mockery of the male power that was used against them.

## A Caution: Beyond Simple Explanations for "Self-Blame"

Throughout this chapter we have seen women going to great lengths to avoid naming their own painful experiences with such labels as rape, battering, victimization, or abuse. Yet, as their abstract convictions demonstrate, their reluctance to use such labels does not stem from a lack of awareness of hetero-relational abuse in women's lives. Nor do their attributions of personal responsibility derive from a general tendency to blame women for their own victimization. These young women live and study in a profeminist setting and are quick to defend women's entitlement to respectful treatment in their hetero-relations. Most also voice strong sexual desires and generally advocate progressive sexual politics. But their *personal* attributions and strategies certainly do not conform to any stereotypical feminist "party line" about victimization. Even as they critique hetero-relational inequality, these young women devise individualized, psychological strategies and tend to excuse men from accountability by forming internal attributions to explain their own mistreatment.

In reflecting on these women's decisions, we must not confuse their individualized strategies, resistance to name abuse, or attributions of personal responsibility with such problematic and oversimplified notions as low self-esteem, masochism, denial, or learned helplessness. These terms suggest that the social world is just fine, and that it is women who demonstrate poor adjustment, cognitive deficits, or self-destructive impulses. Such assumptions, so prevalent in traditional psychology, presume that it is the individual woman, rather than her social circumstances, who needs to be changed (Fine, 1983; 1989; Phillips, 1989). Rather than attributing young women's decisions to some flaw in their characters, we must appreciate the meanings of these strategies for the women who have constructed them. In order to do this, we must remember to situate our understandings in an analysis of the cultural contexts and ongoing social and developmental challenges with which they live. As these young women's stories demonstrate, what may appear to be simple self-blame or denial may actually be an effort to take psychological control of their often uncontrollable circumstances.[3] Far from passivity, low self-esteem, or learned helplessness, these women's strategies represent active attempts (however partial and problematic) to preserve a sense of self in an alienating social arena that fails to provide frameworks for being both victim and agent. The primary problem, then, lies not in the minds of these individuals, but in constraining hetero-relational contexts that deny them adequate terms to name their experiences, and adequate avenues to find advocacy when "things go badly."

7

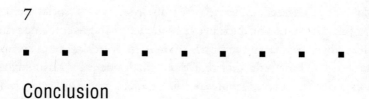

# Conclusion

It has been a simple task for women to describe and criticize negative aspects of sexuality as it has been socially constructed in sexist society, to expose male objectification and dehumanization of women, to denounce rape, pornography, sexualized violence, etc. It has been a far more difficult task for women to envision new sexual paradigms, to change the norms of sexuality. The inspiration for such work can only emerge in an environment where sexual well-being is valued.

—bell hooks, *Feminist Theory from Margin to Center*

IN THIS PASSAGE, bell hooks describes naming and criticizing the negative aspects of sexuality as a simple task. However, the stories young women have shared here suggest that even naming, alone, is not so simple, at least when it comes to assessing one's personal experiences. Although feminist theorists, researchers, and activists have long documented and denounced male coercion and violence against women, the young women I interviewed had much more difficulty making straightforward claims about their own victimization. While they were eager to share complex stories filled with recollections of violence, fear, and manipulation, they found it overwhelmingly challenging, and often impossible, to name their experiences examples of abuse. Intellectually and politically, they were able to speak with great conviction against male sexual aggression. But their reflections suggest that it was no simple task to identify male sexual domination as victimizing in *their own* lived experiences.

I agree with hooks that envisioning new sexual paradigms may pose an even more difficult task. Making their way through such constraining cultural discourses and social and developmental challenges, and lacking a discourse of female pleasure without penalties and a discourse of male accountability, these young women found it difficult, indeed, to develop a sense of entitlement to insist on hetero-relations in which their own agency and well-being were fostered. But whereas both hooks and traditional attribution theorists seem to suggest that women first recognize victimization and then attempt to explain it or develop more empowering possibilities for their sexual well-being, the stories presented here suggest that young women's meaning-making processes for their *own* experiences may work in reverse. That is, young women appear unable to name their own victimization precisely *because* their cultural contexts make it so difficult to insist on male accountability and to envision and experience hetero-relational pleasure without penalties.

We have seen that although the participants expressed a powerful awareness of male violence and coercion, and although they attributed women's victimization to such abstract villains as a "patriarchal society," "sexism," "cultural misogyny," or "men in general," only two women, Diana and Wendy, translated those acknowledgments and attributions into a willingness to name victimization in their own lives. And even they referred to other violent or painful encounters or coercive relationships they endured as simply "weird," something they "didn't want," or a "bad experience." When contemplating their own circumstances, women were much more likely to attribute encounters or relationships that "went badly" to faults in their own judgment or to psychological wounds or ignorance underlying a man's actions, rather than naming and holding him accountable for his abusive behaviors.

These findings raise at least three important questions. First, while we have seen that young women perceived certain psychological *benefits* from accepting personal responsibility and disqualifying themselves as victims, what are the *costs* of not naming victimization? Second, how can these women's experiences shed light on recent debates about women's supposed eagerness to adopt a "victim identity"? And third, the classic (and by far the toughest) question, what can we do? How might these women's stories and struggles propel us to transform current hetero-relational realities so that women, as well as men, are safe and entitled sexual subjects? In this final chapter I explore these questions and consider their implications for broader social and political understandings of agency and victimization in hetero-relations.

## Personal Responsibility and the Costs of Not Naming

As we have seen, these young women are engaged in an admirable struggle to preserve their personal integrity both within and after victimizing experiences. Their stories reveal many compelling reasons for choosing not to name their own experiences victimization, and for forming attributions that support their resistance to use such labels when "things go badly." While we can now appreciate young women's reluctance to acknowledge their own victimization, we must also consider the costs of not naming abuse.

As with their strategies for entering, managing, and making an exit from their encounters, the participants' strategies for explaining their own abuse leave dominant hetero-relational power asymmetries essentially intact and even reinforced. In lieu of naming their painful sexual experiences abuse, confronting men, or seeking social support or legal recourse, these young women use individualized, psychological strategies in an attempt to control the damage after the fact. Unfortunately, by strategizing privately, any critiques of male behavior occur out of earshot of the very men whose conduct needs to be challenged. At best, men who are simply ignorant of their mistreatment of women are protected from knowing the negative effects of their actions, making it highly unlikely that they will learn to treat women more respectfully. Worse, men who knowingly exploit and abuse are free to continue victimizing these or other women, safe in their assumption that they will not be confronted about their harmful and sometimes criminal behaviors.

We have seen that the strategies these young women turn to derive from dominant hetero-relational discourses that constrain their options and normalize the daily assaults on their gendered and sexual integrity. But by offering only individualized, psychological means of making it all go away (which it never does), those very strategies also reproduce these problematic discourses. As young women use the cultural tools available to them to participate in and make sense of their own hetero-relations, they also unwittingly participate in their own entrapment. Lacking access to a discourse of male accountability and a discourse of female pleasure without penalties, they have no culturally acceptable framework in which to critique their stories of pain, humiliation, and confusion without losing themselves as active subjects. As they attempt to situate their experiences in the available discourses—none of which offer them room for ambiguity or an entitled subject stance—their only apparent avenue for preserving subjectivity amid victimization is to take personal responsibility and dismiss men from accountability. While they can certainly get angry, and a few try to get even, these women have not felt able to name, report, or seek social redress for the abuses they have endured. Indeed, in a culture that dichotomizes consent and coercion, that presumes female guilt, and that promotes individualized "solutions" for social problems, these participants have developed a painful awareness that women who do speak out are vilified as "bitches." Rather than finding sympathy or support, they are often treated with contempt.

These psychological strategies, and the discourses that inform them, decrease the likelihood of young women coming together in solidarity to publicize and politicize the wrongs that have been done to them. Indeed, recall that several participants refused even to look at their own transcripts, and many said that they had never uttered these stories before. Although they expressed feminist views, an awareness of the prevalence of woman abuse, and a strong belief that victimized women deserve advocacy, they tended not to apply these abstract convictions to their actual personal lives. Finding that their experiences defied the dominant cultural script for victimization, and thus reluctant to name their own abuse, these young women silenced their own stories, refusing even to read them themselves. Each woman's privatized story is a lost opportunity for women to gather collectively to challenge and rewrite that dominant script to embrace the complexities of their lived experiences. Thus, while young women may advocate strongly for women's rights, their own textured stories typically remain outside the public discourse and thus unable to transform social awareness of women's actual hetero-relational needs and experiences. In short, we see a circular process whereby gendered power asymmetries and the cultural denial of male accountability promote women's individualized strategies—which in turn promote the very cultural denial and power imbalances from which those strategies arise.

In addition to these social and political costs, women's difficulty naming abuse exacts an intrapersonal toll. Although these women have created psychological strategies to preserve their sense of safety and agency, their attempts to deny their pain have been only partly successful. While the participants have succeeded, to some extent, in avoiding the potential stigma, insecurity, and disillusionment that come with acknowledging victimization, their stories reveal a great deal of residual pain, both from their victimizing encounters and from their inability to access help in processing them. Many also describe a lack of trust in their subsequent hetero-relations, as well as a reluctance to inform their partners when they feel hurt or objectified. Unable to find the words or the courage to confront or educate their partners, many women have resigned themselves to letting their own sexual desires go unsatisfied. Without a socially recognized name for "things that went badly," they tend to tell few people, if any, about their experiences, least of all the men involved. Forced to deal privately with their often overwhelming emotions, many are plagued by feelings of shame, confusion, and self-doubt years after their victimization. As Henna put it so powerfully,

> I really tried to put it all behind me, to just pretend like it never happened. I just try not to think about it. It's better now, but I still think about it just about every day. And still maybe once or twice a month it really, really gets to me. I'll be thinking everything's fine, but then something will set me off and I'll just get so angry. I just feel so confused, like why did I let this happen to me? And I wonder if I'm even normal. You know, a normal person would just put this behind them. They wouldn't be still obsessed with this so many years after it happened. But I can't ever seem to resolve it in my mind. How could this have happened, and why am I still so messed up about it? I sort of feel like it ruined me. Like all my relationships will always be affected by it. I just can't get it out of my mind. Like, I was so stupid to let this happen to me, and now I'm too messed up to let it go. I sometimes worry that I never will. (Henna, 21, "heterosexual," "Korean")

If young women who wish to have hetero-relationships are to find entitlement to enter into and find pleasure in them, they also need to know that they can choose *not* to participate in encounters that threaten their well-being or deny their needs. And if they are to survive abusive encounters with a sense of integrity, rather than guilt and self-doubt, they need to know that their victimization does not erase them, and that they need not take on men's responsibility by excusing them for their exploitive behaviors. While the feminist emphasis on naming women survivors rather than victims has been an important step in that direction, the victimization script itself must be rewritten so that women who are ambivalent, sexually assertive, or "in over their heads" can feel entitled to seek advocacy and redress. Young women need space to be sexual and still be "good girls," to be "together women" and still be confused, to be victims and still be agents, and, conversely, to be active agents without forfeiting their right to be "true victims." They need to know that when they are victimized, even their most complex and paradoxical stories will be heard with both compassion and respect.

## Reexamining Victim "Status"

Recent claims from the Right suggest that contemporary women have embraced a "victim identity," capitalizing on a "politics of victimization" that has, presumably, been forced on them by feminists and others on the Left. According to this line of thinking, the feminist movement has encouraged women to view themselves as victims and even to claim a paradoxical position of power by adopting a victim stance. In such a framework, women are thought to be somehow seduced by feminists, obsessed with victimization, into inventing or exaggerating instances of abuse, so that innocent men are persecuted and the label "victim" becomes diluted beyond meaning. Consistent with the normal/danger dichotomy discourse and the true victim discourse, proponents of this view claim that the label "victim" must be reserved for clear-cut cases in which women try to resist but are physically forced to submit to violence.[1]

While the view that women are increasingly contriving claims of victimization appears to be gaining in popularity, this perception suffers from at least two serious misconceptions. First, as the participants' narratives have demonstrated so poignantly, instances of hetero-relational abuse and exploitation are seldom straightforward, so that in many women's experiences, the search for clear-cut "true victims" approaches impossibility. Furthermore, dominant cultural perceptions of what counts as victimization are so deeply woven with problematic assumptions about race, class, and disability that those women who are granted a victim label are likely to represent a very skewed portion of the women who suffer the consequences of male domination.[2]

A second assumption underlying this perspective is equally problematic—that is, the assumption that women do, in fact, wish to lay claim to a victim identity. While recent highly publicized cases of sexual harassment, battering, and acquaintance rape may suggest, at first glance, that women are emerging eagerly to charge men with abuse, the results of this study suggest that the opposite is true. Contrary to concerns on the Right that women are eager to make false claims of victimization, the women in this study were remarkably reluctant, indeed often adamantly opposed, to considering themselves victims—despite friends sometimes labeling them as such, and despite their own acknowledgment that they would describe another woman in the same scenario as a victim. Recall that of the twenty-seven women who recounted experiences involving violent force or coercion, twenty-five (93 percent) refused to label any personal experiences abuse or victimization. While these participants may not represent the entire population of U.S. women, their overwhelming resistance to claim victimization is quite compelling. In fact, given their access to feminist ideas and information about violence against women, the conservative argument would suggest that these women would be *more* likely to claim victimization if, indeed, they had somehow been brainwashed by feminists into adopting a victim identity. As we have seen, this is not the case. Indeed, these findings suggest that it is not women's claims of victimization, but rather the Right's *fears* of such claims, that are grossly exaggerated.

## What to Do? Envisioning Possibilities

How might we move from an understanding of the participants' complex and often troubling articulations toward transforming social conditions in ways that would enable women to develop more authentically agentic visions and experiences of/in their hetero-relations? As hooks (1984) notes in the quote above, envisioning new sexual paradigms is no easy task. My reflections on these young women's stories, however, have prompted me to ponder several possibilities. These involve building on social change efforts already begun in the overlapping areas of education, institutional change, collective action, and research. Each of these possibilities requires us to shift the focus of societal attention, and thus the burden of responsibility, away from individual women and onto social practices and assumptions that promote or deny mutual hetero-relational entitlement and accountability.

## On Early (and Ongoing) Education

Although I have focused here on young women's perspectives, their stories point to the need for greater attention to hetero-relational complexities in the early educations of both girls *and* boys, young women *and* young men. If young women's subjectivities are culturally constructed, so too are young men's. Like young women, they no doubt internalize (and, of course, may also resist) the discourses available to them as they construct their own ideas of what is acceptable and desirable in hetero-relations. Unfortunately, the very discourses that constrain young women's options and critique also position men as entitled to unconditional sexual fulfillment, even at great physical and/or emotional cost to women. They encourage young men to incorporate the same dichotomies (good girl/bad girl; normal/danger) into their thinking while also normalizing coercion with suggestions that "boys will be boys." By suggesting that only "pleasing women" are "true victims" and that other women "ask for it," these discourses promote the idea that women (other than sisters, mothers, or perhaps girlfriends) should be seen as "conquests" in the construction of hetero-sexual male identity. They further skew the hetero-relational balance by suggesting not only that men are driven by their "hormones," but that it is women's responsibility (rather than men's) to act as the brakes—to prevent men from acting on their sexual "instincts." By endorsing the notion that "love hurts," these messages encourage a societal resignation to the fact of male insensitivity and female disappointment. Of course, many young men resist such notions and do not choose to exploit their socially condoned privilege. But the stories these young women have shared suggest that all too often, even the "good guys" misuse power and exploit (consciously or unconsciously) young women's subordinated position in the available cultural discourses.

The participants' recollections of their early hetero-relational lessons point to a need for a profound reshaping of the messages sent to children from a very young age. Those who are educators, advocates, community organizers, and parents or other caregivers must work with children to problematize the terms of current hetero-relational discourses. If the next generation of young women and men are engaged in early and critical examinations of how social practices and institutions reflect and reproduce sexist, racist, classist, and homophobic ideologies, they may be better able to recognize and critique the socially constructed nature of their individual experiences as young adults. Adults must look critically at the messages communicated to children and adolescents, not only through words, but also through actions and silences.

Families, educators, advocates, and community members must press for sexuality education (both in and outside schools) that incorporates exploration of social structures and hetero-relational practices that normalize male domination, privilege male entitlement, and deny or pathologize female desire (Phillips and Fine, 1992; Sears, 1992; Whatley, 1992). Both boys and girls need opportunities to problematize dominant constructions of "masculinity" and "femininity" and to explore the roles of sexism, racism, classism, and hetero-sexism in maintaining those constructions (Ward and Taylor, 1992). Unfortunately, as we saw in chapter 3, lessons learned both at home and at school often perpetuated, rather than challenged, dominant assumptions about "good" women, "normal" male sexuality, "true" victimization, and what is "inevitable" in hetero-relationships. To the extent that adults entertained issues of female pleasure and desire in these women's early experiences, they made it clear that fully sexual women (but not men) lacked self-respect, good judgment, or "class." Many women's experiences fueled race, class, gender, and sexuality stereotypes already lurking in the dominant culture. Often shrouded in secrecy and framed by warnings to "just say no," these early educations failed to speak to the lived realities of young women (and young men) needing information and guidance through their sexual encounters and relationships. Rather than sidestepping these issues by telling adolescents to "be safe" or "just say no," adults need to discuss gendered and developmental challenges, critically and openly, in ongoing conversation with young people.

Implicit in this vision is an invitation for children and adolescents to raise questions that stem from their own experiences and developing curiosities. Instead of controlling the terms of discussions to make "controversial" questions and assumptions off limits, we must create families, classrooms, community groups, and other contexts that are psychologically safe and respectful enough for young people to voice their misunderstandings so that they may engage in collective explorations of the problematic ideologies woven through them. Rather than silencing young people's questions and avoiding the complexities of their experiences and perspectives, adults need to listen respectfully, acknowledge, and work with them to help them critique and transform the cultural discourses they have already absorbed. Only with an appreciation of their multiple, culturally situated, and often problematic understandings may we help children grow into young men and young women who can envision other possibilities.

## On Institutional Change

In addition to reshaping early hetero-relational messages, both women and men must work to disrupt institutional practices and assumptions that support woman-blame and deny male, as well as societal, accountability for female victimization. Rather than encouraging women simply to *maneuver around* male domination and potential violence, we must challenge the very inequalities and structured silences that condone male aggression and endorse only individualized strategies for preventing or coping with abuse. In order to promote a more just and empowering vision of hetero-relations, we need to press for a discourse of male accountability and a discourse of female pleasure without penalties. These currently absent or marginalized discourses must be infused into sexual harassment policies in workplaces and schools; laws against rape, battering, and sexual harassment; and scholarly and applied work on violence against women.

While policies, laws, scholarship, and practice have been developed over the last few decades and represent constructive changes in the hetero-relational landscape, many of these societal mechanisms continue to reproduce problematic assumptions about the nature of victimization and culpability. Laws and policies based on the true victim and normal/danger dichotomy discourses leave little, if any, room for the complex and contextualized nature of many women's hetero-relational circumstances. Current institutionalized expressions of these discourses either dissuade women from naming their own textured experiences victimization or force them to rewrite their nuanced stories to fit dominant, straightforward scripts if they wish to seek advocacy or redress. Practices that presume (rather than disrupt) the pleasing woman, love hurts, and male sexual drive discourses "normalize" the everyday domination so many women endure, and they place the onus on women to prevent, work around, or simply tolerate male aggression. To the extent that institutions such as the legal system do advocate for women, those that incorporate the pleasing woman and true victim discourses often privilege the claims of certain women (read: white, middle-class or affluent women), especially when those claims are against men of color, and dismiss or downplay the claims of others (read: women of color and/or poor women) (Fine, 1983; Fine and Weis, 1998). Sources of "support" that endorse the love hurts and love conquers all discourses encourage women to stick it out and find higher meaning, rather than expressing outrage and working toward collective action. Support mechanisms that promote the together woman discourse expect women to somehow extract themselves from structured inequalities and complex social contexts to advocate individually (and preferably without "making a fuss") for their own fair treatment. In short, while institutional vehicles increasingly acknowledge female victimization and offer women some "official" means of redress, at present they do little to disrupt (and often actually promote) the structured power imbalances and problematic discourses that help give rise to that victimization in the first place.

If women are to be safe and entitled subjects in their hetero-relationships, they need more than individual encouragement to "just say no," "just leave," or "just report" unwanted male behavior to "the proper authorities." They need to be able to experience and express their entitlement to say "yes," "no," "I'm not sure," or perhaps "yes to this, and no to that"—and they need to be able to do so without being punished for trying to navigate the skewed and contradictory discourses that contextualize their experiences. To get to this point, women need to be positioned in educational, legal, scholarly, and popular discourses as *co-subjects* and active *initiators* in their own sexualities, rather than simply respondents to men's requests or demands for sex. At the same time, notions of male accountability must go much further than telling men that "no means no." We need to challenge and reshape existing cultural discourses and power asymmetries that underlie cross-gender encounters so that hetero-relational decision making is not viewed as a matter of "working a yes out"

(Sanday, 1990), but rather as a *process* in which both men and women must be fully engaged. Central to this is a critique of the male sexual drive discourse, which encourages young men to express (and young women and societal institutions to accept) male sexualities as inherently aggressive, and male desires as needing/deserving to be fulfilled at any cost. This also requires that we critique the normal/danger dichotomy discourse for its tendency to excuse men from responsibility for their mistreatment of women, as long as they can perceive and portray themselves as exempt from such traditionally constructed categories as rapist, batterer, or sex offender. We must simultaneously challenge the normalizing of force and coercion in hetero-relations, and push for schools, workplaces, and the legal system to address the often aggressive elements of "typical" encounters. And we must work to illuminate the ways the true victim discourse and the pleasing woman discourse underlie the racist, classist, and homophobic discrepancies in determining which women get advocacy and which men get punished.

## On Collective Action and Safe Spaces

Underlying the previous two possibilities is the clear need for collective action. This includes not only pressing for policy and educational reform and rethinking individualistic scholarship and practice. It also means carving out spaces where women (and concerned men) can come together within and across race, class, sexuality, and community, to critique existing ideologies, share their stories, envision other possibilities, and work together toward constructive social change. This might take the form of speak-outs, poetry readings, group artwork, demonstrations, creative organizing efforts, and discussion groups in which young women are able to probe the political nature of what has, for far too long, been kept personalized.

Whereas women coming of age during the early second wave of the feminist movement had access to such forums for expressing collective indignation and finding support, the current generation of young women is entering adulthood at a time when increasing conservatism and antifeminist backlash threaten to shrink safe spaces for vocalized critique. They have come through adolescence in a context where they were often told that the women's movement was over, that women had essentially reached equality, that racial inequities were all but solved, and that neither private nor public forums were needed to ensure women's rights. Certainly, such forums have not disappeared entirely. Take Back the Night marches are now annual events in many communities, providing a much-needed sense of personal and collective empowerment, conviction, and renewal. Peer education and advocacy groups thrive in some schools and communities, offering adolescents and young adults opportunities to build on one another's knowledge and discuss their experiences. Women's studies programs are alive and well on many college campuses (although threatened by budget cuts and hostility on many others), inviting at least some young women and men to examine gendered power and male violence. But too often even these progressive and/or feminist spaces focus on "clear-cut" forms of violence against women, inadvertently crowding out discussions of young women's secret struggles to "control the damage" when "things go badly." As Evelyn said of her reluctance to use the word "rape" to describe her own experience of forced intercourse, "to say my experience was rape maybe waters down the cases of real victims—it feels, I don't know, kind of unfeminist." Compounding the fear of seeming "unfeminist" is the equal (or perhaps greater) fear of seeming "unfeminine." Indeed, those who speak out collectively against even extreme cases of violence are often chastised as "bitches," "whiners," and "bitter" women who "can't get a man."

Without safe spaces in which to give voice to the complexities of their stories and find connections across their own and others' experiences, young women are left to fend for themselves—to strategize individually, to form internal attributions, and to choose between agency and an acknowledgment of their own victimization. But with access to such spaces, women might be able to pool their collective strengths and insights, envisioning (and demanding) next steps toward hetero-relational equality. Fine and Weis (1996) refer to this work as "homesteading":

> —finding unsuspected places within and across geographic communities, public institutions, and spiritual lives—to sculpt real and imaginary spaces for peace, struggle, and personal and collective identity work. These spaces offer recuperation, resistance, and the makings of "home." They are not just a set of geographic/spacial arrangements, but theoretical, analytical, and spacial displacements—a crack, a fissure in an organization or a community. Individual dreams, collective work, and critical thoughts are smuggled in and then reimagined. Not rigidly bounded by walls/fences, these spaces

often are corralled by a series of (imaginary) borders where community intrusion and state surveillance are not permitted. These are spaces where trite social stereotypes are fiercely contested. That is, young women and men—in constantly confronting harsh public representations of their race/ethnicity, class, gender, and sexuality—use these spaces to break down these public images for scrutiny and invent new ones. (261)

As we saw so powerfully in the 1970s and 1980s, consciousness-raising groups and collective action helped fortify second-wave feminists to push for the creation, reform, and enforcement of laws against rape, battering, and harassment; the establishment of victim support services and shelters; the increase in sexuality education programs; and the expansion of reproductive options. Such collective action might allow current and future generations of young women (and, hopefully, young men) to push this work even further. With an understanding of hetero-relational complexities, social and developmental challenges, and the conflicting cultural discourses that simultaneously confound and dichotomize consent and coercion, women and men, young and old, can move toward establishing discourses of male accountability and female pleasure without penalties. We can work toward developing language that more faithfully captures the textured realities of hetero-relations, power, and victimization. We can fight collectively to transform societal institutions and cultural practices to better speak to the lived experiences and needs of women across various races, ethnicities, classes, ages, sexualities, and communities.

## On Further Research

Finally, if we are to heed bell hooks's call for women (and, I would add, men) to envision new sexual paradigms, we need further research that ventures beyond individualistic analyses of women's thoughts and behaviors and instead probes the social construction of both women's and men's decision-making processes. This entails critical interrogation of the contexts in which their decisions take shape—including the institutional and interpersonal practices that constrain women's options, privilege certain claims over others, and endorse male entitlement to use aggression and coercion while simultaneously locating accountability for that aggression and coercion in women rather than men. Such research might include analysis of laws, policies, and court cases involving sexual harassment; stranger, acquaintance, and statutory rape; battering; and child molestation and incest.[3] It might also include content analyses of television news and print media reports of such cases, women's and teen magazines' articles and stories about these issues, and sexuality education curricula. Also helpful would be ethnographic studies of cross-gender student dynamics and teachers' practices in classrooms and on playgrounds, at school dances and field trips, in school and community sports programs, in sexuality education programs, and in other organized and informal settings where norms about gender roles and appropriate hetero-relational dynamics are communicated to young people, whether silently or through words and (non)actions.[4]

As important as research that investigates the problematic messages and social practices that inform women's and men's understandings of hetero-relations is research that explores sites of possibility—that is, spaces where young women and young men find encouragement to critique existing cultural discourses and begin envisioning new sexual paradigms based on mutual pleasure and mutual responsibility. Research that sheds light on conditions (including parenting practices, progressive sexuality education programs, peer education groups, gender studies programs, and so forth) that promote boys' and young men's resistance and critique of unproblematized male entitlement may point toward new ways of helping them construct hetero-relational subjectivities in which male hetero-sexual identity does not presume license to use coercion, manipulation, or force in the pursuit of sexual pleasure or ego fulfillment. Similarly, research is needed to illuminate conditions that encourage consciousness-raising, resistance, and collective action among young women.[5] Particularly helpful is collaborative research with/in community organizations, grassroots organizing groups, sexuality education programs, women's centers, informal support groups, and other spaces where women come together to struggle with the meanings of agency and victimization. Also important is research that explores aspects of girls' and young women's lives beyond sexuality (such as academic and athletic programs, families, after-school and summer programs, and so on) that affirm girls' and women's senses of themselves as entitled and multidimensional subjects and that thus implicitly or explicitly critique the pleasing woman and love conquers all discourses' notion that women find fulfillment and self-worth through being desirable to men and finding the "perfect" hetero-relationship.

Particularly important is respectful exploration of the possible tensions between/within/among various cultural values, practices, and expectations as young women and men construct their hetero-relational subjectivities at the intersections between "home" and "dominant" cultures. While both home and dominant cultures may promote male entitlement and female accountability, pressures from the various cultures in which young women and men are situated may exacerbate and/or clash with one another in ways that compound/confound the messages of either culture. As important (although even less straightforward and less studied) is greater understanding of how the unmarked category "whiteness" helps to shape women's and men's understandings of appropriate hetero-relational dynamics and expectations.

Although I have focused in this text on *hetero*-relationships, more research is needed to explore how issues of power and aggression might filter through same-sex relationships as well. However, such work must be positioned carefully in a critical sociopolitical framework so that discussions of problematic dynamics in such relationships do not fuel the already virulent cultural pathologizing of gay, lesbian, bisexual, and transgendered individuals and relationships. Whether studying same-sex or hetero-relationships, researchers should work in collaboration and respectful dialogue with advocates and activists who sit on the front lines of movements against violence and victimization, and who know so well the volatile politics of this work.

The possibilities offered above only scratch the surface of the work that is needed. Although raised in a different generation than the women I interviewed, I too am a product of the problematic cultural contexts in which I am situated. As such, I am probably as yet unable to envision possibilities that may some day seem obvious. But efforts to reshape early hetero-relational educations, to fight for institutional change, to create safe spaces and foster collective action, and to conduct respectful activist-research seem to me good places to focus attention if we want to move past problematic dichotomies and structured silences that hold women accountable for their own abuse.

In the months I spent listening to young women reflect on their pains and possibilities, their fears and their fantasies, I found myself developing a fantasy of my own—that some day, many years from now, I would conduct another study, much like this one. But this time, the results would be different. In my fantasy, young women would speak of their sexual desires without guilt or apology, and very few would have tales of victimization to tell. I would also speak with young men to learn how they think about hetero-relations. While I might enter into this new study with trepidation, pessimistic about the stories I would hear, in my fantasy, I would be happily surprised. I would hear young men speak of respect, reciprocity, and open communication in their relationships and encounters. Of course, everyone would practice safer sex, and partners would see themselves as mutually responsible for ensuring that all parties found pleasure in a context of sexual justice and sexual health. Reflecting on their early educations, young women and men would remember concerned adults who welcomed their questions, invited their input, and encouraged their critique. Women would feel entitled to resist, rebel, and relocate accountability where it belonged. But in fact, I would not be able to write about "controlling the damage," because in my fantasy, there would be little, if any, damage to control. And while young women could flirt to their hearts' content, no one would need to flirt with danger.

Of course, this is all just a fantasy, far removed from the lived realities these young women have shared. But it is a fantasy born of my hope that we can move, however slowly, toward a future where young women as well as young men are active and entitled sexual subjects, where they find pleasure and respect in their hetero-relations, and where, if things do "go badly," they do not feel compelled to rewrite their stories, blame themselves, and bury their pain. If we are to move from the often troubling stories young women have shared in these pages, toward a place where safety and reciprocity prevail, we, *as a society*, have a great deal of work to do. We must move beyond dualistic preconceptions of hetero-relations and instead listen closely to the nuances and contradictions in young women's lived experiences. We must situate our understandings in a critical analysis of larger cultural contexts, but we must also endeavor to *transform* those contexts. And we must carve out spaces in which young women can speak their minds, voice their confusion, and "control the damage" not through self-blame, but through collective critique and social action.

■  ■    ■     ■    ■    ■    ■    ■    ■

# Afterword

*Lingering Dilemmas: How Much Do We*
*Want to Know?*

If feminist scholars do move to reinstitutionalize our work on violence
against women, we must be sure to collect the diverse voices of women,
harmonious and disharmonious, across races, ethnic groups, classes, dis-
abilities, sexualities, communities, and politics, and, together with activists, create forums in which ideas, nodes of agreement, and fault lines
of dissension can be aired, studied, resolved, or worked around. In the
absence of such collaboration, feminist scholarship will retreat (if unwittingly) toward individualism, to be ignored or, perhaps worse, used
against those women whose social contexts we seek to transform.
—Michelle Fine, "The Politics of Research and Activism"

MY AIM IN WRITING THIS BOOK has been to stimulate discussion of
hetero-relational nuances often overlooked in both traditional and feminist social science literature. My hope throughout this project has been
that in hearing the participants' stories and considering the contexts in
which they took shape, researchers, advocates, activists, educators, policy

makers, and perhaps most important, young women themselves would gain insights that might further efforts to confront male aggression and coercion as it plays out in women's daily lives. As a researcher, an educator, and an advocate for women and girls, I take seriously Fine's call to "create forums in which ideas, nodes of agreement, and fault lines of dissension can be aired, studied, resolved, or worked around." I hope that this book will contribute to the development of such forums by stimulating further discussion about how those interested in promoting sexual justice might study, envision, and promote young women as active, entitled sexual subjects who can find both pleasure and safety in their hetero-relations.

And yet, sitting alongside these hopes are some nagging concerns. Having listened to, theorized, and written about these young women's perspectives, I am left with residual questions about the implications of conducting and presenting (as well as of *not* conducting and presenting) this type of research in the politically charged arena of sexuality and violence against women. As I have attempted to "work the hyphen" (Fine, 1994) between activism and research in this project, I have spent countless hours sorting through my hopes and my worries about how these findings might be interpreted and used in debates about male aggression and female victimization.

While I hope that this study has made clear the importance of exploring with young women the contradictions and paradoxes woven throughout their hetero-relational subjectivities, I continue to grapple with difficult questions about the relationship of such work to the efforts of anti-violence movements. On the one hand, I anticipate that some might argue that the findings uncovered here should be kept silent—that it is politically dangerous to make public women's acknowledgment of confusion, ambivalence, or tendency to self-blame. Indeed, it might be argued that highlighting the contradictions in women's experiences threatens to unravel important statements about violence that the women's movement has worked so hard to establish. This concern is particularly powerful given the victim-blaming tendencies of the dominant culture and the current political context of enormous right-wing backlash. In a culture that assumes that women "ask for it," in a culture that asks, "Why don't women just leave?" rather than "Why do men rape, harass, and batter?" it has been critical to assert that women see aggression, exploitation, and domination as neither normal nor desirable. Such assertions have been important not only in raising public consciousness in general, but also in prosecuting men for rape, battering, and harassment and advocating for battered women who have killed or injured their abusive partners in self-defense. In a context of zero-sum guilt (Fine, 1990) and without a discourse of male accountability, such cases require demonstration that women are completely innocent, "true victims" who say and mean "no" and who never confuse sex or love with coercion or domination. Indeed, given the androcentric ideologies that inform public thought, it is difficult enough to persuade judges and juries to take seriously women's claims of "straightforward" cases of rape, battering, and harassment. It certainly will not help a woman's case any if her lawyers and advocates encourage her to come forward and name her experience as "just a bad night" or give voice to her perception that "I really only have myself to blame."

In a culture that is often indifferent, if not hostile, toward women's claims and eager to deny the prevalence or significance of male violence, there may be much to be gained from declaring that consent and coercion are mutually exclusive. Having worked in both the battered women's and the rape crisis movements, I have found myself on many occasions relying on clear-cut declarations that women hate male aggression, find harassment humiliating, and never wish to be dominated. When conducting workshops on college campuses, when working as a psychotherapist with sex offenders, or when explaining to those curious about my work why women do not "just leave," I have insisted to would-be victim-blamers that women find aggression, exploitation, and domination antithetical to normal sexuality and relationships. Indeed, as I stated in the opening lines of this book, I even own a political button that asks, "What is it about 'no' that confuses you?" suggesting that women find nothing ambiguous about the word "no."

On the other hand, having listened closely to the stories of these participants, as well as the stories of women in my classrooms, my office, and my casual conversations, I am persuaded that keeping young women's hetero-relational complexities and contradictions out of the public discourse may bring even greater long-term costs. Political efforts to bifurcate consent and coercion have indeed brought much-needed attention to violence against women. But I worry that they work within and around, rather than challenging, the assumptions of the pleasing woman discourse, the true victim discourse, and the normal/danger dichotomy discourse. As such, they may unwittingly alienate young women like those in this study from an ability or sense of entitlement to name, express outrage, and seek redress for harmful experiences that are not so clear-cut as "true victimization." Lacking a space for complexity and contradiction in either the dominant or popularized feminist discourses of victimization, women may continue to keep their stories buried. Rendered mute, these stories lose their ability to transform public consciousness about the nature and extent of hetero-relational abuses.

Research and political strategies that *illuminate* the textures of women's lived experiences, rather than smoothing them over, may help fuel efforts to critique and transform existing problematic discourses and to develop and amplify new discourses that more faithfully speak to women's often nuanced experiences of victimization in their hetero-relationships. But to conduct such studies thoroughly and responsibly, researchers must always be careful to embed explorations of women's subjectivities in an analysis of unequal gender, race, class, and sexual power relations. Care must be taken to problematize hetero-relational contexts and dominant understandings of victimization so that it is not women themselves who continue to be problematized or pathologized. In any research or writing that brings young women's perceptions and strategies to light, it is essential to stress that their acknowledgment of confusion and acceptance of personal accountability are not indications that they have not been abused, or that men should not be held responsible for their misdeeds because women, after all, "don't know what they want." These perceptions and strategies should be framed as powerful evidence of the ways gendered inequalities both translate into danger for women and pressure them to manage and accept blame for that danger rather than speaking out, seeking advocacy, demanding that men take responsibility for their actions, and demanding that societal institutions see that they do.

By honoring the complexities in women's stories, such research and activism may enhance advocacy efforts for girls and women struggling to position themselves as sexual agents in societal and interpersonal contexts that threaten to marginalize or silence their own perspectives. It is my hope that research that listens closely to women's nuanced perceptions and strategies, and offers critical analyses of the problematic contexts in which they take shape, will further the efforts of advocates, activists, educators,

young women, and others working to transform dominant scripts of hetero-relations and victimization. It is my hope, too, that in hearing, reading, and giving public voice to those stories too often kept privatized,
young women may be both comforted and catalyzed by the knowledge
that they are not alone.

■    ■    ■    ■    ■    ■    ■    ■    ■

# Appendix A

*Individual Interview Guide*

## A. Background Information

1. In order for me to get to know a little bit about you, can you tell me how you would describe yourself? How would people who know you describe you?

2. How would you describe the values of the people around you (family, school, community, friends) growing up? What were their values like in general? What were their values/expectations regarding sexuality and relationships? Regarding *your* sexuality and relationships?

3. How would you describe the values of those around you now about these things? If there was a change, how does that feel for you? Does/did that affect your feelings about yourself/body/sexuality? How are your views the same as or different from the views of others you know?

4. Can you describe your early education about sexuality? What were your sources of information (family, school, friends, religion, boyfriends, girlfriends, siblings, books, magazines, pornography, personal experimentation, personal victimization, witnessing others' relationships, etc.)? Was the information you got technical, social, personalized? How did you learn

to feel about desire, passion, flirtation, your body, males/females, sexuality, romance, danger (what were you warned about)?

5. How did your education (formal and informal) about sexuality and relationships change over time? Do you feel you have the kinds and amount of information you want and need about sexuality and relationships at this point in your life? With whom do you feel most comfortable/uncomfortable discussing these issues or asking questions?

6. Can you tell me about the relationships/encounters you've had? Start with your first crush, relationship, sexual experience, etc. Can you describe the feelings you had (expand these questions according to the stories/histories offered)? How did your relationship(s) end?

## B. Images of Womanhood and Femininity

1. Where did you learn about "femininity"? What does this mean to you (appearance, behaviors, attitudes)? How were these lessons communicated? Do you/have you ever dressed/altered your appearance or behavior for men? For women? For a lover? For general strangers (the male/female gaze)? For a potential lover? How so, and why?

2. Do you/have you ever read women's or teen magazines? Which ones? Why those? What do you think are their images of the "ideal woman"? Do you agree with them? How do they affect you? What should you look like, aspire to be like, with men/women? Do these magazines make you feel better or worse about yourself, or both/neither?

3. Do you/have you ever read romance novels? What are they about? What's the attraction? Do you find them arousing? Why/why not? What parts of them do/don't you like? Is it romantic/erotic to be swept off your feet? What is the difference (if any) between romance novels and pornography?

4. Do you/have you ever read how-to books about sex or romance? What ones? What are they like? What did you think of them? Have you ever tried their strategies? Did they work? What does that mean?

5. Do you/have you ever read/watched pornography? What kinds? How does it make you feel? Can you describe the first time you saw pornography? How did you feel? What do you like most/least about pornography? How do you feel about men/women using pornography? Is there

anything erotic about the taboo surrounding pornography? Do you identify with the women/men in the scenes?

6. Who are/were your role models (real or fictional) as women? Why
are/were you drawn to these women? Do they make you feel better or
worse about yourself/about being a woman?

## C. Attitudes about "Normal" Sexuality and Relationships

1. Have you had any serious relationships? What does "serious" mean
to you? If you have had a serious relationship, please describe the person
and the relationship. How did you meet? How did you know it was serious? What are/were the best/worst parts of the relationship? What is/was
most complicated about it?

2. How would you describe your ideal relationship? How would you
describe your ideal lover? Have you ever experienced these? Do you imagine yourself getting married or being in a long-term relationship with a
partner? Why/why not?

3. People often talk about wanting equal partnerships: what does this
mean to you? Have you ever experienced this? If so, what are the positive
and/or negative aspects of this type of relationship? What does being "in
control" in a relationship mean to you? Would you want either partner to
be dominant in your relationships? Why/why not?

4. How do you experience a sense of personal power in your relationships? What does this feel like?

5. Can you describe a relationship you have had or seen (serious or casual) that you would consider unequal? Have you had any sexual encounters that felt unequal? If so, please describe.

6. Do you ever have "uncommitted sex" or "one-night stands"? What
do/don't you like about this? How do you/others communicate what
you/they want in these situations? Is it easier to feel pleasure in a one-
night stand or in an ongoing relationship? Why?

7. How entitled do you feel to make your needs and desires known in
your relationships? Does it get easier or harder as a relationship progresses?
Have you ever faked your own pleasure (e.g., faking orgasms, etc.)?
Why/why not? Do you know other women who have done this?

## D. Attitudes and Definitions of Abuse

1. How would you describe an abusive relationship? How (if at all) does it differ from just a "bad" relationship? Do you think women ever want to be/don't mind being abused?

2. Why do you think some people stay in abusive relationships? What would you recommend to someone who was being abused by her lover? Are women ever at fault for their own abuse or rape? Why/why not?

3. What is acquaintance rape or date rape? Is there a difference between this and "rough sex"? If so, what are the lines separating the two? Do you think this happens much? Does it worry you (why/why not)? Has this ever happened to you? If yes, please describe.

4. Have you ever had sex when you really didn't want to? If yes, what happened, and how did you feel at the time? How do you feel about this now? If no, can you imagine this happening to you (why/why not)? Has anyone you know ever experienced acquaintance rape? What do you think a woman should do in such a situation? What (if anything) should she do afterward?

5. How do you feel about the statement "no means no"? Does this hold true for you/women you know? Are there ever times when you're not sure if you're "allowed" to say "no" or to say "yes"? If so, please describe. How do you think men hear "no" or "yes" from women?

6. Have you ever been victimized by any kind of male violence or known anyone who has (family members, friends, etc.)? Have you ever been psychologically abused or exploited by a lover, or witnessed this? If yes, please describe.

7. What is the line between "normal" interactions and "abuse" or "victimization"? Are the lines clear when you are in a situation? Are they any clearer or less clear in retrospect? Can you give an example/explain?

8. Have you ever had a sexual experience that you thought would give you pleasure but didn't? What did you do? What did you want to do?

9. Have you ever had sex when you wanted to but the other person/people did not? If yes, did you know this at the time, or did you find out afterward? Please describe your feelings about this.

10. Have you ever entered into a relationship or encounter with someone you really weren't interested in? If so, what led you to do this? Have you ever stayed in a relationship longer than you wanted or longer than

was healthy for you? If so, why? Would you do it again? If you are no longer in the relationship, how did the relationship end?

## E. Flirtation and Seduction

1. Can you tell me about flirtation? Do you flirt? If so, with whom, and what does it mean for you/them? Are you more likely to flirt with strangers or people you know? Why?

2. Is teasing an element of flirtation? What does this mean? Is it ever fun to "flirt with danger"? What does that mean for you? Have you ever worried that flirtation would "go too far" or lead to problems? Has this ever happened? If so, please describe what happened and how you felt.

3. Is seduction different from flirtation (if so, how)? What is your ideal seduction scenario? If you are attracted to both genders, would you seduce a man differently than a woman? How/why? Would you seduce someone differently than you would like to be seduced yourself? How/why? Is wanting to seduce someone the same as wanting to have sex with them? If not, what is the difference?

4. How do you feel about being the "object" of male attention? How do you think most women feel about it? How do you go about attracting someone to you? Who typically initiates your sexual interactions?

5. Have you ever felt like you should "follow through" if you arouse someone? If so, please describe. Have others ever compelled you to do so? If so, how, and how did you feel/what did you do?

6. Can you describe your own romantic/sexual fantasies? Would you want them to come true if you had a chance? Why/why not? Are there any differences among people you find arousing, people with whom you would actually have sex, and people with whom you would have a relationship? If so, please explain.

7. Do you ever feel aroused by things/people you wish did not affect you that way? What kinds of things? How do you feel about this? Can you describe where this sense of eroticism comes from?

8. Is it easier or more pleasurable for you to give or receive sexual/romantic pleasure? What kinds of pleasure are easy/difficult for you to give/receive? Why?

9. What are the differences for you between flirtation/seduction and sexual harassment? Have you ever been harassed (in workplaces, at school,

on the street)? How does it feel? Do you ever have more than just one set of feelings about this? If so, please explain.

## F. Closing Questions

1. Do you consider yourself a feminist? What does that mean? Why are/aren't you a feminist? How do you/people in your life feel about feminism?

2. Are there any other stories or issues you can tell me about that would shed more light on the kinds of things we've been discussing?

3. Are there questions I haven't asked you that you think would be important for me to ask you or other women?

4. Do you have any other questions?

# Appendix B

*Group Interview Discussion Topics*

## Session 1

Introductions, description and update on the project, expectations (payment of ten dollars, confidentiality, group dynamics, etc.).

Discussion topic: Early socializing influences and expectations for femininity, bodies, self-image, and sexuality. Role of families, peers, educators, etc. in forming expectations.

## Session 2

Discussion topic: Early messages about hetero-relations—what to expect, what to desire, what to fear. Media images of women, men, and hetero-relations.

## Session 3

Discussion topic: Experiences of clear-cut and less clear abuse, exploitation, or domination from men/women. Lines between "normal" and "abusive" hetero-relations. Feelings about nearing/crossing over those lines.

## Session 4

Discussion topic: Interpretations of men's exploitive, harassing, and/or abusive behaviors. Interpretations of own and other women's responses to such behaviors. Similarities/differences between abstract and more personalized feelings about such behaviors.

Wrap-up: Thoughts on the focus groups and overall project. Resources for further reading or discussion. Final questions/comments.

## Appendix C

*Analysis: Working with the Data*

Although this study was not ethnographic in terms of data collection or setting, my organization and interpretation of the data were guided by assumptions associated with ethnographic analysis. That is, rather than testing specific hypotheses developed prior to data collection, I used an inductive method of analysis that allowed themes and analytic categories to emerge from the data (Patton, 1980). My approach to the data was further guided by Glazer and Strauss's (1967) work on "grounded theory," in which the generation of theory is grounded in continuing, systematic, and detailed analysis as patterns emerge through the research process. Like ethnographic analysis, grounded theory analysis moves from data toward the development of theory, rather than using data to test preestablished hypotheses. Such orientations are also consistent with feminist approaches to research, which tend to emphasize the diverse meanings participants make of their own experiences rather than attempting to structure their responses into previously defined categories (Farganis, 1989; Fine and Phillips, 1990; Gergen, 1988; Lather, 1986; 1991; Linton, 1989).

As I noted in chapter 2, I entered into this study hoping that the participants would collaborate with me in the analysis of their own transcripts.

Since (for a variety of reasons) participants resisted this idea, I was left to analyze the data on my own. The following is a description of the steps I took to analyze the findings.

## A.

Immediately following each interview and group meeting (each of which was audiotaped), I took field notes regarding (a) prominent themes that emerged in the interview or group session; (b) tensions that were raised in/by me and/or the participant(s); (c) any modifications that should be incorporated into future interviews; and (d) general conditions under which the interview or group session was conducted. Tapes of all individual interviews were transcribed in their entirety; tapes of group sessions were partially transcribed (due to difficulty in distinguishing individual voices on the group tapes).

## B.

Once the individual interviews were transcribed, I worked with the data in four phases:

1. I first read through each transcript individually and made summary notes, working with each interview as a complete unit. In their preliminary stage, these notes took the form of a four-paragraph summary for each interview, with one paragraph dedicated to summarizing the major issues for that participant in each of the following categories: (a) a general description of the participant, her life situation, her educational background, and the conditions of her family and childhood; (b) early messages and experiences regarding gender, relationships, sexuality, and male aggression; (c) romantic and sexual experiences that the participant and/or I considered abusive, exploitive, or empowering; (d) the participant's general feelings and opinions regarding such issues as violence, domination, and consent, noting any contradictions among the woman's thoughts on these matters.

2. I then combed through each transcript, searching for instances of tension or contradictions between abstract beliefs ("I would never stay with a man who dominated me"; "Women have a right to have sex or not, whenever they want to") and personal experiences ("My boyfriend is very controlling, but I know it's because he loves me"; "I don't feel entitled to

say no if it seems like I might have led him on"). I searched for further tensions or contradictions *within* women's subjective experiences of any particular hetero-relational encounter ("I felt really scared, but also excited at the same time"; "I felt humiliated, but the attention was also flattering").

3. I searched for themes running through the early messages young women received as well as their current thoughts and attributions about their negative encounters. From this analysis, four dominant sets of messages, each with two competing discourses, emerged (described in chapter 3). I then went back through the transcripts to note places where these discourses overlapped or sat in tension with one another in women's experiences. This analysis revealed complex interactions of these cultural discourses in four general areas: (a) their construction of ideas about hetero-relations through childhood and adolescence; (b) their current perceptions of the nature of hetero-relational encounters; (c) their decision making and construction of strategies for managing their hetero-relational encounters; and (d) their labels for and attributions about their own and other women's encounters once abuse or exploitation had occurred.

4. Finally, I analyzed moments during the interviews when women shifted positions in their own narrations—that is, when women moved from telling their stories from their own perspectives to taking on the perspectives of the men involved. I further analyzed any changes in women's positioning of themselves as subjects versus objects in their descriptions of their own relationships, thinking, feelings, and behaviors.

Although this summary portrays the steps I took, it should be noted that the process of qualitative data analysis, while certainly systematic, is always more complex than such an overview can convey. Indeed, I spent months working through the transcripts and the notes I took, searching for competing interpretations and gathering feedback from other researchers who were kind enough to look through portions of the data. At times, certain themes seemed to emerge that then did not hold up when I went back through each transcript. At other times, themes I had initially missed seemed to scream out at me as I was working through the data looking for something else. In the end, the cultural discourses, strategies, and attributions I identify throughout this text are those that run consistently throughout the transcripts, although, of course, each woman experienced and articulated them in her own unique way.

# Notes

*Notes to the Preface*

1. By agency I mean a sense of entitlement and ability to advocate for oneself and one's needs. Agency implies taking a proactive stance in attempting to shape one's circumstances. Although we are all constrained by societal institutions and practices, agency suggests a sense of power or desire to critique and resist those forces, and an ability to envision alternatives.

*Notes to Chapter 1*

1. Here I am referring to incidents that involved physical violence or use of coercion and/or institutional power to force sexual contact. I am not referring to cases of "simple" street harassment such as whistles or sexual comments. All thirty of the women in this sample reported experiencing this type of street harassment, and most saw it as an inevitable part of their lives. Such interactions certainly represent abuses of hetero-relational power and often leave women feeling nervous, angry, or humiliated. But because the young women typically experienced these interactions as discrete moments, rather than part of their relationships or sexual encounters, I discuss street harassment as part of a problematic hetero-relational backdrop. Thus, when I say that twenty-seven of the thirty women experienced rape, battering, or harassment, I mean that these women reported encounters that went well beyond street harassment to include physical violence, manipulation, or threats of repercussions if they did not comply with a man's (or men's) sexual demands.

2. I use the word "we" throughout this text to refer to those of us who wish

to gain better understandings of young women's lived experiences and to advocate for their sexual safety and entitlement. "We" may include researchers, theorists, students, activists, advocates, family members, and so on, whether we are
women or men, and whether or not we refer to ourselves as "feminists." Although some of the issues I raise here may be of particular interest to those conducting qualitative feminist research on this topic, I assume that all readers
should be concerned with doing justice to the complexities of women's hetero-
relational experiences, while also ensuring that their rights to advocacy and legal
redress are maintained.

   3. See, for example, Paglia (1992); Roiphe (1993); and Sommers (1994). For
excellent critiques of these views, see Sanday (1996), as well as contributors to
Lamb's (1999) and Maglin and Perry's (1996) edited volumes.

### Notes to Chapter 2

   1. In order to protect participants' privacy, I have changed all names and identifying information (such as where they grew up or names of their partners and
family members).

   2. Some of the most helpful understandings of subjectivity can be found in the
sometimes overlapping schools of postmodernism, poststructuralism, feminist theory, deconstructionism, postcolonialism, and social constructionism. Working
most often in and across fields of philosophy, critical social psychology, women's
studies, cultural studies, and education, increasing numbers of feminists are exploring the complexities of the cultural construction of subjectivity. Much of this
work is based on Foucault's (1978; 1980; 1981) provocative work on power and
sexuality as well as insights from critical theory.

   3. Feminists such as Gatens (1992) and Jaggar (1989) have critiqued such traditional Western understandings of subjectivity not only as theoretically insufficient, but also as reproducing dominant liberal and androcentric notions, and thus
reinforcing the status quo. The writings of feminist theorists of color and non-
Western women have been particularly important in disrupting the notion of "self"
as context-neutral. Highlighting the cultural embeddedness of identity, authors
such as Patricia Hill Collins (1991); Oliva Espin (1984); bell hooks (1984; 1990);
Audre Lorde (1984); Chandra Talpade Mohanty (1992; 1993); and Uma Narayan
(1989) have revealed not only the extraction of identity from culture in the traditional social sciences, but also the absence of attention to race, class, sexuality, and
ethnicity in much feminist writing on subjectivity. Probing the multiple intercon-
nections among race, class, gender, culture, and sexuality, these theorists articulate
a vision of subjectivity that is inherently fluid, multidimensional, and culturally and
historically situated. This work has pushed forward notions of subjectivity by insisting that explorations of identity be anchored in critical analyses of varying cultural positionality.

   4. Consistent with this perspective, Henriques et al. (1984) conceptualize the
individual as "not a fixed or given entity, but rather a particular product of histor-

ically specific practices of social regulation" (12). Similarly, Young-Eisendrath (1988) writes, "there is no knowledge or experience of being a person that is first learned alone and then attributed to others. In order to see ourselves as persons, we need the reflections, definitions, and perceptions of others. Personal experience is originally and continually a shared experience" (157). Marecek and Hare-Mustin (1990) advocate replacing the idea of a true self with "the idea of a human actor with a subjectivity constituted by social relations. Such an actor is not fixed in a unified identity, but rather her subjective experience is constituted by multiple positions available in the different social relations she is involved in" (13).

5. Of course, this practice continues in many courtrooms today, and laws criminalizing battering, rape, and harassment are not always effective. However, the very creation of such laws suggests that the women's movement has indeed had an impact on public consciousness, at least to the extent that such laws have received enough public and legislative support to be enacted.

6. In Andrea's and Paula's self-descriptions, the dashes (Andrea) and question mark (Paula) noted for their sexualities represent what they wrote on their survey, rather than my notations. No participants left any of these questions blank.

7. Throughout this text I quote the participants extensively so that readers may have a better sense of their own thinking and the language they used. However, in cases where narratives contained a great deal of repetition, hesitations, or other interruptions of their thought process (such as "um," "you know," "like"), I did edit the quotations to enhance clarity (although I did not change their words). In instances where participants' thoughts on a particular subject were interrupted by a tangential idea or story, I have brought together the two aspects of the original thought and connected them with ellipses to note where other words were deleted.

### Notes to Chapter 3

1. Throughout this discussion I use such expressions as "lessons learned," "messages received," and "ideas encountered" by the participants in their childhood and adolescence. My use of such language is not meant to imply that they necessarily agreed with what they learned or that they incorporated entire lessons to the exclusion of others. To say that a woman learned a certain hetero-relational lesson does not necessarily mean that she consciously "buys into" this notion or that this is all she believes. Rather, it is to indicate that she was exposed to certain pervasive cultural messages that impressed her (positively or negatively, or both) at least to the extent that this is what she remembered about her early exposure at the time of her interview.

2. I use the past tense here because I am referring to the period in which the participants were in middle school and high school. However, it should be clear that the conservative climate to which I refer was by no means limited to the Reagan/Bush era. Indeed, in the time since these young women left high school, we have seen a continued shift toward conservatism. With the election of a Republican Congress, severe budget cuts, and continued pressure from the

Religious Right, school-based sex education faces perhaps even greater threats at the time of this writing than it did when the participants were in middle school and high school.

3. Although the availability of sex education has increased dramatically in the last fifteen years, still only twenty-three states and the District of Columbia required sex education as of 1997 (NARAL Foundation, 1997). Moreover, the types of sex education offered remain problematic. In 1997, twenty-six states required abstinence education, yet only fourteen of those states also required education about pregnancy, contraception, and disease prevention (NARAL Foundation, 1997). As of 1995, eight states recommended or required schools to teach that homosexuality is a crime according to their state's laws or that it is an unacceptable lifestyle (NARAL Foundation, 1995). That same year, five states (Connecticut, Illinois, Louisiana, Michigan, and South Carolina) explicitly restricted or prohibited discussion of abortion in schools (NARAL Foundation, 1995).

4. I use the term "virginity" throughout the text because it is the word young women used to describe those who have not had hetero-sexual intercourse. I do not mean to imply, however, that women or men who have not had such experiences are asexual or that women's sexual lives begin at the moment of penile/vaginal penetration. Similarly, since participants typically characterized their first experience of hetero-sexual intercourse as "losing" their virginity, I use that expression in this writing. However, I remain uncomfortable with casting virginity as a commodity or personal virtue that is forfeited at first intercourse, as well as with the use of the passive voice to convey this "event" (since losing one's virginity implies that something is taken from a young woman; she is not seen as an active participant). Therefore, when writing of women's "loss" of virginity in this text, I put words such as "losing" and "lost" in quotation marks.

5. "Megan's Law" is named for Megan Kanka, an eight-year-old New Jersey girl who was raped and murdered by her neighbor, a convicted sex offender. This controversial law requires police notification/registration by all paroled or released sex offenders returning to the community. At the time of this writing, several other states have enacted or are debating enactment of variations on such a law.

6. I do not mean to imply here that rape and other forms of violence against women are normal/healthy. I do, however, wish to problematize the literature's characterization of "abusive" relationships/sexuality/men as inherently distinct from those that are "typical," since such large numbers of hetero-relationships contain elements of domination, exploitation, or abuse.

7. It is interesting to note that Wendy is the only woman in the study who used words like "molesting" and "rape" when referring to sexual abuse committed by family members. It is also interesting to note that she described later sexual experiences involving force that she did *not* characterize as "rape" or "abuse."

8. Although Chloe did not use the word "rape" to describe her experience, I use that word here, since he forced her to perform oral sex on him and to have intercourse against her will. In later chapters I discuss some of the reasons Chloe and

other women refused to use words like "rape" or "victimization" to describe such experiences.

9. Writers such as Roiphe (1993); Paglia (1992); and Sommers (1994) have become notorious for advocating this position.

*Notes to Chapter 4*

1. I refer here to women's social development rather than biological maturation. In examining where the participants are situated developmentally, I am not suggesting that we revisit the "nature/nurture" debate. Rather, I am suggesting that their transition from adolescence to adulthood in a society that privileges adult status (but lacks clear and consistent markers for "arrival" at that status) poses socially constructed challenges that are particularly poignant at this time in the participants' lives.

2. It is interesting to note that when women discussed their identities in more abstract terms, they seldom mentioned such concerns. Speaking in a general sense about the orienting themes in their lives, participants were more likely to speak in characterological rather than developmental terms. When I asked how they would describe themselves overall, they said such things as "I try to always be honest with myself and other people," "I'm basically a happy person," or "I think I'm very down to earth." In fact, none of the women described herself, in the abstract, as trying to appear grown-up. Yet, as women shifted to descriptions of the thinking that motivated or accompanied their hetero-relational behaviors throughout their adolescence and young adulthood, each woman, at some point in her interview, referred to the need to seem "together," "like a grown woman," or "not a little girl."

3. Some readers of this excerpt have wondered whether Gloria's referral to being "pretty mean" was meant to describe her own choice to have oral sex rather than intercourse, or her partner's decision to give her an ultimatum. While her transcribed words make this reference seem ambiguous, in the interview her affect and body language suggested strongly that she was referring to her choice to opt for oral sex. As she began the phrase, "which was pretty mean, now that I think about it," she paused, giggled, and rolled her eyes sheepishly, as though she were both apologizing and taking a certain pride in her decision.

4. Although many girls experience sexual danger and victimization long before they reach adolescence or decide to enter into sexualized relationships willingly, their transition through adolescence and into adulthood marks a time when they must grapple with decisions about how to position themselves as sexually mature while also maneuvering around the sexual dangers about which they have been warned.

5. See Fine, Powell, et al. (1996) for a fuller discussion of "whiteness" as the unmarked, "Other" category.

6. Interestingly, women reported these feelings regardless of how they described their sexual identities. Although women may have had a range of reasons

for privileging male pleasure, there was no discernible difference in the responses of women who identified themselves as hetero-sexual, bisexual, or lesbian/bi.

7. It is important to recognize that the challenges and themes discussed throughout this chapter are not necessarily exclusive to women in this age group. Certainly older women may struggle with many similar issues. However, these dilemmas may be particularly poignant for adolescent women, as their senses of maturity and sexuality, as well as the expectations others may have of them, are undergoing intense shifts, and are often being tested for the first time. The point, then, is not that these social and developmental challenges occur *only* during adolescence, but rather that these challenges, first encountered during this period, provide an important dimension of the ongoing context from which young adult and older women may draw in understanding their later hetero-relational experiences.

### Notes to Chapter 6

1. Although participants sometimes referred to "generic" derogatory comments from unknown men on the street as "harassment," they did not use this term to refer to sexually explicit/demeaning comments or unwanted sexual advances from teachers or supervisors. When the man was known to them, they insisted that such behavior did not "count" as harassment, even when the man had institutional power over them.

2. While Diana was willing to describe this particular relationship/man as "about abuse," she was unwilling to use this term to describe another experience with a man who appeared similarly forceful and frightening. For an example of a "terrible night" that Diana was *not* willing to label abuse, readers are referred to her quote in the section "Making Higher Meaning," later in this chapter. Also, while Wendy was willing to say she was "raped" by her uncle (see chapter 3), she did not use language of victimization to describe any painful relationships with partners.

3. Previous studies of victimization indicate that forming such individualized attributions may be an adaptive coping mechanism among individuals who have experienced negative events beyond their control (Janoff-Bulman, 1979; Silver and Wortman, 1980; Thompson, 1981). While "self-character blame" (internal, stable attributions based on a negative view of one's character) appears correlated with depression and negative coping (Janoff-Bulman, 1979; Peterson, Schwartz, and Seligman, 1981), studies of "self-behavior blame" (internal, unstable attributions based on a critique of one's actions) have yielded mixed results. Some researchers have found that coping is unrelated to "self-behavior blame" (Janoff-Bulman, 1979; Major, Mueller, and Hildebrandt, 1985), while others have found that such attributions are inversely correlated with depression (Peterson, Schwartz, and Seligman, 1981). Further, studies suggest that *external* attributions are related to a *negative* ability to cope (Janoff-Bulman and Wortman, 1977; Janoff-Bulman, 1979). There may be many reasons to want

young women to make external attributions (i.e., blame the men who victimized them) for their victimization. However, these studies suggest that internal, unstable attributions such as those found in the present data may actually help victims cope, at least in the short term, with painful life events by enabling them to feel a sense of control over their circumstances.

### Notes to Chapter 7

1. Please see note 3 to chapter 1.

2. For an excellent (and deeply disturbing) analysis of the interplay of race, class, gender, and disability in constructing notions of female victimization and male entitlement, see Fine, Genovese, et al. (1996).

3. Provocative examples of such analyses include Fine, Genovese, et al. (1996); Lefkowitz (1997); Sanday (1990; 1996); and Morrison (1992) and contributors to her edited volume.

4. See Cohen and Blanc (1996); Stein (1995); Thorne (1993); and Ward and Taylor (1992) for examples of such research in school settings.

5. For some compelling examples of such studies, see Ward (1996); Pastor, McCormick, and Fine (1996); Sullivan (1996); Rhodes and Davis (1996); Robinson and Ward (1991).

# References

Abma, J. C., A. Chandra, W. D. Mosher, L. S. Peterson, and L. Piccinino. (1997). Fertility, family planning, and women's health: New data from the 1995 National Survey of Family Growth. National Center for Health Statistics, *Vital and Health Statistics*, 23 (19).

Adisa, O. P. (1997). Undeclared war: African-American women writers explicating rape. In L. L. O'Toole and J. R. Schiffman (eds.), *Gender violence: Interdisciplinary perspectives* (194–208). New York: New York University Press.

Bartky, S. (1990). *Femininity and domination: Studies in the phenomenology of oppression.* New York: Routledge.

Benjamin, J. (1988). *The bonds of love: Psychoanalysis, feminism, and the problem of domination.* New York: Pantheon.

Benson, P. (1990). *The troubled journey.* Minneapolis: Search Institute.

Blackman, J. (1990). *Intimate violence: A study of injustice.* New York: Columbia University Press.

Blume, J. (1971). *Are you there, God? It's me, Margaret.* New York: Bantam Doubleday Dell Books for Young Readers.

Bordo, S. (1989). The body and the reproduction of femininity: A feminist appropriation of Foucault. In A. Jaggar and S. Bordo (eds.), *Gender/body/knowledge: Feminist reconstructions of being and knowing* (13–33). New Brunswick: Rutgers University Press.

Borgida, E., and N. Brekke. (1985). Psycholegal research on rape trials. In A. W. Burgess (ed.), *Rape and sexual assault: A research handbook* (313–42). New York: Garland.

Boston Women's Health Book Collective. (1984). *The new our bodies, ourselves.* New York: Simon and Schuster.

Britzman, D. (1988). Paper presented at the *Ethnography in Education Forum,* Philadelphia.

Brodkey, L., and M. Fine. (1988). Presence of mind in the absence of body. *Journal of Education,* 170 (3), 84–99.

Browne, A. (1987). *When battered women kill.* New York: Free Press.

Brownmiller, S. (1975). *Against our will: Men, women, and rape.* Toronto: Bantam Books.

———. (1984). *Femininity.* New York: Fawcett Columbine.

Butler, J. (1990). *Gender trouble: Feminism and the subversion of identity.* New York: Routledge.

Caraway, N. (1991). *Segregated sisterhood.* Knoxville: University of Tennessee Press.

Carli, L. L., and J. B. Leonard. (1989). The effect of hindsight on victim derogation. *Journal of Social and Clinical Psychology,* 8 (3), 331–43.

Castelano, C. (1996). *Safe and healing places for women survivors of domestic violence: Immigrant Asian Indian women's perspectives.* Unpublished manuscript, City University of New York.

Christian-Smith, L. K. (1993). Voices of resistance: Young women readers of romance fiction. In L. Weis and M. Fine (eds.), *Beyond silenced voices: Class, race, and gender in United States schools* (169–89). Albany: State University of New York Press.

Clover, C. J. (1987). Her body, himself: Gender in the slasher film. *Representations,* 20, 131–72.

Cohen, J., and S. Blanc. (1996). *Girls in the middle: Working to succeed in school.* Washington, DC: American Association of University Women Educational Foundation.

Cole, M., and S. R. Cole. (1993). *The development of children.* 3d ed. New York: Scientific American Books.

Collins, P. H. (1991). *Black feminist thought: Knowledge, consciousness, and the politics of empowerment.* New York: Routledge.

———. (1994). Shifting the center. In D. Bassin, M. Honey, and M. Kaplan (eds.), *Representations of motherhood.* New Haven: Yale University Press.

Dobash, R. E., and R. P. Dobash. (1992). *Women, violence, and social change.* New York: Routledge.

Dworkin, A., and C. A. MacKinnon. (1988). *Pornography and civil rights: A new day for women's equality.* Minneapolis: Organizing Against Pornography.

Espin, O. (1984). Cultural and historical influences on sexuality in Hispanic/Latin women: Implications for psychotherapy. In C. Vance (ed.), *Pleasure and danger: Exploring female sexuality* (149–64). Boston: Routledge and Kegan Paul.

Ewing, C. (1987). *Battered women who kill.* Lexington: D. C. Heath.

Farganis, S. (1989). Feminism and the reconstruction of social science. In A. Jaggar and S. Bordo (eds.), *Gender/body/knowledge: Feminist reconstructions of being and knowing* (207–23). New Brunswick: Rutgers University Press.

Fine, M. (1982). An injustice by any other name. . . . *Victimology: An International Journal* 6 (1–4), 48–58.

———. (1983). Coping with rape: Critical perspectives on consciousness. *Imagination, Cognition, and Personality: A Scientific Study of Consciousness*, 3 (3), 249–64.

———. (1988). Sexuality, schooling, and adolescent females: The missing discourse of desire. *Harvard Educational Review*, 58 (1), 29–53.

———. (1989). The politics of research and activism: Violence against women. *Gender and Society*, 3 (4), 549–58.

———. (1990). Ventriloquy, voices, and activism: Repositioning politics inside social research. Keynote address, *Ethnography and Education Forum*, Philadelphia.

———. (1994). Working the hyphens: Reinventing the Self and Other in qualitative research. In N. Denzin and Y. Lincoln (eds.), *Handbook of qualitative research* (70–82). Newbury Park, CA: Sage.

Fine, M., T. Genovese, S. Ingersoll, P. Macpherson, and R. Roberts. (1996). Insisting on innocence: Accounts of accountability by abusive men. In M. B. Lykes, A. Bannazizio, R. Liem, and M. Morris (eds.), *Myths about the powerless: Contesting social inequalities* (129–58). Philadelphia: Temple University Press.

Fine, M., and L. M. Phillips. (1990). Activist feminist research: On mistakes and possibilities. Paper presented at the annual meeting of the *American Psychological Association*, Boston.

Fine, M., L. Powell, L. Weis, and M. Wong (eds.). (1996). *Off-white: Readings on society, culture, and race*. New York: Routledge.

Fine, M., and L. Weis. (1996). Writing the "wrongs" of fieldwork: Confronting our own research/writing dilemmas in urban ethnographies. *Qualitative Inquiry*, 2 (3), 251–74.

———. (1998). Crime stories: A critical look through race, ethnicity, and gender. *Qualitative Studies in Education*, 11 (3), 435–59.

Finkelhor, D., and J. Dziuba-Leatherman. (1994). Victimization of children. *American Psychologist*, 49 (3), 173–83.

Foucault, M. (1978). *History of sexuality*. New York: Pantheon.

———. (1980). *Power/knowledge: Selected interviews and other writings, 1972–1977*. New York: Pantheon.

———. (1981). The order of discourse. In R. Young (ed.), *Untying the text* (48–78). New York: Routledge and Kegan Paul.

Frye, M. (1983). *The politics of reality: Essays in feminist theory*. Freedom, CA: Crossing Press.

Furnham, A., and B. Gunter. (1984). Just world beliefs and attitudes toward the poor. *British Journal of Social Psychology*, 23 (3), 265–69.

Gatens, M. (1992). Power, bodies and difference. In M. Barrett and A. Phillips (eds.), *Destabilizing theory: Contemporary feminist debates* (120–37). Stanford: Stanford University Press.

Gee, J. P. (1987). What is literacy? Paper presented at the *Mailman Foundation Conference of Families and Literacy.* Harvard Graduate School of Education, Cambridge, MA.

Gergen, K. (1985). The social constructionist movement in modern psychology. *American Psychologist,* 40, 266–75.

Gergen, M. M. (1988). Toward a feminist metatheory and methodology in the social sciences. In M. M. Gergen (ed.), *Feminist thought and the structure of knowledge* (87–104). New York: New York University Press.

Gilligan, C. (1982). *In a different voice.* Cambridge: Harvard University Press.

Glazer, B., and A. Strauss. (1967). *The discovery of grounded theory.* Chicago: Aldine.

Gordon, L. (1988). *Heroes of their own lives: The politics and history of family violence.* New York: Penguin.

Griffin, S. (1981). *Pornography and silence: Culture's revenge against nature.* New York: Harper and Row.

Gruman, J. C., and R. P. Sloan. (1983). Disease as justice: Perceptions of the victims of physical illness. *Basic and Applied Psychology,* 4 (1), 39–46.

Haavind, H. (1984). Love and power in marriage. In H. Holter (ed.), *Patriarchy in a welfare society.* New York: Columbia University Press.

Halson, J. (1990). Young women, sexual harassment, and heterosexuality: Violence, power relations, and mixed sex schooling. In P. Abbott and C. Wallace (eds.), *Gender, sexuality, and power.* New York: Macmillan.

Hare-Mustin, R. T. (1991). Sex, lies, and headaches: The problem is power. In T. J. Goodrich (ed.), *Women and power: Perspectives for therapy* (63–85). New York: Norton.

Hare-Mustin, R. T., and J. Marecek. (1990). *Making a difference: Psychology and the construction of gender.* New Haven: Yale University Press.

Haug, F. (1987). *Female sexualization: A collective work of memory.* London: Verso.

Henriques, J. (1984). Social psychology and the politics of racism. In J. Henriques, W. Hollway, C. Unwin, C. Venn, and V. Walkerdine (eds.), *Changing the subject: Psychology, social regulation, and subjectivity* (60–89). New York: Methuen.

Henriques, J., W. Hollway, C. Unwin, C. Venn, and V. Walkerdine (eds.). (1984). *Changing the subject: Psychology, social regulation, and subjectivity.* New York: Methuen.

Hoff, L. A. (1990). *Battered women as survivors.* New York: Routledge.

Hollway, W. (1984). Gender difference and the production of subjectivity. In J. Henriques, W. Hollway, C. Unwin, C. Venn, and V. Walkerdine (eds.), *Changing the subject: Psychology, social regulation, and subjectivity* (227–63). New York: Methuen.

————. (1995). Feminist discourses and women's heterosexual desire. In S. Wilkinson and C. Kitzinger (eds.), *Feminism and discourse: Psychological perspectives* (86–105). London: Sage.

hooks, b. (1981). *Ain't I a woman: Black women and feminism*. Boston: South End Press.

————. (1984). *Feminist theory from margin to center*. Boston: South End Press.

————. (1990). *Yearning: Race, gender, and cultural politics*. Boston: South End Press.

————. (1996). Dissident heat: *Fire with fire*. In N. B. Maglin and D. Perry (eds.), *Bad girls, good girls: Women, sex, and power in the nineties* (57–64). New York: Routledge.

Jaggar, A. (1989). Love and knowledge: Emotion in feminist epistemology. In A. Jaggar and S. Bordo (eds.), *Gender/body/knowledge: Feminist reconstructions of being and knowing* (145–71). New Brunswick: Rutgers University Press.

Janoff-Bulman, R. (1979). Characterological versus behavioral self-blame: Inquiries into depression and rape. *Journal of Personality and Social Psychology*, 37 (10), 1798–1809.

Janoff-Bulman, R., and C. B. Wortman. (1977). Attributions of blame and coping in the "real world": Severe accident victims react to their lot. *Journal of Personality and Social Psychology*, 35 (5), 351–63.

Jones, A. (1994). *Next time she'll be dead*. Boston: Beacon Press.

Jones, A., and S. Schechter. (1992). *When love goes wrong*. New York: HarperCollins.

Kahn, A. S., and V. A. Mathie. (1999). Understanding the unacknowledged rape victim. In C. B. Travis and J. W. White (eds.), *Sexuality, society, and feminism: Psychological perspectives on women*. Washington, DC: American Psychological Association.

Kidder, L., and M. Fine. (1986). Making sense of injustice: Social explanations, social action and the role of the social scientist. In E. Seidman and J. Rappaport (eds.), *Redefining social problems* (49–64). New York: Plenum.

Kitzinger, C., and A. Thomas. (1995). Sexual harassment: A discursive approach. In S. Wilkinson and C. Kitzinger (eds.), *Feminism and discourse: Psychological perspectives* (32–48). London: Sage.

Kitzinger, C., S. Wilkinson, and R. Perkins. (1993). Theorizing heterosexuality. *Feminism and Psychology*, 2 (3), 293–324.

Koss, M. P. (1985). The hidden rape victim: Personality, attitudinal, and situational characteristics. *Psychology of Women Quarterly*, 9, 193–212.

————. (1993). Rape: Scope, impact, interventions, and public policy responses. *American Psychologist*, 48 (10), 1062–69.

Kurz, D. (1990). Interventions with battered women in health care settings. *Violence and Victims*, 5 (4), 243–56.

Ladner, J. (1971). *Tomorrow's tomorrow: The Black woman*. Garden City, NY: Doubleday.

Lamb, S. (ed.). (1999). *New versions of victims: Feminist struggles with the concept.* New York: New York University Press.

Langan, P. A., and C. W. Harlow. (1994). *Child rape victims, 1992.* U.S. Department of Justice crime data brief. Washington, DC: Government Printing Office, June.

Lather, P. (1986). Research as praxis. *Harvard Educational Review,* 56 (3), 257–77.

———. (1991). *Getting smart: Feminist research and pedagogy with/in the postmodern.* New York: Routledge.

LeCompte, M., and A. Bennet. (1988). Empowerment: The once and future role of the gringo. Paper presented at the annual meeting of the *American Anthropological Association,* Phoenix, AZ.

Lefkowitz, R. (1997). *Our guys: The Glen Ridge rape and the secret life of the perfect suburb.* Berkeley: University of California Press.

Lerner, M. J. (1980). *The belief in a just world: A fundamental delusion.* New York: Plenum.

Lerner, M. J., and D. T. Miller. (1978). Just world research and the attribution process: Looking back and looking ahead. *Psychological Bulletin,* 85 (5), 1030–50.

Linton, R. (1989). Toward a feminist research method. In A. Jaggar and S. Bordo (eds.), *Gender/body/knowledge: Feminist reconstructions of being and knowing* (273–92). New Brunswick: Rutgers University Press.

Lips, H. (1991). *Women, men, and power.* Mountain View, CA: Mayfield.

Lorde, A. (1984). *Sister/outsider: Essays and speeches by Audre Lorde.* Freedom, CA: Crossing Press.

Lykes, M. B. (1989). *The caring self: Social experiences of power and powerlessness.* New York: Praeger.

Maglin, N. B., and D. Perry. (eds.). (1996). *Bad girls, good girls: Women, sex, and power in the nineties.* New Brunswick: Rutgers University Press.

Major, B., P. Mueller, and K. Hildebrandt. (1985). Attributions, expectations, and coping with abortion. *Journal of Personality and Social Psychology,* 48 (3), 585–99.

Marecek, J., and R. T. Hare-Mustin. (1990). Toward a feminist poststructural psychology: The modern self and the postmodern subject. Paper presented at the annual meeting of the *American Psychological Association,* Boston.

Marsh, C. E. (1993). Sexual assault and domestic violence in the African-American community. *Western Journal of Black Studies,* 17 (3), 149–55.

Meyer, J. (1988). Feminist thought and social psychology. In M. Gergen (ed.), *Feminist thought and the structure of knowledge* (105–23). New York: New York University Press.

Miller, J. B. (1986). *Toward a new psychology of women.* Boston: Beacon Press.

Mohanty, C. T. (1992). Feminist encounters: Locating the politics of experience.

In M. Barrett and A. Phillips (eds.), *Destabilizing theory: Contemporary feminist debates* (74–92). Stanford: Stanford University Press.

———. (1993). On race and voice: Challenges for a liberal education in the 1990s. In B. W. Thompson and S. Tyagi (eds.), *Beyond a dream deferred: Multi-cultural education and the politics of excellence* (41–65). Minneapolis: University of Minnesota Press.

Morrison, T. (1992). *Race-ing justice, en-gendering power: Essays on Anita Hill, Clarence Thomas, and the construction of social reality.* New York: Pantheon.

NARAL Foundation. (1995). *Sexuality education in America: A state-by-state review.* Washington, DC: NARAL Foundation.

———. (1997). *Who decides? A state-by-state review of abortion and reproductive rights.* Washington, DC: NARAL Foundation.

Narayan, U. (1989). The project of feminist epistemology: Perspectives from a nonwestern feminist. In A. Jaggar and S. Bordo (eds.), *Gender/body/knowledge: Feminist reconstructions of being and knowing* (256–69). New Brunswick: Rutgers University Press.

Paglia, C. (1992). *Sex, art, and American culture: Essays.* New York: Vintage.

Pastor, J., J. McCormick, and M. Fine. (1996). Makin' homes: An urban girl thing. In B. J. Ross Leadbeater and N. Way (eds.), *Urban girls: Resisting stereotypes, creating identities* (15–34). New York: New York University Press.

Patton, M. Q. (1980). *Qualitative evaluation methods.* Beverly Hills: Sage.

Peiss, K., and C. Simmons. (eds.). (1989). *Passion and power: Sexuality in history.* Philadelphia: Temple University Press.

Peterson, C., S. Schwartz, and M. Seligman. (1981). Self-blame and depressive symptoms. *Journal of Personality and Social Psychology,* 41 (2), 253–59.

Phillips, L. M. (1989). Resources for battered women: A critical examination of "options." Paper presented at the annual meeting of the *American Psychological Association,* New Orleans.

———. (1996). Constructing meanings in hetero-relations: Young women's experiences of power and desire. Paper presented at the twenty-sixth *International Congress of Psychology,* Montreal, August 16–21.

Phillips, L. M., and M. Fine. (1992). What's "left" in sexuality education? In J.T. Sears (ed.), *Sexuality and the curriculum: The politics and practices of sexuality education* (242–49). New York: Teachers College Press.

Rhodes, J. E., and A. B. Davis. (1996). Supportive ties between nonparent adults and urban adolescent girls. In B. J. Ross Leadbeater and N. Way (eds.), *Urban girls: Resisting stereotypes, creating identities* (213–25). New York: New York University Press.

Riger, S. (1991). Gender dilemmas in sexual harassment policies and procedures. *American Psychologist,* 46 (5), 497–505.

Robinson, T., and J. V. Ward. (1991). A belief in self far greater than anyone's disbelief: Cultivating resistance among African American female adolescents.

In C. Gilligan, A. G. Rogers, and D. Tolman (eds.), *Women, girls and psychotherapy: Reframing resistance* (87–103). Binghamton, NY: Harrington Park Press.

Roiphe, K. (1993). *The morning after: Sex, fear, and feminism on campus.* Boston: Little, Brown.

Ross, L. (1977). The intuitive psychologist and his shortcomings: Distortions in the attribution process. In L. Berkowitz (ed.), *Advances in experimental social psychology,* vol. 10 (174–220). New York: Academic Press.

Rotheram-Borus, M. J., S. Dopkins, N. Sabate, and M. Lightfoot. (1996). Diversity in girls' experiences: Feeling good about who you are. In B. J. Ross Leadbeater and N. Way (eds.), *Urban girls: Resisting stereotypes, creating identities* (35–52). New York: New York University Press.

Russell, D. (1982). *Rape in marriage.* New York: Collier Books.

Sanday, P. R. (1990). *Fraternity gang rape: Sex, brotherhood, and privilege on campus.* New York: New York University Press.

———. (1996). *A woman scorned: Acquaintance rape on trial.* New York: Doubleday.

Sawicki, J. (1991). *Disciplining Foucault: Feminism, power, and the body.* New York: Routledge.

Schechter, S. (1982). *Women and male violence: The visions and struggles of the battered women's movement.* Boston: South End Press.

Sears, J. T. (1992). Dilemmas and possibilities of sexuality education: Reproducing the body politic. In J. T. Sears (ed.), *Sexuality and the curriculum: The politics and practices of sexuality education* (7–33). New York: Teachers College Press.

Shweder, R. A. (1995). Culture: What is it? In N. R. Goldberger and J. B. Veroff (eds.), *The Culture and psychology reader* (41–86). Cambridge: Cambridge University Press.

Silver, R., and C. Wortman. (1980). Coping with undesireable life events. In J. Garber and M. E. P. Seligman (eds.), *Human helplessness: Theory and applications* (279–340). New York: Academic Press.

Snitow, A. (1983). Mass market romance: Pornography for women is different. In A. Snitow, C. Stansell, and S. Thompson (eds.), *Powers of desire: The politics of sexuality* (245–63). New York: Monthly Review Press.

Snitow, A., C. Stansell, and S. Thompson. (1983). Introduction. In A. Snitow, C. Stansell, and S. Thompson (eds.), *Powers of desire: The politics of sexuality* (9–47). New York: Monthly Review Press.

Sommers, C. H. (1994). *Who stole feminism? How women have betrayed women.* New York: Simon and Schuster.

Stanko, E. (1985). *Intimate intrusions: Women's experience of male violence.* London: Routledge and Kegan Paul.

———. (1990). *Everyday violence: How women and men experience sexual and physical danger.* London: Pandora Press.

Stein, N. (1995). Sexual harassment in schools: The public performance of gendered violence. *Harvard Educational Review*, 65 (2), 145–62.

Steiner-Adair, C. (1990). The body politic: Normal female adolescent development and the development of eating disorders. In C. Gilligan, N. P. Lyons, and T. J. Hanmer (eds.), *Making connections: The relational worlds of adolescent girls at Emma Willard School* (162–84). Cambridge: Harvard University Press.

Stoltenberg, J. (1990). Pornography and freedom. In M. Kimmel (ed.), *Men confront pornography*. New York: Crown.

Sullivan, A. M. (1996). From mentor to muse: Recasting the role of women in relationships with urban adolescent girls. In B. J. Ross Leadbeater and N. Way (eds.), *Urban girls: Resisting stereotypes, creating identities* (226–49). New York: New York University Press.

Summers, G., and N. S. Feldman (1984). Blaming the victim versus blaming the perpetrator: An attributional analysis of spouse abuse. *Journal of Social and Clinical Psychology*, 2 (4), 339–47.

Sunday, S., and E. Tobach (eds.). (1985). *Violence against women: A critique of the sociobiology of rape*. New York: Gordian Press.

Taylor, J. M. (1996). Cultural stories: Latina and Portuguese daughters and mothers. In B. J. Ross Leadbeater and N. Way (eds.), *Urban girls: Resisting stereotypes, creating identities* (117–31). New York: New York University Press.

Thompson, S. (1995). *Going all the way: Teenage girls' tales of sex, romance, and pregnancy*. New York: Hill and Wang.

Thompson, S. C. (1981). Will it hurt less if I can control it? A complex answer to a simple question. *Psychological Bulletin*, 90, 89–101.

Thorne, B. (1993). *Gender play: Girls and boys in school*. New Brunswick: Rutgers University Press.

Tiefer, L. (1995). *Sex is not a natural act and other essays*. Boulder: Westview.

Tolman, D. L. (1996). Adolescent girls' sexuality: Debunking the myth of the Urban Girl. In B. J. Ross Leadbeater and N. Way (eds.), *Urban girls: Resisting stereotypes, creating identities* (255–71). New York: New York University Press.

Tolman, D. L., and T. E. Higgins. (1996). How being a good girl can be bad for girls. In N. B. Maglin and D. Perry (eds.), *Bad girls, good girls: Women, sex, and power in the nineties* (205–25). New Brunswick: Rutgers University Press.

Unger, R. K. (1988). Psychological, feminist, and personal epistemology: Transcending contradiction. In M. M. Gergen (ed.), *Feminist thought and the structure of knowledge* (124–41). New York: New York University Press.

———. (1989). Sex, gender, and epistemology. In M. Crawford and M. Gentry (eds.), *Gender and thought: Psychological perspectives* (17–35). New York: Springer-Verlag.

United Nations. (1995). *United Nations human development report, 1995*. New York: United Nations.

Valverde, M. (1987). *Sex, power, and pleasure*. Philadelphia: New Society Publishers.

Vance, C. (1984). Pleasure and danger: Toward a politics of sexuality. In C. Vance (ed.), *Pleasure and danger: Exploring female sexuality* (1–27). Boston: Routledge and Kegan Paul.

Vazquez-Nuttal, E., I. Romero-Garcia, and B. DeLeon. (1987). Sex roles and perceptions of femininity and masculinity of Hispanic women: A review of the literature. *Psychology of Women Quarterly*, 11, 409–25.

Walker, L. E. (1979). *The battered woman syndrome.* New York: Harper and Row.

———. (1989). Psychology and violence against women. *American Psychologist*, 44 (4), 695–702.

Ward, J. V. (1996). Raising resisters: The role of truth telling in the psychological development of African American girls. In B. J. Ross Leadbeater and N. Way (eds.), *Urban girls: Resisting stereotypes, creating identities* (85–99). New York: New York University Press.

Ward, J. V., and J. M. Taylor. (1992). Sexuality education of immigrant and minority students: Developing culturally appropriate curriculum. In J. T. Sears (ed.), *Sexuality and the curriculum: The politics and practices of sexuality education* (183–202). New York: Teachers College Press.

Warshaw, R. (1988). *I never called it rape: The Ms. report of recognizing, fighting, and surviving date and acquaintance rape.* New York: Harper and Row.

Weeks, J. (1985). *Sexuality and its discontents: Meanings, myths, and modern sexualities.* New York: Routledge and Kegan Paul.

Whatley, M. H. (1992). Whose sexuality is it anyway? In J. T. Sears (ed.), *Sexuality and the curriculum: The politics and practices of sexuality education* (78–84). New York: Teachers College Press.

White, J., and M. Niles. (1990). Social construction of consent: Sexual scripts and acquaintance rape. Paper presented at the annual meeting of the *American Psychological Association*. Boston.

Young-Eisendrath, P. (1988). The female person and how we talk about her. In M. M. Gergen (ed.), *Feminist thought and the struture of knowledge* (152–72). New York: New York University Press.

Yllo, K., and M. Bograd (eds.). (1988). *Feminist perspectives on wife abuse.* New York: Sage.

# Index